101 SOLUTIONS FOR SURVIVING OFFICE INSANITY

Am I the only SANE ONE working here

ALBERT J. BERNSTEIN, Ph.D.

New York   Chicago   San Francisco   Lisbon   London   Madrid   Mexico City
Milan   New Delhi   San Juan   Seoul   Singapore   Sydney   Toronto

The **McGraw·Hill** Companies

Library of Congress Cataloging-in-Publication Data

Bernstein, Albert J.
   Am I the only sane one working here? : 101 solutions for surviving office insanity /
Albert J. Bernstein.
      p.   cm.
   ISBN 978-0-07-160872-5 (alk. paper)
   1. Psychology, Industrial.   2. Career development—Psychological
aspects.   3. Office politics—Psychological aspects.   4. Employee motivation—
Psychological aspects.   I. Title.

HF5548.8.B393   2010
650.1'3—dc22   2009000691

For Clara

Copyright © 2009 by Al Bernstein. All rights reserved. Printed in the United States of America. Except as permitted under the United States Copyright Act of 1976, no part of this publication may be reproduced or distributed in any form or by any means, or stored in a database or retrieval system, without the prior written permission of the publisher.

2 3 4 5 6 7 8 9 10 11 12 13 14 15 16 17 18 19 20 21 22   DOC/DOC   0 9

ISBN 978-0-07-160872-5
MHID   0-07-160872-9

McGraw-Hill books are available at special quantity discounts to use as premiums and sales promotions or for use in corporate training programs. To contact a representative, please e-mail us at bulksales@mcgraw-hill.com.

This book is printed on acid-free paper.

Contents

Acknowledgments

FIRST AND FOREMOST, I'd like to thank the hundreds of people who, over the years, were almost driven crazy by their jobs until we figured out what was going on and what to do about it. Their stories are the basis for this book.

I am grateful also to my agent, Janet Rosen, of Sheree Bykovsky and Associates, who persuaded me that if I wrote all this stuff down, people would want to read it, and to my editor, John Aherne, who guided me through this project with high style, an open mind, and a grand sense of humor.

I am obliged to my sister, Joyce Howell, to Mindy Ranik, Bob Poole, Yvonne Edes, and Donna Sherwood, friends, helpers, and muses, who have graciously shared their ideas, inspiration, and encouragement.

My daughter, Jessica, suddenly an adult, provided invaluable help with youthful perspective and surprisingly erudite literary criticism. That college education sure paid off!

Thanks also to the rest of my family, Luahna, Josh, Melvin, and baby Clara, who have put up with my rising before dawn to write and falling asleep in my chair by dusk.

Last, a pat on the head to Molly and Mocha, who got up with me every morning to guard me as I wrote.

Introduction

IF YOU FEEL CONFUSED and frustrated by the insanity at your office, you are not alone. Sometimes it seems as if the whole world of business has gone crazy.

The CEO is handing out slick-paged reports to the board showing an excellent return on investment, but in your department the work is piling up and everyone is stressed out because of the hiring freeze. The network is down, and the people in IT aren't answering their phones. The guys in sales have made impossible promises to customers, and now they're yelling that it's your job to deliver. The VP has called a meeting to improve communications, but you know that if you say that anything is wrong, the real problem will turn out to be your attitude.

Your boss, the micromanager, has no idea what she wants but is absolutely certain that whatever it is, you won't do it right. The people in your work group seem to have forgotten the meaning of the word *deadline*.

The worst part is that no one with the power to do anything seems to notice, much less care.

Each day, you try your best to get some work done, but the woman in the next cube is screeching at her kids on the phone, and the guy behind you keeps popping his head up to tell you what he saw on TV last night. Another staff meeting starts in ten minutes. Meanwhile, you have 736 unread e-mails in your in-box, 700 of which have nothing to do with you.

You stare blankly at your screen and wonder, "Am I the only sane person working here?"

The secret to preserving your sanity lies in how well you understand the craziness going on around you.

When you pay close attention, you can see that the crazy situations at work, like all other human behaviors, follow predictable patterns. The patterns are not rational, in that they often operate at cross-purposes from getting the job done efficiently and well, but that doesn't mean that they make no sense. If you understand the patterns, you can make choices about whether to follow them. The choices you make can keep you sane.

All the behavior patterns discussed in this book are interactive. This means that when things get crazy, you may not be able to control the situation, but you can control how you respond to it. How you react can keep things from getting crazier. Your internal responses, how you think and feel, and your actions, what you say and do, will determine how much damage the general insanity does to you. If you understand what is going on, you can keep the craziness from bothering you, you can keep things from getting worse, and sometimes you can even make them better.

This book outlines 101 difficult and crazy-making people and situations that you are likely to encounter at work. The scenarios range from dealing with irritating coworkers like liars, slackers, bullshitters, control freaks, and passive-aggressives, to surviving worst-case scenarios like getting chewed out, facing a bad review, or the chance of being laid off for political reasons. There are also short pieces on organizational psychology and philosophy that may help you to understand the reasons for corporate behaviors that don't seem to make rational sense. Each scenario stands by itself with clear, concise explanations about what is going on and what you can think, do, and say to survive with your reason and your job intact. You may choose to read them straight through in order, or use the titles or the index to find the ones that are most relevant to you.

You may not be able to stop the insanity at your office, but with a little help you may be able to keep it from driving you crazy also. You have considerably more power and control than you think. This book will show you how to use it.

Part 1

Lies and Bullshit

AT WORK, people who say what they mean and mean what they say are almost as rare as spotted owls. Here are some ideas about how to deal with coworkers who play fast and loose with the truth.

SURVIVAL SCENARIO 1 Bullshit or Just Plain Lying

Chris has done it again. He's the golden boy in sales, who will tell customers anything to get them to sign on the dotted line to meet his sales quota. He knows the turnaround time for orders is close to two weeks, but he's been telling everybody you can get the shipment out in two days. Already this morning, you've had four angry calls from customers wondering why you're dragging your feet, and there's an e-mail from the sales manager asking about "problems with shipping."

You've talked to Chris, and he swears he told all his customers how long it would take to get their orders out. Like that really happened.

You've talked to your boss about it, but there's nothing she can do.

The thing that drives you crazy is wondering how Chris can keep getting away with—and getting praise for—such blatant bullshit.

Bullshit or just plain lying, Chris gets away with what he does simply because he makes money. In many companies, selling is the most important function. If Chris's numbers are good, management is less likely to question how, and at whose expense, they got to be that way. It's unfair, shortsighted, and just plain wrong, but there's not much you can do about it—except learn from it. For that reason, Chris's bullshit is as good a place as any to begin our discussion of how to stay sane in a world of corporate craziness.

First, there is absolutely no percentage in confronting Chris about the error of his ways in hopes that guilt will cause him to stop lying and become a good citizen. Chris probably doesn't believe he is doing anything wrong, since he's being praised by his boss for his impressive sales figures, and even if he does think he's wrong, he's never going to admit that to you. Also, by confronting Chris, you will have set up a situation in which he has to acknowledge wrongdoing in order to give you what you want, namely, a little more honesty with customers. This is a profoundly difficult negotiating position, as most people would rather kill you than admit they're wrong, not to mention the mayhem they'd do to keep from losing a commission or bonus.

Second, even though perhaps there should be, there is no one in your company whose job it is to make Chris tell the truth. If you go to your boss, his boss, or (God forbid) the CEO, you will get in more trouble for tattling than he will for lying.

SURVIVAL SOLUTION *1*
Wading Through Somebody Else's Bullshit

So, how do you deal with Chris's (or anybody else's) dishonesty yourself?

Know Your Goal. We have already established that you will not be able to make Chris stop slinging bullshit. A more realistic objective would be to minimize the damage his duplicity will do to you. Everything you do should be directed to that end.

Backfill, Even If You Didn't Dig the Hole. For the calls coming in today, all you can do is politely apologize for the misunderstanding and let your customer know when the order will actually arrive. You might be tempted to slightly underestimate the arrival date to make the customer feel better. Don't. If you must play fast and loose with the truth, as we all do, it is much better to overestimate and have the customer be pleasantly surprised when the shipment arrives ahead of time.

Look for the Pattern. Your best tool for minimizing future damage is the knowledge that most difficult behaviors follow predictable patterns. Chris will lie again. He may blindside you the first time, but the second time you should be ready for him.

Get Out of the Middle. Your most effective strategy will be to devise some way of getting yourself out of the uncomfortable place in between a liar and the person he lied to. You might do this by sending a courteous informational e-mail about the proposed shipping date to every customer as soon as the order arrives in your system. The e-mail should say that any questions can be referred to their salesperson, whose address and phone number you have been kind enough to supply. The more automatic this process appears, the better it will work. Also, you would do well to send the e-mail via an account to which the customer cannot reply.

SURVIVAL SCENARIO 2 Dog-Ate-My-Homework Liars

Joey, the schlemiel from marketing who got assigned to your project team, is supposed to be working on the PowerPoint for the presentation next week. He says it's almost done, but you have your doubts. He's choked in the clutch before.

All he needs to do is tell you in advance if he won't finish it in time, so you can do it yourself. You've done most of the work yourself anyway.

You keep asking how it's going, and he keeps saying, "No problemo!"

There is a problemo. Joey is the basic dog-ate-my-homework type of liar, who will say anything to avoid a confrontation. His transparent deceptions, hardly worthy of being called lies, are made up on the spot and seldom thought out in advance. Joey never does anything in advance. Like a ten-year-old, he doesn't stop to think that dissembling now will lead to a much bigger confrontation later on.

When later on comes, he will apologize for messing up and promise that it will never happen again. But it will, and you know it.

SURVIVAL SOLUTION 2

Forget the Dog; Get the Homework

Here are some ideas about how to keep low-skill liars like Joey from driving you crazy:

Recognize That the Problem Is Immaturity, Rather Than Deception. At some level, Joey *is* a ten-year-old. He lives in the moment, doing whatever comes easiest, and ignoring anything that is difficult. Like the parent of a ten-year-old, you may be tempted to tell him that he will always get into more trouble for lying than he would for not doing the PowerPoint. You did not believe this line when you were ten, and neither will he. Immature people have only a hazy conception of cause and effect and almost no ability to predict the future.

Just as with a real ten-year-old, grounding him—or any other form of punishment—will not work; it will only teach him that he is bad or that you are mean. This he already knows.

Never Ask Why. For more mature people, the punishment of choice is guilt induction. If you made an error in judgment, and someone questioned you about why you did what you did, the chagrin over admitting your own failing and the effect it had on others might influence you to be more careful in the future. *Chagrin* is not a word in Joey's vocabulary. If you question him about why he didn't get his work done, he will come up with a flimsy rationalization. He may say that it wasn't really his fault, because no one gave him the information he needed. This may pull you into an argument about who sent him what and when, but that won't get you the PowerPoint any more quickly, nor will it change Joey's view of events. He will not learn anything from your lectures or his own mistakes, except that he is a screwup, to which he readily admits, because it is easier than doing something about the problem.

An important thing to remember about Joey, and all the other difficult people at your office, is that they are difficult because they don't think in the same way you do. What works on you may not work on them.

Get Him to Show Rather Than Tell. Don't give Joey a chance to lie about whether the PowerPoint (or anything else) will be done. Demand that he show it to you, and let him make up a story about why it isn't done. This approach will minimize the damage by giving you more usable information, and enough time to do the job yourself if necessary.

If you want someone like Joey to do his homework, you will have to sit him down at the kitchen table and watch him, just as you would with a recalcitrant ten-year-old. At the office, you'll have to stop by frequently to see that he's doing his work rather than surfing the Net. It will probably be easier to do his work yourself, which is what he's counting on. If it is your misfortune to have to supervise someone like Joey, nothing will work like frequent spot checks.

If You Don't Have Control, Get It by Becoming a Jewish Mother. If a liar like Joey is your peer or even above you in the food chain, you will have to exert some informal power. Learn how to do this from an expert, my mother. Here are some of her secrets:

- **Induce guilt with food.** Schedule progress-review meetings to which you always bring something to nosh. A schlemiel like Joey, or even a momzer like the guy from IT who's never around when something needs fixing, would have a hard time eating your food and bringing nothing to show you.

- **Tell everybody.** Send e-mails on how the project is going and who is doing what as if they were reports on how your grandchildren are doing in school. The liar's section will be the shortest, with his pitiful excuses prominently featured—something like, "Poor Joey is working so hard, but the dog keeps eating his homework." Other people might call this damning with faint praise. My mother would say, "I'm just telling people what happened." Go with that.

- **Noodjie.** Just as Eskimos have a hundred words for *snow*, Yiddish has almost as many terms for *nagging*. *Noodjieing* is gentle but persistent. Keep bringing up what needs to be done, making it absolutely clear that the only way to get you to stop is to do it.

SURVIVAL SCENARIO *3* Pathological Liars

"Byron, Ed from GOCO called me mad as hell. He says he e-mailed you two weeks ago to cancel his order."

"I never got an e-mail."

"He says he's got a confirmation from you."

"No way. Somebody else must have sent it."

Chris's and Joey's lies are annoying, but Byron's do real damage. Chris may exaggerate and cover his tracks, but Byron blatantly alters reality in a way that benefits him and harms others. He promises customers things that he knows can't be delivered, and he delivers anyway when a cancellation might cut into his commission, hoping it will take too much time and trouble to send it back. He also lies about the hours he puts in, where he is during the day, his personal life, and just about everything else you can think of.

Pathological liars do not view communication in the same way that normal people do. For most of us, our words are a means of imparting more or less accurate information. For pathological liars, every word they say is simply a device for creating an effect. Liars like Byron try to convince you how cool they are by telling you that they party with rock stars or are dating the best-looking woman in the next department. They may play on your sympathy by confiding that they have been diagnosed with some dread disease or that they suffered unspeakable abuse as children. These days, almost all pathological liars "ran with gangs" as teenagers.

After a few such revelations, you begin to wonder, as well you should, if anything they say is true. Hold that thought, because that is one of the best ways to defend yourself.

It is tempting to ascribe pathological lying to low self-esteem, but that tells you nothing useful. Low self-esteem can "explain" most psychological disorders. Any concept that explains everything ends up having no meaning. With most difficult people, it is far more constructive to understand what they do and how they do it than it is to ask why.

The most important concept to remember about pathological liars is that, unlike you, they are not thinking in terms of truth or falsehood but about the momentary effect their words might have on you. Lie and truth are moral concepts that have a great deal of meaning to honest people, but they have far less relevance to liars. This dichotomy is what makes liars dangerous. If we dissemble, we feel guilt according to degree; a little lie that hurts no one is more acceptable than a big lie that hurts everyone. Pathological liars make no such distinction, so they feel no guilt.

If one thing a liar like Byron tells you is suspect, suspect everything. This advice does not apply to the dog-ate-my-homework type of liar we discussed in the previous section. They do what is easiest and seldom exert enough effort to make up believable excuses.

SURVIVAL SOLUTION *3*
He Lies Only When His Lips Are Moving

Here are some ideas about how to protect yourself from pathological liars:

Trust Your Gut. Usually, the first inclination you have that someone is lying is the feeling that something is wrong. Pay attention to that feeling, as it usually arises from preconscious analysis of what a person is saying. If at some level you are wondering whether a story is true, it probably isn't.

People who are telling the truth are usually congruent in what they are saying, how they are saying it, and what their body is doing as they talk. When people are lying, often one of the parts doesn't quite fit. They may smile as they're telling you a sad story, or scowl as they protest their love.

Many liars are adept at controlling their faces. Most of us believe that someone who is lying can't look you in the eye. This belief is flat-out untrue. Liars are often very good at holding your gaze without even blinking. Too much eye contact is a better cue than none.

Facial cues are less useful in picking out lies than are movements in the rest of the body. As liars talk, they tend to make unusual movements with their hands and, especially, with their feet. No one cue is a sure indicator that someone is lying. Intuition usually beats conscious analysis in spotting deception.

One more thing to remember: liars are usually very good at figuring out what you want to hear. If something sounds too good to be true, it is.

Pay Close Attention to Details. Liars are more likely to focus on big events rather than small details, especially if they are cutting their story out of whole cloth. Often, especially in the retelling, they will slip up on issues of who, what, where, and when. This is why police interrogations focus on asking for the same details over and over. If you ever have to interrogate a liar, take a tip from the cops. Let your questions cover the same ground a couple of times. Let inconsistencies be a warning.

If Possible, Ignore Rather Than Confront. Almost everything pathological liars say is untrue, but most of it is unimportant. If you set yourself the task of catching these liars in their lies, your work will never be done. Being caught in one lie will have no effect on them, so why waste your breath? Remember, pathological liars do not think in terms of truth and falsehood. Focus on lies with potential to do damage, and ignore the rest, regardless of how outrageous they seem.

If You Go After a Liar, Use Firsthand Evidence. If a pathological liar is doing harm, tell someone who can do something about it. This is more effective if you never accuse the person of lying. Encourage the person in charge to check the facts and let them speak for themselves. In Byron's case, you might give the appropriate manager a list of lost customers and suggest that he or she call them to find out why they are no longer doing business with the firm.

SURVIVAL SCENARIO 4 People Who Lie to Themselves

Janelle is never wrong, and she never makes mistakes. She always follows directions explicitly, so if you didn't want it done that way, why didn't you tell her? Janelle doesn't get angry either, unless you criticize her unfairly or forget to praise her for all the hard work she does.

Actually, a lot of Janelle's hard work has to be done over, because she doesn't pay close attention. Even though she is the weakest member of the team, she still rates herself as excellent and believes she should be paid as much as her boss, because she works longer hours.

Janelle is in denial, but don't try to tell her that, because she'll deny it.

To deal with her effectively, you need to understand how denial works. For you, denial is probably like wishful thinking. You may try to convince yourself that three weeks of fast food and skipping workouts won't really affect your weight all that much, but when it does, the pretense evaporates. Janelle will think there is something wrong with the scale.

Denial, for people like Janelle, consists of dividing her self-awareness into two parts: what she approves of, and what isn't there. No amount of evidence will convince Janelle that she and all her actions are anything less than wonderful. Usually, this splitting of awareness is learned fairly early in families in which appearance is more important than substance, and the consequences of looking bad are literally unthinkable. Once learned, denial is very resistant to change.

Though Janelle's denial may be caused by low self-esteem, it manifests itself as unrealistically high self-esteem. There is a cultural element here as well. At least some of Janelle's perceptual distortion is the product of the late-twentieth-century notion that most psychological problems and social inequalities can be cured by raising self-esteem. This also raises an interesting question: Is Janelle the unhappy victim of this societal misconception, or are you?

The research in this area is equivocal. In most studies, shallow people who pay little attention to their own motivation turn out to be happier and more psychologically healthy than people who are more internally focused.

As a therapist who spends considerable time helping people unravel their internal tangles, I have some misgivings about these results. Most were achieved by self-report measures. As you might imagine, people who are in denial are more likely to *say* they are happy, regardless of what they actually feel. That fact, however, raises the inconvenient question of whether there is a difference between really being happy and merely believing that you are happy.

I bring this issue up for two reasons. First, since you are reading a book aimed at self-improvement, you do not use denial as your major defense. Second, I'm sorry to report that there are more of them than there are of you, so you'd better learn how to interact with the Barbies, Kens, and Janelles of this world before they drive you crazy.

SURVIVAL SOLUTION 4
How to Avoid Denying Denial

Here are some suggestions for dealing effectively with the Janelles in your life:

First, Realize That Unconscious Is Unconscious. Janelle is not pretending. She really cannot see the parts of herself that she considers negative, regardless of how apparent they are to everyone else. Do not waste your time trying to expand her awareness. Put your effort into changing her actions rather than her view of herself.

If You Must Point Out a Mistake, Devise a Face-Saving Excuse. Your first goal with a person like Janelle is to get her to listen. If you start off being critical, she will close her ears. Begin by acknowledging her view of herself, no matter how unrealistic. Say, "Janelle, I can see how a conscientious person like you might have interpreted this differently, but . . ." The fact that the excuse is totally transparent does not matter. People who use denial are not big on internal consistency.

Before anything can change, you will need to get Janelle's attention. You will never get it by telling her she is wrong. Approach mistakes by saying she was right but could be even righter.

Never Ask Why. Her explanations will only give you a headache.

Convey Information in Unambiguous Written Form. Regardless of whether you have supervisory responsibility over someone like Janelle or not, you should clearly specify exactly what you need from her and when you need it. Never do this verbally, because her mind will automatically change your instructions to conform to whatever she is already doing. If you are explaining something to her, don't rely on her to take notes; provide them for her. If you send her information in an e-mail, always get acknowledgment in writing. If you don't, she will say you never sent it. Her computer automatically deletes things she doesn't want to read.

Evaluate by the Numbers. If you have to manage someone like Janelle, you will need to adhere slavishly to a written system of goals and objectives. Try to avoid subtle evaluative terms such as *excellent*, *good*, *fair*, and *needs improvement*. If you use them, she will argue that her performance is always excellent. Anchor any ratings to the number of goals accomplished on time, and keep editorial comments to a minimum.

SURVIVAL SCENARIO 5   High-Power Bullshit

What is it with Dave, the VP of your division, and motivational speakers? He calls a meeting to improve communications, but instead of discussing any real issues, he plays a video of some hyperactive guy in an expensive suit who seems to be saying that, contrary to the laws of physics, you can simultaneously work faster, improve quality, increase production, and lower cost. All it takes is the right motivation and knowing where they put your cheese.

According to Dave, everything is fine all the time, and if you don't think so, you're just not motivated enough.

Though what Dave and his motivational speaker are suggesting isn't really true, it isn't exactly a lie either, nor is it really bullshit. It is more like the expression of a religious belief.

I don't usually make a habit of questioning other people's religions, but in the case of motivation, I'll make an exception. Nowhere do business and psychology diverge further than in their understanding of this elusive concept.

In many corner offices, motivation is not merely positive thinking; it is the magical force that turns good into great without anyone's having to specify details. It is the spark of desire that can be fanned into flames of performance by listening to a retired athlete shout about how he won the big game by having faith in himself, even though he was a sickly kid who almost died of starvation, and everybody told him he'd never amount to anything.

The magic of motivation must constantly be stimulated by slogans that end with exclamation points and be inspired by photographs of flying eagles and racing sailboats, emblazoned with one-word statements of key elements of Western philosophy that believers hang on their walls in lieu of art.

Motivation, to members of its cult, is a powerful force yet so fragile that it must be guarded from any doubt by carefully hiding negative, de-motivating information about the company in piles of positive rhetoric while at the same time withholding positive information about an individual's day-to-day performance lest he or she forget that one can always do better.

To a psychologist, motivation is not located in the soul; it comes from outside, in the form of rewards and punishments. The problem with the spiritual notion of motivation espoused by many businesses is that it leads management to divert more resources toward inspirational speakers, slogans, and posters that have, at best, a temporary effect on performance and to ignore the day-to-day rewards and punishments that actually determine behavior in the long run.

SURVIVAL SOLUTION *5*

Religious Sensitivity

Deal with the cult of motivation as you would with anyone's religion—carefully and conspicuously. Here are some suggestions:

Watch Your Language. Try to sound motivated, especially when you have your doubts. Never say that anything is wrong or bad, only that with a little effort, what is good now can be made great. Always present ideas in terms of the positive goal you would like to achieve, never as a remedy to a problem. Motivated people don't see problems, only good things that can be made better.

Show Respect. Clap enthusiastically for motivational speakers, and never, ever roll your eyes.

Cultivate Patience. Your suffering may be rewarded in heaven.

SURVIVAL SCENARIO *6* **Bearers of Bad Tidings**

Becky from HR says her friend in purchasing told her she overheard one of the engineers on your team saying you didn't have a clue about how to run a project. He's been bad-mouthing you all over the building. She has no idea why he's doing it, but he is. She solemnly swears she is telling the truth.

Before you start wondering which engineer Becky is talking about, stop and think: Why is she telling me this? Actually, you should ask yourself this question about everything you hear or read at work. Some messages are merely attempts to convey information, but most have other purposes as well. Most of us pay more attention to the content of messages—*what* people are saying—than we do to the context—who is saying what, how they are saying it, and why. Throughout this book, we will be doing contextual analyses of comments people make as a way of gaining useful information about their intentions.

Let's start with Becky. Is she a friend who is trying to help you or a gossip who delights in being the first to deliver the bad news? Just thinking about what she has done in the past should yield valuable information about what she is telling you now.

People who share negative comments about you are usually not doing so out of the goodness of their hearts. Often, they're trying to mess with your head or attributing their own opinions to other people. Sometimes they're trying to turn you into a guided missile to attack someone they don't like.

Becky's rather vague and indirect approach suggests that at the very least, she is more interested in stirring things up than calming them down. People who are trying to be constructive usually encourage direct communication rather than bearing tales.

Another clue that Becky is not being totally up front is that, in general, only liars swear they're telling the truth. Honest people expect to be believed. It never crosses their minds that someone would think they were lying.

Paying attention to the context of Becky's message should alert you that she is not trying to help. Even if you are unsure of her exact intention, or of how much truth there is in what she is saying, you should be careful about how you respond.

SURVIVAL SOLUTION 6
Consider the Source, Not the Message

Say, "Thank You for Sharing." Don't show too much interest in the gory details that Becky is aching to tell you. Remember, she is probably messing with your head. Any response you give, especially something negative about any of the people involved, will be the next piece of bad news she will spread.

Resist the Urge to Investigate. In other chapters we will consider the discussion of rumors and gossip. For now, consider the fact that by investigating a rumor about yourself, you are also spreading it and giving it more power. Stay calm, and be alert. If there is any truth in what Becky is saying, you will hear similar stories from other people.

SURVIVAL SCENARIO 7 Sleaze

Kyle, your boss's boss, puts a hand on your shoulder and leans close to your ear. "You make us look good on this project, and there could be some big things in store for you. I can't say who told me, but I just thought you'd like to know."

As mentioned previously, the two questions you must always ask yourself when anybody says anything to you at work are: *What did he actually say?* and *Why is he telling me this?*

Before you get too excited about big things in store, dissect what Kyle actually said. That's right, nothing. But it is the particular kind of nothing that is the hallmark of sleazes everywhere. Though it has no substance, it sounds like a promise. It is not a lie—sleazy bosses are usually too smart for that—but it is still deceptive. If you believe there is some sort of guarantee in what he said, the problem is yours, not his.

Sleazy bosses know when you are hoping for a raise, a promotion, or simply some acknowledgment of your efforts, and they will use that knowledge to exert subtle control. They also know that they can get far more out of you more times by making vague almost-promises than by actually giving you what you want.

SURVIVAL SOLUTION 7
Don't Let the Sleaze Stick to You

Don't Believe It Unless It's in Writing. There is always value in pleasing your boss, or anyone above you on the organizational chart, but remember one of the first rules of business: unless there is a specific contract, there is no way of knowing what you will get for what you do. In this case, there isn't much information about what those big things are or what you'd have to do to "make us look good." Are you being asked to downplay anything that would make the company look bad? Vague comments may have dark undertones.

Do What You Would Do Anyway. Just do your best on the project, as you were intending to do all along. Unless your boss is willing to be specific with you about what you need to do to get a particular reward, be careful about believing that any promises were made. Just give him a thumbs-up and go on about your business.

SURVIVAL SCENARIO 8   The Dark Side

They don't call Elaine, the CFO, "Ice Queen" for nothing. The temperature drops at least ten degrees as she steps into your cubicle.

"Your figures are way off," she says. "Run them again. Now."

The figures are accurate but not very heartening. You've run them six ways to Sunday, and you're dead certain. There is no way short of cooking the books that can make the numbers more favorable. Elaine also knows that the figures are accurate. Is she suggesting that you change them, without actually saying anything incriminating?

If you respond to a vaguely threatening suggestion like this, the Ice Queen will own your soul.

Think back on all the corporate scandals you've read about over the last few years. It is in ambiguous conversations like this that they all began.

Facts, especially in the financial area, are facts. Always let your work show that they are. Never let anyone else persuade you to alter numbers. This is a real moral issue worth losing your job over. If you make even a tiny change now, the Ice Queen's demands will never end.

The only real question is how to say no to the Ice Queen.

SURVIVAL SOLUTION *8*
Fighting the Forces of Darkness

If you are in a situation in which you believe that someone is pressuring you to do something immoral or illegal, here is what I recommend:

Play Dumb. Do exactly as the Ice Queen asks—no more, no less. Run the figures again, and tell her you got the same result. If she wants something besides deniability, make her ask for it.

Don't Keep Secrets. When you are confronted with a moral dilemma, always share it with someone you trust. Your own moral compass may be influenced by the magnetic pull of the Ice Queen's demands. A close friend, preferably one outside the company, can help you keep your bearings.

I am not suggesting that you inform on the Ice Queen or that you talk about her with coworkers or managers. You have nothing but easily denied speculations. If you make them public without an airtight case, she will know, and she will eat you alive.

Be Smart. Don't merely accept purportedly new numbers or any other new information you may be offered; check everything thoroughly. Ask how numbers were calculated and where new information came from. Ignore implied threats or promises. Take strength in knowing that if you refuse to alter anything, she can do you far less damage in the long run than if you comply. Also remember that no matter how hard she makes it for you, it's easier than being indicted.

Don't Be Afraid to Say No. If she gives you a direct order that is unethical, tell her no directly. If she orders you to alter the figures, say you're sorry but you are unwilling to do that. This will take courage, because she may fire you on the spot. If she can get away with that, you are probably better off being gone, because it is likely that the rest of the management team supports her clandestine maneuvers. If her illegal activities come to light, it will be people at your level who take the blame and take the fall.

Before You Go Further, Call an Attorney. If you are thinking of informing, contact an attorney. If you are considering blowing the whistle on the Ice Queen, you will need sound legal advice. Find an expert before you say anything to anyone in the company.

SURVIVAL SCENARIO *9*	To Protect Yourself from Liars, You Have to Think Like One

Chris, Byron, and Elaine the Ice Queen are all first-rate prevaricators. You can't lie your way out of a wet paper bag, and even if you did, your conscience would bother you, you could never keep your story straight, and you're sure you'd get caught. Sometimes you wonder how they manage to pull it off so easily.

Experienced liars know how to lie effectively, and you should also. Not that I'm suggesting that you would use their techniques to deceive people, only that you should recognize their strategies to keep from being deceived yourself and to limit the damage their deceptions do to you.

These techniques might also come in handy if someday you consider running for office.

SURVIVAL SOLUTION *9*

How to Lie

The most dangerous liars are, in a word, calculating. They think carefully about what they are doing. They assess the gains versus the risks and tailor their lies to the goals they are trying to accomplish. Here's how they go about it. Follow these directions and you too can lie like a pro:

Know Your Goal. Sometimes liars want to be believed, and sometimes it doesn't matter to them whether you believe or not; they just want to avoid being caught in a lie.

If you want people to believe you, all you need to do is tell them what they want to hear or expect to hear. To do this, liars assume that everyone operates as they do, totally in their own self-interest. More often than not, they are right. If there is the tiniest scrap of larceny in anyone's heart, liars will find it and use it to their advantage.

Assess the Situation. Liars know that certain situations are ripe for deception because it will be almost impossible to get caught. Unlike you, liars often do not care whether you know that they are lying; they just want to make sure you can't prove it. In the following situations, it is relatively easy to get away with lying:

- ◆ When it's your word against someone else's
- ◆ When there is no clear way to check up
- ◆ When someone else is lying or trying to cover something up

Choose Your Words Carefully. Politicians in government and business are particularly adept at answering questions deceptively without telling out-and-out lies. Here are some of their favorite techniques:

- ◆ Exaggerate. If you're good enough, you can turn a grain of truth into a whole waterfront development.
- ◆ Avoid answering questions by changing the subject.
- ◆ Leave out important details.

- Answer a totally different question from the one that was asked. You can say that there are no layoff plans on your desk if they actually are on the credenza.
- Obfuscate. If you say enough words fast enough, the details can miraculously disappear.
- Imply that it is treasonous to even ask such a question.

Groom Your Victims. Everybody who exploits other people knows that you start slowly and work your way up. Sexual abusers start with just a touch, physical abusers with a few sharp words. Liars know if you let their small deceptions go by now, they can get away with whoppers later.

Use Your Imagination. The most effective liars use the same techniques as fiction writers: they make up stories and then work out all the details and implications. If liars are to be accepted, their lies have to fit into the context of a believable narrative. Once liars have created a story, they stick to it by accepting the basic premises themselves and telling it as if it were true. They also need good memories.

Draw a Mental Curtain Around Your Actions. People who consciously choose to do things that they know are wrong deal with their consciences by compartmentalizing. They focus on one event at a time and pretend that it exists in total isolation just this one time and that it has no relation to anything or anyone else in their lives. Liars are also masters at persuading themselves that the end justifies the means.

Repeat Lies as Often as Possible. The more often people hear something, the more likely they are to believe it.

If You're Caught, Change the Subject. Even the most skilled liars sometimes get caught. When they do, they use all sorts of techniques to distract the people who catch them. Here are some favorites:

- Get angry.
- Never, ever admit to a lie. Call it something else, such as poor judgment. Whatever you do, stick to your story.

- Give your reasons as if they justify your actions. Caught liars often claim that they lied because they were afraid to tell the truth or they didn't want to hurt someone's feelings.
- Accuse your accuser.
- Claim executive privilege.

This is how liars do it. If you don't have the stomach to use these techniques, better adhere to the truth.

SURVIVAL SCENARIO *10* Getting the Straight Story

After reading this section, you feel surer of something you already suspected: business is full of lies and bullshit. Sometimes you wonder if you can trust anyone to give you the straight story—to just come out and tell you what he or she really wants or thinks or what is really going on.

Actually, people give you the straight story more often than not. To hear it, first and foremost, you have to expand your definition of the straight story beyond the truth, the whole truth, and nothing but the truth. As I hope you've learned by now, in business—and just about everywhere el.se, for that matter—the unvarnished truth is a rare commodity indeed. Sometimes, however, the varnish itself can give you most of the information you need. To make sense of it, you have to listen very carefully.

Listening carefully means more than hearing the words another person is saying. The process is more like trying to understand a poem. It involves interacting with the material, asking yourself why people are expressing themselves in a particular way. Of all the things they could be saying, why this and why now? Therapists call this listening with the third ear. Straight answers don't necessarily come from questioning other people. The most important questions are the ones you ask yourself.

Of course, if you are asking yourself the questions, the answers must come from you also. This is just as well, because other people may not be admitting their thoughts and intentions to themselves, much less to you. If nobody is admitting anything, how do you know that the answers you're coming up with are correct?

To have faith in your interpretations, you need to realize that everybody's view of every situation is biased. All of us distort our perceptions of reality to fit with our hopes, fears, and expectations. Most of our interpersonal difficulties arise from these distortions. To figure out whose distortions are whose, look for repetitions. When someone keeps getting into the same difficulties with different people, there is apt to be a distortion involved. This is as true of you as it is of them. If you keep seeing the same thing from one person after another, the problem may be your perception rather than their actions. The more honest you are with yourself, the more likely you are to interpret other people accurately.

SURVIVAL SOLUTION *10*
How to Listen

Listening means more than hearing; it includes asking yourself probing questions about what you hear. Here are some questions that will help you figure out the straight story:

Why Is She Telling Me This? We have encountered this question before, but it is so important it bears repeating. What is the other person's purpose in saying anything to you at all? In the world of psychology, everything has a purpose. Is she trying to persuade you? Does she want you to do something or feel something? What is it she wants you to know, and why does she want you to know it? People seldom talk without a purpose, even if they are just trying to be friendly or to pass the time. When you talk with people, especially people with whom you have problems, always ask yourself about the purpose behind the words.

Does This Person Want Something from Me or Want to Give Me Something? This question presents another way to get at the purpose of the conversation. Sometimes, paying attention to the content alone will give you an incorrect answer.

Asking for something may really be a gift. When an intelligent person asks for your advice, make no mistake: you are being complimented. If people ask you to do something, it usually means they think you are competent enough to get it done. When people tell you a secret, it is usually a sign of trust. Many people feel starved for praise because they don't recognize a compliment when they hear one. Often, the biggest compliments lie in the requests others make of you.

Giving may not be what it seems either. People may try to flatter you into doing something for them or owing them something. People who are trying to deceive you usually fill their conversations with gifts. They give you compliments; they defer to your opinion and generally treat you like you are the most interesting person in the world, because they think this will help them get what they want from you. Undeserved gifts often have strings attached. People who are too nice, especially when you don't know them very well, may well have a hidden agenda.

As I mentioned in a previous scenario, liars are more likely to swear they are telling the truth. People who aren't trying to deceive you just expect to be believed.

If You Have Strong Feelings, Where Are They Coming From? Strong feelings, either positive or negative, should alert you that something is going on below the surface of a conversation. Try not to act on those feelings until you know their source.

If you listen carefully with your third ear, you may be surprised at how often people actually tell you the straight story. For more ideas on how to listen and what to listen for, read the next section.

Part 2

Understanding Craziness

PEOPLE ACT CRAZY when they are paying more attention to their own irrational thoughts and feelings than they are to objective reality. If you understand this phenomenon, you can deal with them from their point of view rather than your own. This will make you more effective and less likely to be driven crazy yourself.

SURVIVAL SCENARIO 11   Why People Do Stupid and Annoying Things

Kinesha is bright and articulate and has good ideas, but she turned down a promotion because in the new job she would have to make presentations in front of large groups. To Kinesha, that is a fate worse than death.

Roger's management philosophy is: If people are doing a good job, leave them alone; if they mess up, ream 'em a new one. Everyone lives in fear of being summoned to Roger's office, because it's never for a pat on the back.

Why are the people you work with so messed up? Why do they act irrationally? Can't they see that they're only creating more problems for themselves and everybody else?

To understand why these people do what they do, think of human motivation as a pile of thoughts, feelings, fears, and desires. You've probably noticed that people often say one thing and do another. This occurs because they are aware only of the conscious intentions at the top of the pile, even though the driving force for most of their actions bubbles up from the depths. To be effective with difficult people, you have to understand what is motivating them even when they don't. Especially then.

SURVIVAL SOLUTION *11*
Know What Moves People Even When They Don't

The way motivations stack up has direct bearing on everything people say and do. To protect yourself from crazy-making behavior, you have to know where it's coming from and how it operates:

Recognize Instinctive Patterns. At the bottom of the pile of motivations are the instincts that are hardwired into the oldest parts of the brain. Like other animals, we are programmed to protect ourselves from danger by either fighting back or running away. We also share instincts for dominance, territoriality, and sexuality, all of which ensure individual and species survival, but not necessarily success in the modern world.

Instincts are located well below the verbal parts of our brains, yet they speak to us in a language of hormones and neurotransmitters that is hard to ignore.

Kinesha, operating based on her internal programming for fear, and Roger, whose lower brain centers are telling him to be dominant, are not consciously aware of the messages their instincts are sending, but they are still receiving them loud and clear and are acting on them. Instincts typically have most power when they operate outside awareness.

Instincts that involve interacting with other people, such as fighting, dominance, and the dance of courtship, typically follow rigid patterns that are, at an unconscious level at least, recognizable to everyone involved. Patterned behavior in one person automatically brings out patterned behavior in others. If you pay conscious attention to instinctive behavior patterns, you can choose whether or not to participate in them. If you do not consciously recognize the patterns, your lower brain centers will make your choices for you.

See Through Perceptual Filters. Because our worlds, external and internal, are too complex to be experienced whole, we must sort out what is relevant and what to ignore at the neurological level. Socialization trains our brains to filter reality through the sieve of what we have learned. We see what we expect to see, sometimes regardless of what is actually there. Through socialization, our emotional responses are shaped to maintain our beliefs, and vice versa.

Often, the filtering process simply supports what our instincts tell us. To Kinesha, an audience is every bit as dangerous as a hungry tiger. Roger hardly gives a thought to what his subordinates feel when he is chewing them out. It's not his problem; they're prey.

Even if our beliefs filter instinctual messages out of our awareness, this doesn't stop us from acting on them; it only stops us from knowing that we are doing so.

Recognize Their Habits—and Yours. In order to carry out complex tasks, we learn to link behavior sequences. Once actions are hooked together, we no longer have to pay attention to each individual link in the chain. Do you remember how difficult it was to learn to drive when you had to think about everything at the same time?

Habits are essential, but they can cause problems if there is a faulty link in the chain. You know what I mean if you have ever had to change your golf swing or tennis stroke. To fix a weak link, you have to take apart the whole chain and rebuild it, all the while experiencing tremendous internal pressure to go back to doing things the way you've always done them. Building a new habit takes courage and persistence; they say it takes a thousand repetitions to change your golf swing.

Habits, like all other behaviors, are shaped by rewards and punishments. Most bad habits have immediate rewards and long-term punishments. Our wiring ensures that the most immediate consequence has the greatest effect on our choices. What we think of as delay of gratification is really a shift to gratification derived from telling ourselves what good people we are for delaying gratification. The basis for real self-control is this grueling struggle to move from external to internal rewards.

Sometimes Bad Habits Yield More Reinforcement Than Good Ones. Most of us fly on autopilot most of the time. This is fine when the air is smooth. When we encounter turbulence, we need to switch off the autopilot and place our hands firmly on the controls. Unfortunately, our habits often tell us to keep doing the same things and hope for different results.

Make Conscious Choices. Evolution has given us the ability to think, and with it the ability to override all the lower levels of motivation. This situation creates internal conflicts between what we feel like doing and what we know we ought to do. Struggling with these conflicts is what makes us grow.

What we ought to do, especially in business, depends on the result we wish to achieve. Which brings us to the reason for this little discourse on human motivation: when people do crazy things, we are likely to choose our responses based on what is happening to us rather than on what is happening with them, even though the latter is always more effective. The secret to staying sane in a dysfunctional workplace is to make rational choices about your own thoughts and actions even when the people around you are not making rational choices about theirs.

SURVIVAL SCENARIO *12* Awareness

Having just read in Scenario 11 about the sources of human motivation, you suddenly recognize what is going on with some of the people you work with. You want to help Kinesha by explaining that her fear is totally irrational and can be conquered by approaching it rather than running away. Maybe you think someone ought to tell Roger that his anger is really just instinct bubbling up like lava from his reptile brain.

You'd think that telling these people what you can see about their behavior that they can't see would help them to understand themselves, but I can guarantee that it won't. It will only hurt their feelings or make them angry at you. Here's why:

In the preceding scenario, we saw that people's psyches are built of layer upon layer of sometimes conflicting motivations that range from primordial instincts to the highest levels of human thought. Please understand that this is the view from the outside.

From inside, the experience is quite different. Imagine a dark tower full of intricate machinery, with awareness as a flashlight whose beam can illuminate only a tiny part of the complex whole at any one time. To the person whose mind is the tower, whatever is in the beam of awareness seems like all that's there. Usually, the flashlight is pointed unwaveringly at the conscious choices at the very top of the pile. People may have a vague sense that there are other disturbing or conflicting sources of motivation in the darkness below, but they prefer not to shine the light into the depths, for fear of seeing something that is inconsistent with their view of themselves as sane and moral people. If you try to point a flashlight in that direction, they will try to knock it out of your hand.

People want to believe that they are consistent from top to bottom, even though no one actually is. We all have internal conflicts and base motivations that we would rather not see. When other people, even therapists, point them out, we react as if they were trying to do us bodily harm. This pattern is what being defensive is all about.

SURVIVAL SOLUTION *12*
Think like a Psychologist, but Don't Talk like One

Nobody likes being analyzed by an amateur shrink. Follow these suggestions to keep from being attacked by people who are defending their incomplete but comfortable view of themselves:

Never Diagnose! Any statement that begins with "You are" not followed by "wonderful" will be taken as an attack. Use psychological terms with the same restraint you would show with four-letter words, because the reaction will be exactly the same. Making an issue of people's issues is, at the very least, equivalent to accusing them of being less sane than you are. At worst, you may hurt or enrage them.

Approach People from Their Point of View, Not Yours. This is the rule real therapists follow. Use your understanding of people's internal dynamics to speak to them in a way that is consistent with their view of themselves. This is the only way to get them to listen.

Do the Unexpected. Recognize patterns, but do not participate in them. Most interpersonal difficulties are dances that cannot continue if one person purposely stays out of step. The rest of this book is a series of lessons in declining dances that will drive you crazy.

SURVIVAL SCENARIO *13* Autopilot

You've done it again, even though you promised yourself you wouldn't. What was it this time? You said yes when you should have said no?

You blurted out more than you wanted to say when you were angry? Or maybe you put off saying something you needed to say until it was almost too late. Maybe it was all of the above. Inside, you're beating yourself up, because you know better. You hope that next time it will be different, but you fear that you will keep making the same mistakes over and over.

Though I'd like you to believe that you have just read a spectacular demonstration of mind reading, I must demur. Thirty-five years of doing therapy has taught me that we all have this kind of internal conversation and that even after a sound self-scolding, we usually do go out and make the same mistakes again. The problem is not stupidity or moral turpitude; it is faulty programming in the autopilot we use to fly through our lives.

We do not think about most of what we do; we just do it. By the time we are adults, we have developed a fully programmed autopilot that consists of habitual ways of perceiving and acting that either came in the box with our brains or that we have learned from experience. Most of the time, an autopilot is an asset, especially for doing familiar, repetitious tasks. We could not drive a car without a mental template that keeps us from having to reinvent the wheel every time we get behind it.

The problem with autopilot programming is that in emotional situations, it usually makes poor choices. The higher the level of arousal, the more likely we are to revert to the oldest, best-learned responses. In stressful situations, unless we do a manual override, we tend to act like children, or even like creatures lower down the phylogenetic scale. Throughout this book, you can see the effects of faulty programming in other people. Now it's time to think critically about how your own autopilot handles stressful situations. The rule of thumb that will keep you from making the same mistakes over and over is simple: Never go with your most immediate response in an emotional situation. This rule applies everywhere but is absolutely essential at work.

How to Override Your Autopilot

Many of our ideas about how to deal with emotional situations came preloaded in our brains or were learned in childhood. They may have helped our ancestors to survive in the primordial jungle, or kept us from being devoured in our families of origin, but today at work, they are likely to get in the way or get us in trouble unless we are able to shift to newer, more adult behavior patterns. To accomplish this shift, we have to know how to switch off our autopilot before we crash and burn. Here's what to do:

Recognize Emotional Situations by Your Level of Arousal. If you are to avoid your most immediate response in emotional situations, you have to know when you're in one. The most reliable cue is physiological arousal. If your heart is perceptibly thumping, or your muscles are tight, you can be sure that something is setting off an alarm. Before you speak or act, you need to know what it is. Another reliable cue is repetitious thinking. If you keep running the same thoughts over in your mind, you know your emotions are trying to tell you what to do. The more they repeat themselves, the more likely you are to obey them.

Another cue of emotional arousal is blanking out. If you know that a situation is important, but you find yourself unable to think about it, that means your autopilot has done a disconnect. Don't allow yourself to shift to some mindless activity, such as snacking, watching TV, surfing the Net, or playing computer solitaire. Tuning out does not relieve stress; it only delays it. If you can't think, do something active to bring down your arousal level, and keep trying to reboot.

Slow Down. Most autopilot programs are designed to reduce our level of arousal as quickly as possible by escape or by transferring it to someone else. Unless a tiger is approaching, your most immediate response is most likely to be wrong. There is always time to stop and think, especially when you think there isn't. Before you decide what to do next, take a few deep breaths, walk around the block to burn off the excess adrenaline, or talk things over with a coolheaded friend.

Make Sure Your Goal Is Realistic. The beginning of any effective response is knowing what you want to happen and that it actually would improve the situation. Once you've slowed down, ask yourself what your goal is. If the answer is something like, "I want to kill this SOB," or "I need to escape," or "I just want to feel better," ask again. Keep asking until you come up with a goal that is possible, is reasonable, and does more than merely get you out of difficult circumstances.

Beware of Habitual Traps. Certain autopilot programs have a way of overriding the override by convincing you that your emotional response is indeed the correct one. Your autopilot can be very persuasive, especially if it is injecting you with performance-enhancing drugs as it talks to you. Watch out for these patterns of thinking, because even as they're steering you wrong, they feel so right:

- ◆ **Blame.** Figuring out whose fault it is encourages punishing the perpetrator rather than fixing the problem. When you allow yourself to become a victim in your own mind, that is all you can ever be.

- ◆ **Anger.** Anger tells you to fight for the sake of fighting rather than for a goal. If you have a goal, fighting is not usually the best way to achieve it. Most forms of anger are at their root an irrational refusal to accept reality. Life is not fair: people don't behave as they should, incompetent managers can tell you what to do, and the road is full of idiots who don't know how to drive. Deal with it, or if you are going to fight, pick a battle you can win.

- ◆ **Avoidance.** Your autopilot will tell you to stay away from what you're afraid of or what you don't want to do. Don't comply. People grow by mastering what is personally difficult or frightening. If you run from these situations, your fears will grow big enough to take over your life. Success at anything depends on the ability to make yourself do what needs to be done, whether you want to or not. Regardless of what your autopilot may tell you, there is no easy way.

- **Being Overly Nice.** Your autopilot may try to convince you that if you are undemanding and do everything people ask, you will avoid conflicts, and your generosity will be reciprocated. It never works out that way. If you don't ask for what you want, you won't get it, and if you don't say no, they will keep piling on the work. Eventually, resentment will poison your relationships and create much bigger conflicts than the ones you were trying to avoid.

- **Perfectionism.** Perfectionism is a vice that masquerades as a virtue. Nothing destroys perspective quicker than obsessive concern about the one detail that is out of place, and nothing is more effective in alienating the people you are trying to inspire.

I will discuss each of these habitual traps later and offer more detailed suggestions about how to avoid them. For now, wake up. Recognize that in difficult situations, your autopilot may give you faulty information. Switch it off and think manually before you run into something.

SURVIVAL SCENARIO *14* Fear and Avoidance

Your boss is a micromanager who questions you incessantly about the smallest details. Half the folks on your team seem to have advanced degrees in procrastination, and you yourself, even though you disagree with some of the ideas advanced at staff meetings, tend to sit quietly, letting other people do the talking.

Despite their diversity, all these annoying and self-defeating behaviors have one thing in common: they are motivated by fear. Your boss, your coworkers, and you may not feel afraid, but fear is still the driving force behind your choices. Fear is an insidious force because it can control our actions even when we don't feel it. Our most self-destructive habits tend to develop as a means of avoiding things we're afraid of.

Fear exists to get us moving. Our brains are programmed to protect us from physical dangers by giving us the energy to fight back or run away. Our adrenal glands inject us with performance-enhancing drugs, our hearts rev up, our minds shift into overdrive, and our muscles throb and tingle, ready for action. If we don't actually fight or run, the fight-or-flight response can be quite unpleasant. This is why we run away not only from what we fear but also from fear itself. We learn to avoid anything close to what we're afraid of. This generalization of the fear response served our ancestors well by keeping them far from dark jungles where tigers might lurk. For us, the tendency to avoid the things we fear is not nearly so helpful.

Most of the dangers we face at work are psychological rather than physical. The same avoidance mechanism that keeps us away from predators is activated by the threats to the ego, such as conflict, criticism, or embarrassment. We tend to stay far enough away from psychological threats that we do not experience the fear at all. As we approach such threats, we begin to feel uneasy, so we invent good reasons to turn around and go in the other direction. The avoidance becomes a habit. All of us have areas in our lives where we do not venture. We may not consciously know why, but we just don't go there.

SURVIVAL SOLUTION *14*
Look Fear in the Face

There are two equally important aspects to overcoming fear and avoidance. The first has to do with other people, and the second has to do with you.

Recognize Fear in Other People. The most annoying things people do are usually a means of avoiding what they fear. If you focus on your annoyance rather than their fear, you will frighten them more and make a bad situation worse. If you reassure them that your actions will not put them closer to danger, you may make the situation better.

Accept Fear as a Part of Life. If you don't take appropriate action, unconfronted fears can rule your life. Look closely at your own choices for evidence of avoidance. If you find it, turn around and face the music. Safety is often an illusion—and an expensive one at that.

Whatever you're doing, if it doesn't scare you occasionally, you're probably not doing it right.

SURVIVAL SCENARIO 15   At the Crossroads of Fear and Boredom

Sarah is the brightest person in the bookkeeping department. She knows more about accounting than her boss, who is a CPA, but she has gone about as far as she can go in this company without an advanced degree. She knows she would like bigger challenges, but bigger challenges mean bigger risks. Sarah may not realize it, but she's standing at the crossroads that will determine the rest of her life.

Take this scenario as a secular sermon, advice on how to make career choices from someone who has seen many people pick the right road—or the wrong one.

At any given moment, we all stand at a crossroads. One fork leads toward being scared, and the other toward being bored. The choice is existential, so there is no middle road.

SURVIVAL SOLUTION *15*

Scary or Boring: Which to Choose?

For Sarah, the scary path involves steps such as going back to school for that CPA or looking for another job. Boring is a whole lot easier road; all she has to do is stay where she is and keep doing what she's doing.

The problem is that it only seems like she's staying in one place. In real life, nothing stands still; we are going in either one direction or another, growing or shrinking.

Don't Shrink Yourself. We shrink when we let our fears dictate what we choose not to do. If we don't extend ourselves, we head down the road to boredom and, eventually, depression.

OK, so Sarah is not the adventurous type. Besides that, she is a single mom and needs her job. She can't afford school and doesn't have the time to look for other work. She can come up with lots of excellent reasons to stay where she is. She's right, too. Unfortunately, being right does nothing to mitigate the effects of the choices she makes.

Your Mind: Use It or Lose It. Sarah's mind is like a Ferrari; if all she uses it for is to drive back and forth to the grocery store, carbon begins to build up in the cylinders, the engine gets sluggish, and eventually that Ferrari begins to perform more like an '85 Yugo.

Even if Sarah isn't able to accept the obvious challenge of going back to school or looking for a new job, she needs to find a way to get her mind out on the road and open it up and see what it can do. The only way Sarah, or any of us, can accomplish that is by doing what is difficult or frightening. If we don't find those challenges in our job, we need to look for them elsewhere. Hobbies, relationships, travel, classes, museums, churches, synagogues, and mosques—the world is full of opportunities for growth. That tingle of fear when we try something new is the sign we are growing.

Think of your own job and the rest of your life as well. You, like Sarah, are standing at a crossroads. Scary or boring: which do you choose?

SURVIVAL SCENARIO 16 Anger

Roger, the hot-tempered sales manager introduced in Scenario 11, glares at you across the table.

"Is there a problem, Roger?" you ask, knowing that there is.

"No," he says, rather more loudly than necessary. "Unless you consider almost losing the RBS account because of someone's stupidity a problem."

You can't believe your ears! He's accusing you of something one of his guys did, right here in front of God and everybody, not to mention the whole management team! Your vision darkens, your spine turns to ice, and you can hardly draw enough breath to gasp out, "It's not my fault!"

Stop! Even though you're bursting with the urge to explain yourself, keep quiet for a minute and think about what is going on.

You have been attacked, but it's your ego, not your body. Your emotions are screeching, "Fight back or run away!" Either response will make the situation worse.

Anger, like fear, is programmed into the oldest layers of the brain. Fortunately, the newer parts of the brain, the ones that think, can override the default settings.

Instincts follow well-worn paths in the brain. Each step leads automatically and mindlessly to the next. Either fighting back or—unless you actually leave the scene—running away, no matter how well disguised, will reinforce the pattern and increase the anger. By doing the unexpected, you break the ancient rhythm of anger, forcing you and your attacker to use newer brain centers to figure out what's going on and how to solve the problem.

SURVIVAL SOLUTION *16*
Defusing Anger

Anger becomes far less dangerous when people are thinking rather than merely reacting. Here's how to take control:

Ask for Time. Instincts are quick and dirty. All you may have to do to disrupt them is slow down. If someone is attacking you, say, "Please give me a minute to think about this." Roger will not get angrier at you for seeming to take what he says seriously. Delay may also subtly encourage him to do a little thinking of his own, which clearly couldn't hurt.

Know Your Goal. The most important thing to think about in the few seconds you've bought for yourself is what you want to happen. Remember, you can achieve only one goal. It is impossible to simultaneously calm someone down, get him back, and convince him that the whole thing is not really your fault. If you send mixed messages, only the most aggressive will register, so choose carefully.

In most cases, the goal you want to achieve is calming the other person down enough to have a rational discussion. Which leads to the next piece of advice.

Never Try to Reason with a Person Who Is Yelling. Yelling and thinking cannot occur at the same time. If an angry person is yelling, you need to get him or her to stop before you can go any further. Getting people to stop yelling is actually easier than you might think. Simply waiting or keeping your own voice soft may do the trick.

Don't Explain. Explanations are usually a disguised form of fighting back or running away. The typical explanation boils down to either a play for dominance ("If you know all the facts, you will see that I am right and you are wrong.") or a blatant attempt to run away ("It wasn't my fault; you should be mad at somebody else."). This may not be what you mean, but it doesn't matter. Whether you recognize the provocative aspect of your explanations or not, Roger certainly will.

Ask, "What Would You Like Me to Do?" This simple, unexpected question is the most useful tool you will ever find for dealing with anger. There are three distinct reasons why this is so.

First, to answer this question, Roger will have to stop and think, which is precisely what you want him to do. When he does, he may realize that all he really wants is an argument that he can win with bluff and bluster. If you shift the focus of the discussion to what needs to be done to solve the problem rather than whose fault it was in the first place, there is much less to argue about.

The second reason is more subtle. In any argument, the person who asks questions has the upper hand. If you ask and Roger answers, you have control of the conversation.

The third reason is even more subtle and devious. It is also the way to win.

Your instincts tell you that the way to beat Roger is to knock him down and kick him. This does not play well in a business setting. At work, the person who stays coolest is usually perceived as the winner of an argument. If you keep your head while Roger is acting pissed off, he will kick himself, so you won't have to.

SURVIVAL SCENARIO *17* Not-So-Subtle Competition

Your boss takes credit for your successes and blames you for her mistakes. You try to be a team player and go along, but when it was time to fill that new position, she promoted someone whose only qualifications were sucking up and playing politics. To make matters worse, you discovered that a guy with less responsibility makes more money than you do. Doesn't she realize she's talking teamwork while blatantly playing favorites?

Throughout the world of business, people say one thing and do another. Nowhere is this more evident than when they talk about teamwork. Everyone believes teamwork is a good idea, but when it comes down to making day-to-day choices, it may not be good enough. In general, people do what they believe will yield the greatest rewards fastest. When rewards are scarce, people automatically compete for them. Business is about competition, and unless the contingencies are carefully arranged to promote teamwork over internal competition, people will vie with one another for scarce rewards such as money and recognition. Never mind that if everybody works together, there will be more of everything to go around. If that happens, it will be sometime in the future. People are more motivated by what is going on now.

Teamwork takes time, effort, and tremendous commitment from the top down. Competition comes naturally and immediately. Wherever you work, unless management is very enlightened, people will be competing with you for scarce resources. Regardless of what people say, and whether you like it or not, you are playing the game.

SURVIVAL SOLUTION *17*
If You're Going to Play, Know How to Win

To win, you don't necessarily have to take advantage of others. You do have to convince them that it is in their best interest to cooperate with you. Here's how:

Know Your Goal. You've seen this advice before in other survival solutions, and you will see it again. The first rule for staying sane is to know what you want to happen, and let your goal determine your actions. The goals must be achievable. If you play well, you may be able to win raises, promotions, recognition of your efforts, and influence over decisions. You will not be able to convince other people to be team players by simply being one yourself.

Know Other People's Goals. The essence of successful competition is getting people to believe that the best way to get what they want is to give you what you want. To do that, you have to know what they want. You can make some general assumptions: People at your level and below, like the guys in the other department, want their jobs made easier. People above you, such as your boss and the CEO, want information they can use to make themselves look good.

Sometimes, people will do things because they are right or because the rules say they should, but all in all, self-interest is a much more reliable motivator. When you want cooperation, think carefully about what you have to offer in return. Always let people know up front what's in it for them.

Learn from Winners. Pay close attention to what successful people do, rather than judging their actions. What did the political suck-up who got your promotion do that you aren't doing? How about that coworker who makes more than you?

Schmooze Upward. In most places, information is the coin of the realm. You won't learn much of value sitting in your cube or gossiping with your buddies in the break room. Never miss an opportunity to chat informally with people above you. You never know what you might learn about them, or what they might learn about you.

Play Your Cards Close to Your Vest. Information is valuable. Get as much as you can, but be choosy about what you give out. You may be tempted to avoid uncertainty by saying, "I'll show you my hand if you show me yours." Bad strategy. The guy who shows last has a definite advantage.

If people need information or cooperation from you, wait to see what they offer for it. Nice, helpful people seldom win at poker.

Be Proactive. Whatever your goal, whether it's the successful completion of a project or the advancement of your career, think carefully about whose help you need and about who might be in competition for the same rewards. When you can, nip their urge to compete with you in the bud.

One of the best ways to do this is to send out e-mail "press releases" about what you're doing that are full of praise for people who might want to steal your credit. Make it sound like it's about them, but make sure your name is at the top.

SURVIVAL SCENARIO 18 Corporate Bullies

Roger, whose exploits led off this section, spots his victim at the other end of the hallway. His eyes narrow; his smile is cold and sharp, merely an excuse for baring his teeth.

"Kevin, I've been looking for you. What the f— were you thinking?" With that, Roger launches into one of his famous public reamings.

The other people in the hall back away, all wishing they were somewhere else and wondering, "What if it happened to me?"

Sadistic bosses get an almost sexual pleasure from pushing their employees around. It's not just the vociferous reprimands in front of other people; it's also all the unreasonable demands, the last-minute changes in schedule, the calls at home and on vacation, the general attitude that you have to do whatever they say whenever they say it—or else.

What can you do if you report to one of these corporate bullies? Obviously, the first and best answer is to look for another job. If this is not an option, then you're left with trying to make the best of a bad situation. Remember that in dealing with a bully, the most important battle you have to fight is in your own head, not the office hallway. The power that bullies have is in the emotion they elicit in you. The less you fear them, the less control they have over you. This is easy to say; it's harder to do, but not as hard as you may think.

SURVIVAL SOLUTION *18*
How to Handle a Bullying Boss

To deal effectively with a tyrant, your head has to win out over your anger and fear. Your emotion is the ultimate source of your boss's dark power. Here are some moves to consider:

Ask Yourself, "Why Am I Still Here?" No one deserves to be treated like chattel. To keep your sanity when you work for a bully, you need to look into your own heart to find the reason you stay, and that reason is what you need to hold on to. If it's for money or power, or because it's a necessary step in your career, go for it. In the dark times, that's what you will need to remind yourself. If the only reason you're staying is that you're afraid to look for another job, it's time to go. Your own fear will do you more damage than any bully ever could.

Be Realistic. Don't expect your boss to change in response to anything you or anyone else might say or do, and don't believe for a moment that if you somehow read his or her mind and do everything correctly, the criticism will come to an end. The criticism is the source of a bullying boss's power. It is an end in itself. Instead of hoping for a miracle, observe carefully and anticipate attacks. Don't be disappointed—be prepared.

Don't Wave a Red Flag in Front of a Bull. When someone in authority is unreasonable, we all have the tendency to display the very behaviors that get under his or her skin. (Of course, we never do these things on purpose.) For example, if your boss is a punctuality nut, coming in two or three minutes late or taking a longer lunch may be temporarily satisfying, but it will leave your boss with a score to settle with you. Follow the rules, no matter how arbitrary.

Become Indispensable. If at all possible, develop competence in an area in which your boss lacks expertise. This knowledge base will make you more valuable and may give you some latitude for bargaining.

Transcend Temper. Most tyrannical bosses delight in criticizing their employees in front of others. When this happens to you need to endure it quietly with dignity. Maintain eye contact, and resist the temptation to explain. Your best strategy lies in listening to what the boss has to say, asking what he or she wants you to do, and getting out of the situation as quickly as possible. Many office tyrants say that they want employees who will stand up to them. I have never known any who would tolerate it, especially in front of an audience.

Keep Your Ducks in a Row. Know what is going on in your department, and be ready at a moment's notice to recite facts and figures. Tyrants love to get their information by cross-examining their employees, rather than by listening to presentations. Be ready at any time to give information when subjected to the third degree.

Warn Your Family. Let your family know that your boss may ask you to do things at inconvenient times, such as the middle of the night or two days into your vacation. Make sure you share your mixed feelings, and your reasons for staying. Resist the trickle-down temptation to treat your family members the way your boss treats you. Likewise, resist the temptation to make your boss into the family villain and to come home every day ranting about the awful deeds perpetrated on you. This will only make you feel worse, and there will be subtle pressure from home for you to stand up to the asshole.

Avoid the Temptation to Gripe. There is nothing more tempting than getting together with fellow employees and talking about atrocities. This feels therapeutic while it's happening, but it makes the situation harder to live with in the long run. Psychological research shows clearly that the more you talk about how bad you feel, the worse you feel.

Keep Records. When you are told to do something, make sure that what you are asked to do is clear. Log conversations and directives. You may need to refer to them later.

Be Able to Assess Your Own Performance. Office tyrants are quick to blame and slow to praise. To keep your own sanity, you have to be able to know how well you are doing without being told. Pay close attention to your goals and objectives and how well you are meeting them. This is partly a way to defend yourself, but it also is a way to convince yourself that you are doing a good job, even if you are unappreciated.

Demand Top Dollar. Many tyrants are willing to pay for the privilege of pushing their employees around. If you are going to stand up and stand firm in any area, that area should be salary. Make a coherent case, and don't be afraid to "push." This is one facet in which your boss is likely to be reasonable.

Forget Justice. The most dangerous strategy I can imagine is going over your boss's head hoping that his or her boss will side with you. Often, tyrannical bosses do quite well with the bottom line, and their bosses tend to allow them quite a bit of leeway. If you do attempt to attack from above, realize that it is a kill-or-be-killed situation. Do not imagine for a minute that the union, a government agency, or a lawyer will be able to bring your boss to justice. It does happen occasionally, but your case will have to be just about strong enough to put your boss behind bars, or at least get him or her fired.

Finally, if after reading these suggestions you find yourself coming up with reasons that they won't apply in your situation, maybe today is the day you should turn in your resignation.

SURVIVAL SCENARIO *19* Bullies Who Are Only Trying to Help

Rita is the soul of political correctness. She never misses a chance to assist people in their moral development by explaining how offensive and insensitive they are. Whatever you think, do, or eat, Rita can tell you what's wrong with it. She says she's only trying to help, but whenever you talk to her, you go away feeling as if you've been beaten up.

She reminds you of your mother.

Some bullies never raise their voices. They can even be friendly and generous, but be careful. There are always strings attached. Their style of bullying—helpfully pointing out the error of your ways— arises from an unconscious competition with you and everyone else to establish who is the most virtuous person on the planet. They get to feel superior by making you feel inferior. If you get sucked into the competition, you will lose, because there is only one rule, and they made it up: You're wrong.

Helpful bullies get the information they need by encouraging you to tell them all about yourself, especially your problems. If you are lured in by their concern, you will soon discover that your problems are actually caused by the inadequate way you run your life. If you then get angry, it only shows how unreasonable you are. If you accuse them of being manipulative, it will be like putting a knife into their heart, and you will never hear the end of it. The only difference between helpful bullies and pit bulls is that pit bulls eventually let go.

SURVIVAL SOLUTION *19*
How to Avoid Being Helped to Death

What you need to remember about helpful bullies is that they can only work with material you give them. Proceed carefully in each and every conversation. For example:

Be Vague. Like any bully, the power these helpful people have over you is in the emotions they elicit. The way they get to your emotions is by asking about the details of your life. If you don't give them any information, they can't hurt you. They might chide you for having trust issues, but that's about the worst they can do.

Being vague may sound simple, but you will find that it is trickier than you think. Helpful bullies are experts at getting you to share your negative feelings without your even noticing until it's too late.

Never Confide Secrets. In the world of helpful bullies, there are no secrets. Be warned. If you are in therapy or are on medication, never tell them. This advice comes from countless experiences my clients have reported over the years. A surprising number of these experiences end with the statement, "Well, you're the one who's taking antidepressants," implying that their opinions have no validity because they are mentally ill.

Don't Give Out Information About Other People Either. The people you talk about will not be pleased when helpful bullies tell them what they heard. The main reason to avoid such discussions, however, is that getting you to gossip about other people is a surefire way to get at your negative feelings.

Think Twice About Accepting Favors. Whatever helpful bullies do for you will cost you more than you ever dreamed. Debts once incurred can never be repaid.

Don't Even Think of Criticizing Them. They have never done anything improper, ever. The angrier you get at their denial, the calmer and more rational they will become, showing all the world that you are the one with the problem.

Don't Think That Being Really Nice Will Make Them Be Nicer to You. Helpful bullies believe that their helpfulness in pointing out your foibles is the very essence of being nice.

SURVIVAL SCENARIO *20* Being Passive-Aggressive Means You Never Have to Say You're Sorry

Janelle, who was introduced in Scenario 4, makes more mistakes than anyone on your team, but she never admits to them. Somehow, it's always someone else's problem.

If you ask her to do something she doesn't want to do (you can tell she doesn't want to do it by the snorting, which she says is from sinus problems, or the eye rolling, which according to her is the result of staring at a computer screen all day), she agrees and then either forgets, misunderstands and goes ahead with whatever she wanted to do in the first place, or does absolutely nothing, because she is sure you gave her the wrong instructions. If you say something to her, she will be offended and explain how it's your fault for not being clear. She may even cry, because you're picking on her.

Janelle gets you every time. You think, "I should have known better." Then the headache starts, and you know she gave it to you just as surely as if she'd hit you upside the head with a two-by-four.

Passive-aggressive people are among the most tedious in the world to work with. They never seem to get angry themselves, but they have no trouble getting other people angry at them. Unjustly.

SURVIVAL SOLUTION *20*

How to Keep Passive-Aggressive Coworkers from Giving You a Headache

How can you work with people like Janelle, who live their lives blithely unaware of their own motivation?

First, You Need to Know She Isn't Lying. If you did the same thing that Janelle did, you'd have to lie to bring it off. She doesn't. The fact that she's angry at you and is fighting back with obstinate behavior may be apparent to everyone else on Earth, but it is indiscernible to her. Totally unconscious, she has divided herself into what is all sweetness and light and what isn't there. Nothing you can say will change that. Forget any attempt to make her admit what she's doing. It will only make her cry and give you a pounding headache.

Be Aware of Your Effect on Her. The more passive-aggressive people like, respect, or fear you, the less inclined they are to say directly, "I'm angry," or, "I don't want to do that." Instead, they have to rely on misunderstanding or forgetting to do the job for them.

Don't Rely on Instruction, Lecture, or Castigation. Clear, explicit directions, while absolutely necessary when dealing with passive-aggressive people, will not work as well as you think they ought. Chewing them out will not work either. It will just give them more reason to fear you or get back at you.

Praise the Hell out of Her. What will work is piling on the praise. Most passive-aggressive people feel underappreciated. They need more praise for doing things right than most other people. Figure on providing at least twice the amount that you yourself would need (four times more if you pride yourself on your toughness or emotional security).

Pay Attention Now or Pay More Later. The best approach of all is talking on a regular basis. Ask what *other* workers might be upset about. Janelle will be only too happy to tell you what she feels disguised as someone else's opinion. If she has a chance to voice concerns, however indirectly, she will have less need to act out.

Passive-aggressive people cause more trouble than they need to. Their dynamics are simple, and they respond well to praise and attention. The problem is that you can get so angry at what they do that you may not be able to think straight about what is most effective. If you try to get back at them, you will only create more trouble for yourself.

SURVIVAL SCENARIO *21* Politically Incorrect

You know Zack well enough to chat in the break room now and then. He seemed nice, until the day he made a derogatory comment about a coworker's race.

The silence was deafening, save for the clunk of your jaw hitting the floor.

When you pick it up, what do you say?

What do you do when a coworker says something offensive—a slur about race or religion, or perhaps an inappropriate sexual innuendo? Bear in mind that what you do in this situation will have both public and private implications. For example, if you are too heavy-handed, the jerk will perceive you as having a stick up your butt and tell everyone. Then again, if you are bothered by the remark and you don't say anything or, worse yet, you just smile politely, what will you think of yourself?

This situation calls for tact with your coworker and clarity in your own mind.

SURVIVAL SOLUTION *21*
What to Say to an Insensitive Creep

What you say depends on a number of factors: how you feel, what you want to happen, and the culture of your company. Think carefully before you speak.

Decide Whether to Say Anything at All. How big a deal is this? Your answer to this question should depend on how important the issue is to you, as opposed to how difficult it might be to speak out. If you don't make sacrifices for your principles, then you don't have any.

Whether and how you respond to the person should also depend upon what you think it is possible to achieve. There's little point in telling a Klansman that the correct term is *African American*.

As in Any Delicate Situation, Know Your Goal. Do you want to make Zack more sensitive, or do you want to punish him for his insensitivity? You should also ask yourself if you are speaking up because he made you personally uncomfortable, or because his comments might be offensive to someone somewhere. Whatever your answers, your goal should determine your actions. Bear in mind that you are always most effective when speaking for yourself.

If You Want to Educate, Say What You Feel, Not What You Think. You may think that Zack is being blatantly racist, but telling him that will accomplish nothing beyond making your name synonymous with political correctness to Zack's homies around the watercooler

If you make a judgmental comment, he'll either deny it or wave his insensitivity in your face like a Confederate flag in front of a bull, enjoying your irritation. Either way, he'll learn nothing.

If instead you were to say something like, "Zack, when you made that comment just now, I was really uncomfortable. Was that your intention?" He has to stop and think about what he's done and the effect it has on you. He can't deny your feelings.

An insensitive person will probably ask you why you were uncomfortable. If you answer, he will argue that your reason was invalid and that you shouldn't get upset at a joke. Respond instead with silence and your mother's best guilt-inducing look. Let him squirm.

For Repeat Offenders, Consider Going the More Formal Route. If Zack persists in making racist comments, it may be time to report him. Don't just threaten, because that will teach him that you don't mean what you say. Check with HR for the correct procedure. Your company should have a written policy. Follow it to the letter, reporting his exact comments and your statements to him. Just the facts, no interpretations.

Bear in mind that reporting Zack will probably make you unpopular with management, so you have to decide if you really want to do it. It may help to recruit others who have heard him. Under no circumstances should you speak for them or, worse still, say something like, "Other people are bothered as well but are unwilling to give their names." Attempting to add reinforcements in this way will merely weaken everyone's credibility.

SURVIVAL SCENARIO *22* That Depressed Coworker

Dina is in your office again, looking like she's lost her last friend.

"I just don't see the point in going on," she says, in her typical monotone.

"Come on, Dina," you say, a bit less enthusiastically than you'd hoped. "Don't think that way. You have a decent job, you have friends who care about you, and it's a beautiful day for a walk in the park. Why don't you take one at lunchtime?"

"I know I should get some exercise," Dina says. "It's just that when I walk in the park, I see lovers hand in hand, and I wonder what's wrong with me that I can't find a relationship. It's probably the way I look."

"That's ridiculous; you look fine."

"If you like fat."

You don't respond, and tears glisten in her eyes. You wonder how you can keep this conversation from dragging on for hours. "I'm really sorry, Dina," you say, "but I don't have time to talk now. I've got to get this report out before the eleven o'clock meeting."

"It's OK," Dina says. "I don't mean to be a burden."

If you've ever tried to make a depressed person feel better, you know firsthand how black holes suck energy out of the universe.

The biggest problem here is not Dina's love life, but your mixed feelings. Neither of you is saying what you actually feel. Your unavailability is not OK with Dina, and you're not particularly sorry you can't talk with her, even though you may think you should be. Dealing with a depressed person like Dina is confusing. One minute, you're irritated at her for being manipulative, and the next, you're beating yourself up for having uncharitable thoughts about someone who is obviously in pain. How do you avoid becoming her twenty-four-hour crisis service without being cold and rejecting?

SURVIVAL SOLUTION *22*
How to Keep from Being Sucked into Someone Else's Depression

Here are some ideas that may help:

Don't Be an Amateur Shrink. First and foremost, you cannot take responsibility for Dina's depression. Depressed people need support from friends, but they also need qualified treatment (not just medication). Your position should be that you are not qualified to treat psychological problems and that she should be seeing a therapist. If she isn't, that should be what you talk about. If she is in treatment, always ask, "What does your therapist say about this?" and support whatever that response is. You can bet that Dina's therapist is telling her that it's better to get up and take a walk than it is to sit around talking about how bad she feels. That's what you should encourage.

As a coworker, rather than as a junior therapist, you will still have to juggle Dina's demands for support, her manipulation, and your own mixed feelings. That combination is more than enough.

If you understand the situation in the way a real therapist would, you may be able to help Dina without hurting yourself.

Know How Depression Works. There are two basic dynamics concerning depression that you need to know. The first is that the more people talk about how bad they feel, the worse they feel. Relief from "getting it off their chests" is a myth. The last thing you want to do is reward them with attention for doing something that will make them feel worse.

The second is that depressed people want to wait until they feel better to do the things that will make them feel better. It is absolutely impossible to make them feel better for more than a few minutes by using words alone. It will only wear you out and create an unhealthy addiction in them. Focus all your energy on getting them to get up and do something, regardless of how they feel. That, ultimately, is the only way they are going to feel better.

Know the Difference Between Hang-up and Handicap. A real handicap, such as being in a wheelchair, physically prevents you from doing certain things. Accommodating a handicap by changing requirements or making physical alterations improves the disabled person's life.

A hang-up is the belief that you cannot do something when you actually can, but it would be uncomfortable. People with psychological problems like anxiety and depression often see these conditions as handicaps that need to be accommodated by avoiding the things they fear or not doing what they don't feel like doing. The problem is that accommodating hang-ups makes them worse.

Dina believes that her need to talk about her problems immediately and her unwillingness to take walks are handicaps that you should accommodate by being constantly available when she feels depressed. If you do accommodate her, it will make her depression worse. Both of you need to get out of this downward spiral as quickly as possible.

Give Only What She Asks for Directly. It's pretty clear that Dina is miffed that you won't abandon your need to get some work done and minister to her. Like most depressed people, she feels too unworthy to come out and ask for your time, so she does the opposite by offering to shuffle off into her personal hell so she won't be a burden to you. You, being a caring person, have a hard time allowing this, so you're tempted to stay, feeling manipulated all the while.

You are being manipulated, but you need to realize that manipulation is, by definition, unconscious. There is no first-person form of the verb *to manipulate*. Dina does not recognize what she is doing and will not, even if you point it out to her.

There is only one way to keep from being sucked into this neurotic morass: take her absolutely literally. Even if she is sending out strong hints that she needs help or attention, giving it to her without requiring her to ask rewards her for being indirect. If she seems to be hinting, ask her directly what she wants. If she says she doesn't want anything, take that literally, regardless of the contradictory nonverbal signals she is sending. What would be healthy for both of you is a relationship in which Dina asks for what she wants, and you are free to say yes or no. Sanity lies in playing by those rules yourself, even if you suspect she isn't. If you reward her for manipulating you with subtle signs of sadness, that is all you will ever see.

Be Clear About What You Feel, Want, and Are Willing to Do. If Dina is a close friend and you want to address what is going on between the two of you, you might say something like this:

"Dina, when you say you're a burden, I feel stuck. If I go back to my work, it's almost as if I'm admitting that you are a burden. If I stay and try to convince you that you're not a burden, then I have to cancel my own plans, and I get upset. I know that none of this is your intention, because you did tell me to go ahead. Still, I end up feeling like the kind of person who lets down a friend in need."

Dina has a face-saving out, and you get to leave without feeling selfish. Generally, and especially if Dina is not a close friend, it works better to skirt the issue altogether. Just tell her what you're willing to do, and let the guilt fall where it may.

Schedule Appointments. If you want to help Dina, you should do it on your own schedule, not hers. Tell her that you have ten minutes at two o'clock. It is much easier to end any conversation at the outset by specifying how much time is available.

If you have a coworker like Dina, it will help both of you to put limits on your availability for discussing emotional issues. I'm not suggesting that you avoid them but that you set specific times for the beginning and end of your talks about how she feels. The rest of the time, do something together, such as going for a walk in the park.

Other Psychological Problems in the Office

The word is out that you are a sensitive and caring person. People come to talk to you about their troubles.

Jane is afraid to speak up to anybody about anything; she's always worried, blowing little things all out of proportion. Even though Ben is bright and competent, his self-esteem is so low that he often needs a confidence transfusion. Judy is having problems with her marriage, and Jack is upset because he can't get his three-year-old to listen to reason. Madison is constantly agonizing about money. Steve has a drinking problem he's only occasionally aware of; in your cube, he admits that alcohol is a concern, but he seems to forget what he said as soon as the gang goes out after work. Then there's Carol, with all her medical ailments that her doctor can't seem to diagnose.

You don't mind talking with these people when you have time, but you sometimes wonder if you're saying the right thing.

SURVIVAL SOLUTION *23*
What to Say to People with Problems

OK, so you are an amateur shrink; you might as well be a good one. Here are some suggestions from a real therapist on how to deal with the psychological problems you might see in a typical business office:

Encourage Frightened People to Face Their Fears. Encourage Jane to speak up and ask for what she wants. Tell her you know she can do it. You might give suggestions about what to say, but do not agree to be her spokesperson. With worries, it's OK to listen once. When she starts repeating herself, though, it's time to change the subject. Don't try to solve her problems for her. Ask her, "What are you going to do about that?"

Don't Try to Raise Low Self-Esteem. When Ben talks about how incompetent he is, or how ugly, stupid, lazy, or whatever, never try to convince him otherwise, because you can't. He'll either discount you entirely or come to you every time he has doubts. Instead of administering confidence transfusions, you can respond, "It must be tough to feel that way." Or ask, "Do you have a plan for feeling better?" or the old standby, "What are you doing to do about it?"

With Relationship Problems, Don't Take Sides. Remember that when Judy talks about her husband, love is totally irrational. Listen, but avoid taking a stand. If you say something against Judy's husband, she may feel compelled to defend him. (This is almost always the case in abusive relationships.) If you're adept at it, you may be able to help her see situations from her husband's point of view. Though sometimes tempting, it's never helpful to get into a conversation about how all men or women are stupid, evil, irresponsible, or whatever. Stick to the situation at hand.

Don't tell her what to do unless she asks directly. It's always OK to say, "I just don't feel comfortable talking about your marital problems, because your husband is a friend of mine too."

With Kid Problems, Advice from a Veteran Sometimes Helps. Tell Jack that three-year-olds don't have the verbal skills to listen to reason. The biggest problem many rookie parents have with children is thinking they are little adults who are just being obstinate. If you are a more experienced parent, you can help by pointing out what is age-appropriate. If a book has been helpful to you in understanding developmental stages, share it.

Also, it helps to remember that other parents have just as hard a time saying no to their kids as you do to yours. Praise them for making an effort.

Don't Give Financial Advice or Lend Money. Listen and commiserate with Madison's money issues. You might tell her what you did in a similar situation, or refer her to a credit counselor. Never, ever lend money.

Take a Stand Against Substance Abuse. Steve's addictive behavior is more urgent. Friends do say, "I think you've had enough" and take away car keys. If Steve brings up his drinking problem, encourage him to get help, and keep encouraging. Realize also that denial is a part of all substance-abuse problems. The time to talk to Steve is when he's sober. If he's drunk, just try to protect him from himself.

Leave Medical Treatment to Doctors. If you're not a doctor, you don't have to listen to physical complaints. Just say that you're not qualified. If you do want to talk about Carol's medical issues, commiserate with her suffering, but don't side with her against her doctor, even if the practitioner sounds like a quack. Some people like to be a mystery to medical science. Don't diagnose or prescribe, and don't refer her to another doctor unless she asks.

If you are an amateur therapist, some of the approaches I've suggested might be hard to do at first, but if you try them, you'll find that it's much easier to handle other people's problems when you don't get enmeshed with them. When all is said and done, the very best help you can offer is to listen. And that's a very important thing indeed.

SURVIVAL SCENARIO 24 Blamers and Complainers

It started out as a really productive morning. You take a quick break to get some coffee. On the way, you meet Becky, who is fuming over yet another atrocity committed by Roger and Chris in the sales department. (You may recall these three folks from their introductions in Scenarios 6, 11, and 1, respectively, as well as Carol, from Scenario 23, who reappears in the following paragraph.) Do you know what they get to declare as expenses? She does, and it's obscene. There's no love lost between you and the guys in sales. As you listen, you feel yourself getting almost as angry as Becky is. This time, somebody has to do something!

As you pour your coffee, Carol wanders in with carpal tunnel braces on each hand. Apologetically, she holds her cup for you to fill. You were planning to e-mail her later this morning about the figures she was putting together for your report. Now, as she tells you far more than you ever wanted to know about her pain and numbness, you feel guilty about even mentioning the figures.

You shuffle back to your cube, somehow drained of the energy you had only a few minutes before.

Every company has its share of negative people—blamers like Becky, who are always mad about something somebody else did, and complainers like Carol, for whom there is always something wrong, usually enough to keep her from getting her work done. Negative people have a peculiar emotional power. They can stir us up and change the way we see people and events. They can get us to change the rules for them. They can suck us into their problems and leave us feeling drained and tired. All we have to do to get ourselves into this fix is keep listening, and the rest seems to happen automatically.

SURVIVAL SOLUTION *24*
How to Keep Negative People from Spoiling Your Day

When people tell us that something is wrong, we are conditioned to respond in a particular way. At the very least, we listen, and often we feel obligated to do something to help them. It is this automatic response that gives blamers and complainers their power. To protect yourself, you need to switch off your autopilot and step out of the expected pattern. Here are some suggestions:

For Blamers, Practice Creative Ignoring. Blamers delight in telling you about bad things other people are doing. They want you to agree and join in with them in whatever battle they are fighting at the moment. If you show the tiniest spark of irritation at their current enemy, they will be happy to fan it into flames of anger. If you agree even slightly, they will add your name to the list of the outraged when they harangue the next person.

There is no percentage in playing along. Instead, practice creative ignoring. Even if you're surrounded by a crowd of people who are screaming and yelling for someone's head, just sit there. This response is much more thoughtful than automatically doing what everyone else is doing.

Answer Bad with Good. Blamers count on you agreeing with them, even if all you're doing is silently listening. If you want them to stop without having to be rude about it, make use of one of their automatic responses. Every time they say something negative, answer with something positive. Even a very slight positive will work. If Becky complains about the guys in sales, you might say that they do seem to be moving product. Doing this a couple of times will usually be enough to send her looking for a more volatile audience.

For Complainers, Don't Change the Rules. Some people are never quite up to speed. They tell us how bad they feel and rely on the social convention of not demanding as much from sick people. This is reasonable if it happens rarely, but in Carol's case, it seems to happen every other week. She never asks directly to get out of anything, because then you'd have a choice. Instead, she just tells you how miserable she feels and lets your guilt do the rest.

Guilt notwithstanding, make her ask. Winston Churchill said, "Most of the world's work is done by people who don't feel very well."

Unless Carol says specifically that she can't do something, assume she can. If she needs accommodation, she needs to specify what it is and how long she needs it. Complainers know from experience that they usually get far more leniency using the automatic approach. That trick doesn't have to work on you.

Ask, "What Are You Going to Do About It?" Both blamers and complainers expect you to make their problem into your problem. Asking what they plan to do will often stop them dead in their tracks. Try it on negative people and you may be amazed at the results. If they respond, "I don't know," hoping that you'll take the cue, just shake your head and say, "I don't know either."

SURVIVAL SCENARIO 25   People Who Are Not as Smart as You Are

Why don't people listen? You tell them exactly what you need. You explain it clearly. You ask if they have any questions, but they never do. They say they understand, but they end up doing something else entirely. Why don't people pay attention? Don't they care about doing a good job?

They do care. The problem is—there is no way to put this delicately—they just aren't as smart as you are.

Often, smart people don't realize that they understand things that other people don't. They think that anyone can do what they do if the person just makes the effort. Somehow to intelligent people, it seems more acceptable to be conceited about how hard they work than about their natural talents.

Intelligence does make a difference. Even though the idea is politically incorrect, any psychologist will tell you that IQ scores are the best predictor of success in any given field with the possible exception of winning elective office.

Since you're reading this book, I assume you're pretty bright. As intelligence is distributed on a bell curve, if you are slightly above average, it means that at least 80 percent of the population is not as quick-witted as you are. Doubtless, a few of those people work at your office.

Most of your frustrations probably arise when you're trying to show others how to do something different from what they are already doing. On average, 20 percent will get it right the first time. Most will stumble along, missing some important details. A few will do absolutely nothing differently. When you ask them about what you just said, they will stare at you blankly and say, "Were you talking?" These results are not indications of a motivation problem; they are exactly what you'd expect with a group in which intelligence is normally distributed.

SURVIVAL SOLUTION *25*
Use Your Intelligence to Your Advantage

Only about 20 percent of the population can learn something new by just being told. The rest need more help to figure things out. Here's how to give it to them:

Be Smart; Don't Just Act Smart. People already know how bright you are, so there is no need to demonstrate further. There is an especially hot help desk in hell for techies who speak only in jargon and then snort and roll their eyes when normal people don't understand. If you really want people to listen to you, speak to them in their language, not yours.

Before You Start, Find Out Where They Are. There is no point in explaining something people already know. There is also considerable value in asking a few questions to find out what they know that isn't so. Listen carefully to their answers rather than composing yours.

Vary Your Techniques. Most of the advice in this solution is standard operating procedure for educators. They know that people process information differently. Some learn new material best by hearing, some by seeing, some by reading, and some by the feel of practice. You will have most success if you provide information through several different channels. Say it, put it on a screen, and give handouts for people to take away with them. If one strategy doesn't work, be ready to switch to another.

Know Precisely What You Are Trying to Teach. Think in terms of a branching program, with clear emphasis on what to do at choice points. Don't assume that because choices are obvious to you, they are obvious to others. Expertise is the ability to make finer and finer discriminations. Choice points are precisely where expertise, or lack of it, makes the biggest difference. A good rule to consider is that if there are more than three choices at a branch point, people have to consult you or some other expert.

At one sitting, most people can handle instruction about no more than two choice points with three branches each. If what you're trying to show them is more complex than this, break it down into separate teaching segments.

Teach Behavior, Not Attitude. Many business learning programs try to instill an appropriate attitude and assume that will lead to correct behaviors. There is no foundation for this assumption. Describe exactly what you want people to do, and tell them what's in it for them to do it your way. Don't worry about what they're thinking while they're doing it.

Don't Be Afraid to Be Redundant. Repeat yourself. Say the same thing over and over. Whatever the channel, people learn by repetition.

Demonstrate. Showing generally works better than telling. Both together work better still. The closer the demonstration is to what people will actually encounter, the more effective it will be.

Practice, Practice, Practice. Did I say redundancy was OK? Learning must involve both input and output. Give people the chance to actually do what you're trying to teach them. People often resist practicing something new in front of others. No one likes to be a beginner. The way most people signal their anxiety is with a surly statement, like "I've got it. Now can I go back to work?" If you get this sort of response, recognize the fear behind it, rather than your irritation. Be gentle, but don't let anyone get away without practicing.

Ask Questions. You never know what people are taking away with them until you ask. Practical questions about what to do in specific situations will clarify ambiguities and encourage problem-solving skills.

Check Back. Most people will forget about half of any new learning in about a week. They will also lose their handouts. If you really want average people to listen to you and use what you say, be prepared to go over everything again a week later.

Be Smart. If you present new material through several sensory channels, give people input, and allow them to learn by practicing and recalling, your results will be considerably better than the 20 percent success rate that comes with merely telling people what to do.

SURVIVAL SCENARIO *26* Slackers

Slackers! You know who they are: people who try to get by, doing as little as possible and then complaining about how overloaded they are. They tell you they're going to do something and never follow through.

When you go to ask them about it, they're either on break or out sick. Where is their work ethic? Somebody ought to throw their lazy butts right out the door.

Maybe someone will throw them out the door someday. Until then, you'll have to try to get some work out of them, at least on your projects. To do that, you'll have to understand some basic ideas about how people learn to work.

The work ethic that is so prized in our culture is created by a shift in reinforcement values. In adolescence, goofing off is a reward, and work is punishment; in adulthood, somehow the opposite becomes true—at least for some of us. This shift happens because of the contingencies that operate in our lives. As we grow up, work is rewarded with praise and acceptance, and goofing off is punished with bad grades, parental lectures, and the threat of eternal damnation. At some point, we come to believe that it's easier to do the work than to live in fear of punishment. It is the fear, not the punishment, that puts us on the road to being good corporate citizens.

Once we start working, the contingencies begin to internalize. We feel virtuous when we are working and fear hell when we goof off. Some of us take this to extremes and become workaholics. Working hard becomes a matter of morality, rather than mere rewards and punishments.

It is the confusion of work with virtue that makes us ineffective with people who do not hold the same beliefs about effort as we do. We get angry and want to punish them or to lecture them, thinking it was punishment and lectures, rather than the avoidance of punishment and lectures, that made us into the upstanding men and women we are today.

SURVIVAL SOLUTION *26*

How to Get Slackers off Their Lazy Butts

The reason that slackers are sitting on their butts is not that they are bad, but that they didn't grasp the contingencies of life the way you did. They didn't recognize that their actions had any effect on the rewards and punishments that came their way. If you want to get them up and working, that is the connection they need to learn. Here are some insights on how to teach them:

Remove Morality from the Equation. Your goal is not to make lazy slackers into better people; it is to make it more likely that they will do specific tasks correctly and in a timely way. Accept the fact that they want to get by with as little effort as possible, and use it to your advantage. To the best of your abilities, arrange contingencies so that it's harder to do the task wrong than it is to do it right. Requiring lots of paperwork when people make mistakes works well for this purpose.

Forget the Sermons. We did not learn our work ethic from parental lectures or pithy sayings. They served only to encapsulate a truth we had already learned through contingencies. As adults, we recall them warmly and repeat them to our children; as teenagers, we hated them.

What you are actually trying to do is shape slackers' behavior. To accomplish this, you will have to establish clearer contingencies than they usually experience. They don't have to understand the rules; they only have to conclude that it is easier to do what you want than to blow you off.

Give Clear Instructions. The first step is to make sure that slackers know precisely what you want from them—that is, exactly what it will take to get you out of their face.

Always Monitor. If getting you out of their face is to have any value, you have to be in their faces. Slackers need to know you will be checking up on what they do. If possible, do this in person rather than by e-mail. Slackers don't read their e-mails.

Ignore Surliness. If your program is having an effect, slackers will show you by being surly. They are trying to make you think that it will be easier to leave them alone than to make them work. Remember, you are shaping them. Don't let them shape you.

Use Rewards. Nothing shapes behavior like positive reinforcement. Unfortunately, it is a tool that is seldom used in most businesses. Use it. Whenever slackers do anything right or on time, thank them, and tell them they are doing a good job. They probably won't realize that you are trying to shape their behavior. They'll think you like them. Remember to reward even the smallest approximations of work ethic, such as showing up.

Use Punishment Carefully—or Not at All. Most slackers believe that they get punished not for what they do or don't do, but because people don't like them. There is no point in confirming this belief. Use punishment as a tool, not for revenge.

If the slacker doesn't report directly to you, you have few options for punishment anyway. Most slackers are already adept at ignoring criticism or at hiding from people who criticize them.

Don't Forget the Jewish Mother Strategy. In Scenario 2, featuring dog-ate-my-homework liars, I described my mother's secrets for getting people to do what they should. In addition to having thousands of years of tradition behind it, the Jewish Mother strategy has a sound psychological basis. Here's how to use it in dealing with slackers:

- **Induce guilt with food.** A few well-chosen and preferably highly caffeinated offerings of food or drink can serve many purposes at the same time. They are a form of positive reinforcement, they give energy, and they set up an unmistakable contingency: no work, no espresso.

+ **Tell everybody.** Make the progress of your project public in any way possible. Mention everybody's stellar efforts, except for those who aren't making stellar efforts.

+ **Noodjie.** Instead of punishing slackers when they mess up, nag them constantly. Remember, it is avoidance that has the power. If you are constantly reminding them of what they need to do, they may just do it to get rid of you. The best way to noodjie is by asking a lot of detailed questions.

Nobody wants to be a nag, because we all hate to be nagged. This means that nagging works! The technical name for it is *negative reinforcement*, a term that is mistakenly applied to punishment. Negative reinforcers are stimuli that are rewarding when they are turned off. If you don't believe me when I tell you how well they work, ask your mom. Chances are that her noodjieing, rather than your dad's lectures, was what developed that work ethic you're so proud of today.

SURVIVAL SCENARIO 27 Control Freaks

Gwen, your boss, is a control freak who tells everybody what to do and how to do it in excruciating detail. Nothing is too small to escape her attention. She corrects the grammar and spelling in your e-mails. She can't make up her mind; when she assigns you a project, she keeps changing the requirements. When anyone makes even a tiny mistake, she sends out a memo changing procedures for the entire department. The list goes on and on.

Why is Gwen so obsessed with control? Does she think she has the only brain on the planet? Why does she insist that everything be done her way even when you can show her that your way works just as well—or better? Why does she need to control everything all the time?

Before you get too worked up, stop and consider: Why *would* a person have such an overwhelming need to control? The answer to this question, and to many others that you might pose about obnoxious and crazy-making behaviors at work, is, simply, fear.

Frightened people devise frightening systems to keep them at a safe distance from whatever it is they're afraid of. What they do to protect themselves almost always causes more damage than the source of their fear.

As frightened managers like Gwen become more controlling, the performance of her team deteriorates. Worrying about Gwen's criticism makes people overly cautious, so they make more mistakes. Then there is always passive-aggressive retaliation from people who don't like being told what to do. Whatever the cause, the poorer performance increases Gwen's need for control, and performance deteriorates further.

SURVIVAL SOLUTION *27*
Controlling Control Freaks

The secret to dealing effectively with micromanaging control freaks like Gwen is to see their fear rather than your irritation. If you want them to be less controlling, you have to calm them down rather than making them more upset. Here are some ways to go about it:

Don't Call Them Control Freaks. Getting irritated and calling them control freaks, whether out loud or in the privacy of your mind, will make the situation worse. Controlling people pay attention to tiny details. They will see your irritation as clearly as if you'd posted it on a billboard outside their office window. Your attitude will serve as evidence that they should watch you even more closely.

Even if you bring it up in the kindest of ways possible, discussing the issue of control directly will backfire. Control freaks, even if they joke about it, never see themselves as *overly* controlling. They are only protecting an ungrateful world from the inevitable mistakes that result from not paying close enough attention. Forget trying to talk them out of it. Even seasoned therapists have trouble convincing the control-obsessed that his or her behavior might be causing more problems than it's solving.

Use Reassurance, Not Recrimination. Take time before you start a job to get a clear and concrete idea of *what* your micromanaging boss wants, *when* she wants it, and *how* she wants it done. Take copious notes. There are two reasons to do this.

The first is simple reassurance. If you look like you are taking her instructions seriously, she will worry less about you making mistakes. Control freaks love to lecture. When they do, listen carefully. Annoying as these lectures may be, they are inevitable. They are far less damaging at the beginning of a project than they will be later on if she thinks you made a mistake.

The second reason for listening closely to this initial lecture is to come away with clear specifications of the end product required. Every task has a product, which is whatever it is that needs to be done, as well as a process, the actual behaviors through which the end product is achieved. At the beginning, negotiate to deliver a highly specific, measurable product at a specific time. This will be crucial later on when Gwen tries to control the process.

Give Progress Reports Before She Asks for Them. Nothing allays a control freak's fears like excess information. Remind her that you are taking the project as seriously as she does.

If Your Boss Tries to Control the Process, Ask if This Means That the End Product Has Changed. The notes you took during that initial lecture will come in handy here. Treat attempts to control the process as requests to change the end product, which any businessperson would have to agree would reopen the whole negotiation. If the end product is not affected, why change the process? Needless to say, you must have some history of delivering the goods for a strategy like this to work.

Keep Up the Good Work. If you follow this procedure several times and actually do what you say you are going to do when you say you will do it, your boss will become less worried about your performance and may go off to micromanage somebody less responsible.

28 Narcissistic Assholes

Clifford, the CEO, is an asshole of the first order. It's not just that he's paid thirty times what you make, even though his incompetence has caused two huge rounds of layoffs. What you can't stomach is the way he treats the people who work for him—as if he's better than they are. If he passes you in the hall, stand aside, because if you don't, he'll run you over. When somebody else is talking, he interrupts or looks at his watch. He always shows up late for meetings, never having glanced at the agenda. It hardly matters, because he'll forget what people said anyway.

Clifford's office is decorated with pictures of him shaking hands with politicians and movie stars. If you aren't one of those, or on the board, he acts as if you don't exist—that is, unless he wants something from you. Then he's full of flattery and vague promises, but only until he gets what he's after. The rest of the time, you're lucky if he remembers your name.

You and your buds often wonder how such an insensitive asshole ever made it to CEO of a major corporation.

Actually, being an asshole sometimes *helps* people get to the top—but it also makes it hard for them to stay there.

Narcissism is the technical term for being an insensitive asshole. It's one of the easiest human traits to resent, but your resentment will only make you miserable, and narcissists won't be affected at all. They flout the rules you live by and get away with it. There's nothing you can do about that. If you try to engineer their comeuppance, they will squash you like a bug. They don't play fair, and guilt has absolutely no effect.

Colloquially, narcissism means loving yourself, but it's not so much self-love as total self-absorption. Narcissists always know what they want and are willing to do whatever it takes to get it, regardless of whom it hurts. It is as if they look at their own needs through the magnifying end of binoculars and at everyone else's needs through the end that makes everything tiny. Their self-absorption is their strength and their weakness. This single-minded focus often leads to high achievement, but at significant human cost.

What bothers people most about narcissists is their attitude of entitlement, the belief that their accomplishments place them above the rules. Unlike the rest of us, they don't wait, they don't take turns, they don't recycle, they don't stand in line, they don't clean up after themselves, and they don't let other people in ahead of them in traffic. They aren't the least bit ashamed of using the system or the people around them for their personal gain. Narcissists break the golden rule without so much as a thought. Does this make them evil, or oblivious? Your answer will determine how much damage they do to you.

If you see narcissists as evil and take their inconsideration personally, your resentment may render you completely ineffective in dealing with them. Never lose sight that unless they want something, narcissists are not thinking of you at all. They may be masters of the world and captains of industry, but when it comes to empathy, they are infants. Like babies, they are at the center of their own universe; the rest of the world exists only to meet their needs.

SURVIVAL SOLUTION *28*
How to Keep Narcissists from Getting You Down

Management everywhere is rife with narcissists. Since there is no place you can go to escape from them, you'd best learn to protect yourself. Here are some ideas:

First, Suck Up. There is no way around this. If you want to communicate effectively with narcissists, you have to admire them, their achievements, and their toys as much as they do. Typically, this won't require any great effort. They'll be more than happy to come up with reasons to congratulate themselves. All you have to do is listen and look interested.

If not sucking up is a matter of principle with you, you will have to live with the consequences, namely being invisible to most of the people who can help your career along. The choice is yours. Should you wish to learn this valuable business skill, there will be pointers throughout the rest of this book.

Know What You Want for Yourself as Clearly as They Know What They Want for Themselves. Narcissists always know what they want, and they're always trying to figure out how to get it. If your own needs are unclear to you, or you stand back and wait for them to give you what you deserve, you'll never get anything.

Make Them Pay Up Front. Never extend credit to, or accept promises from, a narcissist. As soon as they get what they want, they will be on to the next thing, forgetting whatever they said they would do for you. Sometimes they make promises they don't intend to keep, but just as often, they merely forget. Either way, you should keep a ledger in your mind and make sure you get what they dangle in front of you before you give them what they want. With other people, this mercenary approach might seem insulting. Narcissists will respect you for it. Everything in their world is quid pro quo. They will rarely be offended by people looking out for themselves.

Never Share Confidences. Narcissists love to talk about themselves. They may sound as if they're being open and honest, but what they're doing has nothing to do with intimacy. Do not reciprocate with stories about yourself, unless you want to hear them again at the most inopportune moment. Narcissists are experts at getting information out of people and are utterly ruthless about using it for their own purposes.

If You Are in a Position to Advise, Ask What People Would Think. Narcissists are not stupid; there are just things, like other people's feelings, that they rarely consider. If you have their ear, don't tell them how people might react; instead, ask probing questions. Narcissists are much more likely to act on ideas that they think they thought up themselves.

Don't Cover for Them. Narcissists break rules, because they don't believe that rules apply to them. Don't let them maneuver you into rescuing them from themselves. At best, it is a thankless position. At worst, it is setting yourself up to take their fall.

Keep Your Distance. Narcissists sometimes self-destruct in spectacular ways. When they do, they often bring down those closest to them. Even though there are benefits to being in the inner circle, there are big risks as well. You do have to work effectively with narcissists, but you don't have to be their friends.

SURVIVAL SCENARIO *29* Working with Jerks and Idiots

As we have seen in this section, the world of business is full of jerks and idiots who do stupid and inconsiderate things that are bad for you, bad for them, and bad for business. Look around; they're everywhere—in the next cube, in the corner office, on the highways as you drive home, and maybe even at your house when you get there.

Just think how satisfying your job would be if the people around you would just use their heads for once and do what they're supposed to do.

Dream on. While you're at it, you might want to think about what you'll do when you win the lottery.

The rest of us have an existential question to ponder: How do we do our jobs and live our lives in a world in which a good proportion of the people are jerks and idiots who cause all kinds of trouble and can never be counted on to do what they should?

Your answer to this question will, in large part, determine how effective you are in your job and how happy you are in your life. If other people's insanity drives you crazy, you will be miserable from now until the day you retire.

SURVIVAL SOLUTION *29*

How to Keep Other People's Insanity from Driving You Crazy

They don't do it to you—you have to do it to yourself. The following are proven techniques for helping the jerks and idiots at work to drive you crazy. If you want to stay sane, these are the things to avoid:

Labeling. Regardless of how accurate you might be, seeing someone as a jerk or an idiot severely limits your options. Everything you do and say subsequent to that judgment will make a difficult situation worse.

To stay sane, focus on what they are doing and on what you want them to do. Let your goals determine your actions.

Getting Angry. Jerks and idiots certainly deserve your wrath. If it weren't for them, your job would be so much easier and more productive. Of course, if it weren't for gravity, you could fly.

Aside from the fact that anger can eat away at your soul, it can also ruin your career. Angry people are physiologically incapable of thinking, so they do and say ill-considered things that can't be taken back.

The fires of anger require constant stoking. Instead of internally repeating all the reasons you have to be angry, think of something else. Anything else. A good choice would be what you want to happen—and how to get from here to there.

Trying to Get Even. The only advantage of the tit-for-tat strategy is its utter simplicity. You don't have to be particularly smart to use it; in fact, chimpanzees are quite capable of grasping the concept of revenge.

What chimps miss is the law of physics that states, "For every action there is an equal and opposite reaction." The psychological sequence can be stated in this three-part equation: get mad, get even, get retaliation. To stay sane, heed George Herbert's advice: The best revenge is living well.

Help the Poor Fools by Explaining What They're Doing Wrong. This sneaky technique is how people get even without admitting it to themselves. Some may actually believe they are doing a kindness by showing others the error of their ways. This is usually called being passive-aggressive by everyone except the person doing it. There is a special place in the afterlife reserved for the holier than thou, and it's a lot warmer than they expect.

If you sincerely want to help the jerks and idiots around you to behave differently, you have to see the world from their point of view rather than yours.

Making Ironic Comments. This is the witty and sophisticated way of being passive-aggressive. Before you use this strategy, remember that other people are never able to see the humorous contradictions in their own words and actions, just as you are unable to see them in yours. What is ironic to you will be interpreted as sarcastic by everyone else.

To stay sane, if you must make fun of someone, let it be yourself.

Going on a Talk Show and Complaining About Your Favorite Jerk. You can also call in and gripe to a radio host. If there's not a convenient show that will let you on as a guest, create one yourself in the break room. Your coworkers may sympathize with your travails and perhaps add gripes of their own. Remember however: the more you repeat your stories, the better they get, and the worse you feel.

To stay sane, change the channel.

Not Saying Anything to Anybody, but Thinking About Those Jerks and Idiots All the Time. Sitting and stewing is the way people create stress-related physical symptoms for themselves. The people who bother you wouldn't listen, but maybe your allergist will. Instead of sitting there fuming, go for a walk in the park. The exercise will do you good.

Giving Up, Because You Can't Do Anything Anyway. Depression strikes someone every ten seconds. The minute you give up, the next victim could be you.

If there is a point to this book, it is that there is always something you can do. You may not be able to turn jerks and idiots into responsible people like you, but you can get them to treat you differently. To accomplish this, you must focus less on what they are and more on what they do—and what you want them to do differently. Everything you do should be directed toward that end. This book is full of strategies to get you more of what you want and less overall craziness. Even if you are at the bottom of the food chain at your office, you still have more power than you think.

SURVIVAL SCENARIO 30   Your Secret Weapon

Your secret weapon for dealing with jerks, idiots, assholes, bullies, slackers, and control freaks is you. You may not be able to make them into better people, but you can change the way you respond to them, and your different responses may change the way they treat you.

The broadest and most effective changes you can make are inside your own mind, in how you think about the difficult people and situations you have to face at work. In the preceding scenario, we discussed what you shouldn't do; in this one we'll discuss what you should do. Following two simple rules can help keep you sane. If other people can't get inside your head, they can't drive you crazy.

SURVIVAL SOLUTION *30*

The Two Basic Rules for Staying Sane

Regardless of the craziness of the circumstances you endure at work, you can maintain your sanity by following two basic rules. There is no time like the present to start practicing them:

Analyze Before You Judge. Your health and happiness at work will depend upon your ability to fight the automatic tendency to simplify complex situations by turning them into a struggle between good and evil. This struggle happens whenever you try to fit the rich diversity of human behavior into a two-category system, regardless of what you call the categories. Right-wrong, red-blue, and urban-rural all have moral implications, even when the objects they describe have none. Which of the two categories is good and which is evil depends entirely on where you stand.

The main problem with making judgments is that moral issues are easier to conceive of, but far harder to resolve, than differences of opinion. You will, of course, encounter real moral dilemmas at work, but they will be few and far between. Most every situation is some shade of gray.

Life offers us a cruel choice: we can be right or happy, not both. When you classify actions as right and wrong, you will naturally assume that your way is the right way and the other way is wrong. You will never be able to sell this idea to people with whom you disagree, because they also believe that they are right. Most people would rather kill you than admit that they are wrong, so it makes absolutely no sense to set up a situation in which they have to be diminished by acknowledging moral culpability to give you what you want.

People ferociously compete to be right, because two-category systems imply a hierarchy in which the good are on top and the bad are below. The battle rages even more strongly when this hierarchy does not correspond with the organizational chart at your office. Facts notwithstanding, your boss will never be wrong for you, because she does not have to be.

Virtually every interaction at work, regardless of the subject being discussed, is also about where people fit in the dominance hierarchy. At the root of most conflicts is the instinctual struggle to be on top, or at least not on the bottom. It doesn't matter if the people involved are aware of that struggle or not. Actually, when they are unaware, the struggle is apt to be more fierce. When people start arguing about the principle of the thing, stand back. Someone is going to get hurt.

The second problem with moral judgments also stems from the dominance instincts that are programmed into our brains. In the wild, creatures at the top of the hierarchy can attack those below them, but subordinates cannot fight back. Our instincts make us believe in punishing people who do things we consider wrong, not because it works, but because it feels right. Any psychologist will tell you that punishment usually accomplishes the opposite of what we intend. It serves only to satisfy the punisher, not to change the behavior of the person being punished. Still, punishment is, by far, the most used and least effective technique for behavior modification.

What all this boils down to is that the more you judge, the less effective you will be at getting what you want from other people—and from yourself.

I am not suggesting that you should never make judgments; without them there would be no decisions. What I am saying is: before you judge, always analyze. Ask yourself questions about what people are doing and saying—and why. If you can't see the hierarchies implied in conflicting views of a situation, keep analyzing until you do. Try to figure out how both sides can get some of what they want without either having to diminish their status by admitting to having been wrong.

Think Before You Speak. Everybody believes in this rule, but few people actually follow it. Negative judgments have a way of just spewing out and, in the process, indelibly defining us to everyone who hears. Always remember that words cannot be unsaid, and act accordingly, even if you have to put duct tape over your mouth. Imagine you have to rip it off every time you say something. If you have a hard time with this rule, real duct tape may not be such a bad idea.

Businesslike behavior is always goal directed. With your friends, you can talk for the sake of talking. At work, all your actions should be in service of accomplishing specific outcomes. If you don't know what you want to happen, keep your mouth shut until you do.

Following these two rules is difficult, but it will do more to maintain your sanity at work than a carload of Prozac.

Part 3

The Rules

SOME RULES are like the law of gravity: you live by them whether you agree with them or not, and whether or not they make sense. Ignorance of the law is no excuse, so you'd better know them.

SURVIVAL SCENARIO 31 Unwritten Rules

In every business, there are unwritten rules that are that are more important than anything you will find on paper or on your computer screen. Your value to your company and your success in any job will, to a great extent, be determined by your ability to discern and live by rules that nobody will ever tell you.

Let's look in on some people we met in the previous sections. Clifford's job as CEO boils down to one overriding goal set by the board of directors: keep the stock price up. The easiest way to do that is to keep costs down. This sets the tone for all of Clifford's decisions—and everybody else's as well. At meetings, anytime someone brings up a new idea, the first question is always, "How much will it cost?" The second is, "Can it be done cheaper?" The upstairs meeting room is where good ideas that are just too expensive go to die.

Down on your floor, Dave, the VP, arrives at eight thirty every morning and leaves somewhere between five and seven. If you arrive later or leave earlier, you can be sure he will notice—and will ask your boss about it.

Speaking of your boss, as anal-retentive as Gwen is, there are some items she never gets to, such as your annual review. She's already six months late. Her typical excuse, and the one you hear all up and down the line, is that there is so much to be done that some things just have to wait. For people at your boss's level, you've noticed that the standard answer to "How are you?" is "Busy!" You've picked up this habit yourself, even at home.

In your department, every minute and every nickel's worth of equipment have to be accounted for. None of these documentation requirements apply to the guys in sales. The ones with the best numbers, like Chris, can get away with murder so long as they're bringing in the orders. If you don't like it, take it up with Roger, the ill-tempered sales manager from Scenario 11. By the way, the guys whose numbers aren't so good don't work here anymore.

None of the rules these people are following is written down. They are simply the way things are done at the company. In order to be successful, you have to be conspicuously overworked and enthusiastically cost-conscious. The sales department operates by the law of the jungle, with Roger as the five-hundred-pound gorilla. Cost centers, such as HR, are so unimportant in the hierarchy that they might just as well not exist.

SURVIVAL SOLUTION 31

Live by the Unwritten Rules or Die by Them

Every company has its own set of unwritten rules. You will be expected to figure them out for yourself and to live by them. Since they are so important, you'd better have a clear idea of what to look for:

Don't Expect the Rules to Make Sense. Unwritten rules sometimes make little sense, as they have not been thought through or discussed. They are the reflections of personal preferences of the people who hold power. The first and foremost of these rules, and the one on which all others are based, is *please your boss.* It sounds obvious, but you'd be amazed at how many people forget it. Regardless of how hard you work or what a good job you may be doing, if your boss doesn't like you, you'll get nowhere fast.

You get your boss to like you by doing things his or her way. All the way up and down the corporate ladder, people are learning and responding to their bosses' preferences without being told specifically to do so. They pay close attention to what gets rewarded, what gets punished, and what gets ignored. By this process, the preferences of the powerful are codified into rules that are as compelling as if they were carved in stone.

People Don't Have to Know the Rules to Follow Them. The strangest thing about learning the unwritten rules, at least to anyone who hasn't spent years studying human behavior, is that people who are subject to them rarely talk about them and, in many cases, cannot even say what they are. They just follow them.

My thirty-five years as a psychologist have taught me that the rules that carry the most weight in life, the ones on which people base most of their day-to-day decisions, are almost never articulated. Until you step back and look at your own behavior closely—say, in psychotherapy—it's hard to see that you may be following personal rules such as *avoid conflict at all costs* or *don't let anyone tell you what to do.*

To Figure Out the Unwritten Rules, Don't Listen to What People Say—Watch What They Do. Don't expect the unwritten rules to be consistent with the ones that are written.

In business, unwritten rules sometimes contradict what's down on paper. Even though everybody is aware of the discrepancy, it is never acknowledged, except indirectly.

In every meeting room, there is a gold-framed copy of The Mission Statement, which speaks in lofty terms of concepts like Quality, Integrity, and Respect. When anyone below VP level repeats these sacred words, the tone is always ironic, because everyone knows that the real mission is to keep the stock price up by selling a lot and spending as little as possible. Quality, Integrity, and Respect are always a little too expensive for market conditions.

A good indication of the mental health of a company is how closely the written and unwritten rules correspond. In the more dysfunctional companies, corridors are full of elephant-size contradictions that everyone tiptoes around but no one ever mentions.

Unwritten rules are neither bad nor unethical, but if they are not recognized and discussed, all sorts of questionable actions can sneak in under the radar.

SURVIVAL SCENARIO *32* Unwritten Rules in Your Company

Like Diogenes with his lantern looking for an honest man, you wander the corridors knocking on doors and looking into cubes. Is there anyone who will come out and tell you the rules you're actually supposed to follow? Not today.

If no one will tell you the unwritten rules, how do you find out what they are?

As the preceding scenario explained, you mostly will have to figure them out for yourself. Pay attention to the people who are successful at your office, the ones who move up, and ask yourself what rules they are following. Place much more emphasis on what they do than on what they say.

Also, it may be worthwhile to bring up the idea of unwritten rules with a few coworkers and see what you can figure out together. The more clearly you can articulate specific rules, the less likely you are to be unpleasantly surprised by the consequences of breaking one.

SURVIVAL SOLUTION *32*
How to Figure Out the Unwritten Rules

Most companies have unwritten rules about specific issues. Think carefully about how the following questions would be answered by the actions—not necessarily the words—of successful people in your company:

Is Work Supposed to Be the Center of Your Life? Are people expected to put the job ahead of all other commitments, including family and health, or are they expected to be balanced individuals, with work making up only a part of their lives? Ignore all speeches and documents advocating work-life balance; to get the real story, look around you. One way to figure out these rules is to check out who's still there after closing time. If it's the upper-level people, you should be there too if you ever want to be part of the group. If it's only grunts, who cares? Unless you're a grunt yourself. At all levels, at least look at leave policy and flexibility in hours to see how family-friendly your company actually is. But be aware that while leaves and flex-time may be permitted, it may be professional suicide to ask for them.

How Important Is the Bottom Line? In some companies, staying within budget or bringing in money are the only actions that really count. In others, certain goals are valued above immediate profitability, such as research, training, or community relations. To figure out what the rules are here—and in most other areas—follow the money. Companies allocate funds in direct proportion to what they value.

Are People Expected to Walk the Walk? What is the talk-to-action ratio at your company? Do people follow through with what they say, or is saying it enough to get them by? Almost all companies put out press release–type documents that make everything sound better than it actually is. In some companies, you are required to believe the press releases. At your office, do you have to drink the Kool-Aid?

Which Is More Important: Quality or Quantity? The word *quality* is featured in most companies' mission statements. Real quality is not merely a matter of opinion. Regardless of the industry, it involves sampling, measurement, and feedback, all of which take time and cost real money. If the only number that counts is how many units go out the door, quality is based on luck.

Sometimes products or services do not work as advertised. Another way to pinpoint the unwritten rules regarding quality is to pay attention to how customer complaints are handled.

Are Decisions Influenced More by the Long Run or the Short Run? Does your company have overall plans that it sticks to whether times are good or hard, or does every economic fluctuation or new bestseller lead to major changes?

Is There a Conception of Corporate Responsibility? What is your company's attitude toward being a good citizen? Are people encouraged to involve themselves in civic projects on company time, or is community service just for those guys by the roadside who got DUIs?

These days, for example, every company claims to be green. At your office, does this mean more than having fluorescent lights and a recycling bin? To get the real answer here, as usual, follow the money.

How Are You Supposed to Behave Toward Authority? Are you expected to follow orders blindly, or is questioning allowed and encouraged? Are there people you do not question?

Who Is Accountable for What? For what tasks are people held accountable? What is never checked? How high and low does accountability go?

Are There Expectations About Demeanor? Are you supposed to be positive and professional, no matter what, or is displaying emotions tolerated? Remember, among males, anger is often considered to be not an emotion, but a God-given right. Also, in some offices, over-wrought, emotional pleas are looked on not as signs of an unstable personality, but as hallmarks of passion and commitment.

What Is Kept Secret? Are people expected to be open and honest, or is dirty laundry kept hidden at all costs? In all companies, information is power. Can you get what you need to do your job? If there are rumors, is it possible to get the straight story?

Is It Safe to Be Creative? The essence of creativity is seeing things differently. It grows from the same roots as rebellion, and it cannot be turned off when it is inconvenient. Is creativity tolerated and encouraged in your workplace, or is being too different frowned on?

What Is Your Company's Position on Aggressiveness? How aggressive and competitive are you expected to be toward people outside the company? How about inside? Is talking tough a job requirement?

Are Managers Responsible for Employee Relations? Are managers accountable for employees' feelings about them, or are personality problems and disagreements with the boss typically ignored? Are complainers considered evil?

Obviously, the list could continue indefinitely. The gist is that every company has unwritten rules and that your success, and often your sanity, depends on knowing what these rules are and following them.

Regardless of what business you work in, your success will be in large part determined by your ability to discern and follow rules that nobody will ever tell you. Once you figure them out, your life at work will be immeasurably easier if you follow them, no matter how ridiculous they seem. If the rules seem to you to be immoral, it's time to start looking for another job. Other companies might be more ethical, but don't expect their unwritten rules to make any more sense than the ones where you're working now.

SURVIVAL SCENARIO 33 Corporate Mythology

You're on your way out the door when a coworker grabs your arm.

"Don't leave without your ID badge," she says. "You won't get back in."

"But the guards know me," you say.

She shakes her head. "Let me tell you a story."

Besides watching successful people and trying to figure out the rules they follow, you can learn a great deal about the culture of your company by listening to the stories that are passed along from one person to another. As with all myths, the actual events might never have happened. The purpose of stories is to vividly express common beliefs about the way things are.

SURVIVAL SOLUTION 33
Corporate Myths Teach Unwritten Rules

Every story told around the watercooler has a purpose beyond the simple conveying of events. To figure out what the stories mean, you have to analyze them just as you did in English class.

Listen closely to stories, and think about who is trying to tell you what and why.

Once upon a time, there was a new security guard whose job it was to sit at the entrance to a large corporation to make sure that no one got in without an identification badge. One day, a group approached the front door led by a gentleman in shirtsleeves who was not wearing his ID.

As he had been instructed, the security guard stopped the man at the door and would not let him pass without his ID. The man in shirtsleeves, of course, turned out to be the chairman of the board.

What happened to the security guard? Well, in some versions he was rewarded for doing a good job, and in others he was fired on the spot.

Does this sound familiar? It should; every company big enough to have security guards has a similar myth. It doesn't matter if it's true, because it is meant to convey a larger truth about whether some people are above the rules. Every culture, whether ethnic or corporate, has stories that communicate people's perceptions about how things really are.

The security guard story may even be told with different endings by different groups within the same company, each version will express that group's particular beliefs.

Here are a few more corporate myths to consider:

There were two young executives: one was competent and ethical; the other was a backstabbing, rumormongering suck-up. One is promoted, and the other leaves. Which is which?

What about the incompetent manager who's a personal friend of the boss? At your company, does he get away with murder?

Are old workers valued for their experience, or are they set adrift on an ice floe? What happens to people who take medical leave?

Are people prejudiced against assertive women? How about assertive gays or assertive religious folks?

All of these questions and many more are raised and answered by stories shared around the watercooler. You've probably heard most of them and perhaps have even told a few. Did you think you were just shooting the bull, or did you recognize that you were discussing the nature of corporate reality?

Next time, listen carefully. People's perception of reality influences their actions far more than reality itself does.

SURVIVAL SCENARIO *34* The Rule That Isn't a Rule

Your dad used to say that anyone willing to work hard would get ahead. Going home late again, after driving yourself to exhaustion and accomplishing next to nothing for the pittance you are paid, you wonder, "What was he thinking?"

If you believe that your hard work will lead to success, you may be following a rule that isn't really a rule. Hard work by itself isn't worth much. The sheer amount of effort you put in may be recognized in heaven, but on Earth, the true determinant of your rewards is what you're working at, not how hard you're working.

One reason that hard work in and of itself is not appreciated is that the whole concept is so subjective as to be meaningless. Most of us believe that we work harder than most other people. But how would we know for sure? There is no single standard. Which is harder: digging a ditch, managing a ditch-digging company, or doing ten pages of calculus problems? People don't acknowledge your hard work because they think you're not acknowledging theirs.

Even inside ourselves there is some confusion. What passes for hard work can sometimes consist of many easy tasks piled on top of each other. If the tasks are aerobic, they might get you physically fit, but they don't require you to move out of your comfort zone, and they don't get you much but the chance to do them over and over.

SURVIVAL SOLUTION *34*
How to Get Rewarded for Your Efforts

How do you get some return for what you do? First, you have to know that your job and your life offer two totally separate types of rewards—external and internal:

How to Get External Rewards. If you want external rewards, like promotions and big salaries, you have to work hard at what the people you work for think is valuable. In most companies, bringing in new business and instituting aggressive cost-control measures are usually held in much higher financial regard than mere productivity. In bureaucracies, generating paper or words on a screen is right up there as well. In most places, good social and political skills are typically rewarded better than the specific ability to do any job. If you want the money and promotions, you have to know what your company pays for—and do that. Trying to convince the people who have done what it takes to get promotions that what you do is just as important is the very essence of futility.

Doing what is valued by your company is of little value if nobody knows about it. To get external rewards, you will have to publicize your accomplishments. Factual e-mails to your boss mentioning your successes or subtly bringing them up in conversations are good choices. For more suggestions on how to promote yourself without sounding like an egomaniac, see Scenario 90.

How to Get Internal Rewards. Work also provides internal rewards, such as feelings of accomplishment, reliability, and personal growth. These are the rewards you must give yourself. Appreciation is nice, but if you require it to know you're doing a good job, you'll always have doubts about yourself. Also, you'll spend most of your time being resentful of your insensitive boss and coworkers.

Internal rewards increase as you move further from your comfort zone. The greatest thrill comes from doing what you at first believed you would never be able to do. Don't spoil it for yourself by getting mad that nobody notices it or offers you a raise for doing it.

Hard work is fine, but efficiency is better. Organize what you do according to what you want to happen. If you want your work to be rewarding, do what gets rewarded.

What You Have to Do to Be Allowed to Do Your Job

Wherever you go, in your office or anyplace else, it's the same thing: you're hired to do a job, but other less important matters keep getting in the way.

Charlie believes in doing a day's work for a day's pay. He keeps to himself and does his job. He always does what he's told and usually considerably more than his share. His reviews have all been good, but the promotions all seem to go to less competent guys who spend less of their time working and more time socializing and, well, brownnosing.

Kathy is an expert in management information systems technology. She studied it in business school and really knows her stuff. She was hired three months ago to put in a system, but she hasn't even started. All the managers are so old-fashioned in their thinking, and they're so incredibly slow in getting her the information she needs.

Ann is as creative as the day is long. When she joined the advertising agency, she expected to put her considerable talents to work on some real challenges, but all they seem to want is for her to go out and pound the pavement looking for new accounts. You'd think she was a common sales rep.

Ellen is a veterinary assistant. She trained for this job because she wanted to work with animals. That's what she likes, and that's what she's good at. Why, then, does she have to spend so much time at the front desk and on the phone dealing with the pets' owners? It's just not fair.

Jamal has the makings of a first-rate sales rep. He knows his product and has great relationships with the customers. Why do they keep making such a big deal about the reports and other silly paperwork? What if it is a little behind? He was hired to sell, not push paper.

Carla is a manager; she's got the master's in business administration and the job title to prove it. Decision making, strategic planning, and big-time deals, that's what she's paid to do. And she'd do it, too, if her time wasn't so filled up with people coming to her to solve their day-to-day problems.

Gary is not about to play petty games. He's a professional, and a good one. But the quality of his ideas doesn't seem to count for much, because he's always on somebody's bad side. If he'd wanted to be a politician, he would have run for office.

Every day at work, people drive themselves crazy wondering what they have to do to be allowed to do the jobs they were hired for. Maybe you are one of them.

SURVIVAL SOLUTION *35*
Accept the Informal Aspects of Your Job

Every job has both formal and informal aspects, and both are equally important.

The formal aspects are in your job description. The informal aspects are the things you have to do day to day to be allowed to do the things you were hired to do. Every job has its informal aspects, and if you fight them, you will lose. Here's what to do instead:

Blow Your Own Horn. Charlie, the strong, silent worker, and Kathy, the expert, need to recognize that hard work and bright ideas don't count for much by themselves. You have to be able to promote yourself and sell your ideas, or nobody will take much notice. Again, see Scenario 90 for suggestions about how to do this with subtlety and style.

Keep Your Customers Happy. Ann, the creative artist, and Ellen, the animal lover, don't seem to realize that the primary task in any business is not doing the work, so much as it is finding and serving the customers. If you don't have customers, there will be no work to do, and if the customers aren't satisfied, their business won't keep coming for long. Your customers are not just the people who come through the door, but also everyone you work with, especially your boss. If they aren't happy, you won't be either.

Do the Paperwork. Jamal, the sales rep, has never quite understood that no job is finished until the paperwork is done. Maybe if his numbers are good enough, management will look the other way. Until then, he just has to suck it up.

See Interruptions as Part of the Job. Carla was probably never taught in her M.B.A. program that the day-to-day business of a manager is helping people solve their problems. An important source of information for high-level decision making and strategic planning are the problems people have every day. Deal with it.

Develop Political Skills. You can't *not* play politics; you can only play them badly. Gary, who hates all that political stuff, doesn't realize that the only place where relationships don't matter is on a desert island far away from the rest of the world.

The most important parts of your job may not be in the job description. They involve selling, both yourself and your ideas, doing your paperwork, and, most of all, getting along with others. If you don't master these basic skills, your career is apt to be one disappointment after another.

SURVIVAL SCENARIO 36 — Dominance, a Perpetual Source of Conflict

You're in the departmental meeting. The spreadsheet that a guy from marketing handed out has a glaring error that has clearly thrown all his calculations off. You raise your hand and ask, "On line eight, is that number supposed to be fifty thousand or five hundred thousand?"

Instead of answering, the marketing guy glares at you and says, "Maybe you ought to put on your glasses so you can see for yourself."

Most conflicts at work are really about dominance. Content hardly matters; everything is determined by rules of engagement that are literally programmed into our brains. Everybody knows them, not as words in the head, but as feelings in the gut—buttons that, when pushed, activate automatic aggressive sequences. If you don't recognize and avoid these buttons, the conflicts will never end. To stay sane at work, you must understand the rules of dominance.

Dominance is about hierarchies. The rules are simple: Alphas get a bigger share of everything, and they can hit you, but you can't hit back. If you do, it is a clear signal that you are trying to take their place. To maintain their status, they have to knock you down to a position that is clearly below them. There, in a nutshell, is the pattern for most interpersonal conflicts at work.

Usually, the means of asserting dominance are more subtle than hitting. They can be so subtle, in fact, that they are often done seemingly by accident. I say *seemingly* because we all share the same programming. Even if it is only in our thoughts, we all respond with aggression to challenges to our place in the hierarchy.

Some hierarchies are clear and formal, but most are not. Anytime two or more people get together, there is always some question as to who has ascendancy over whom. We avoid unnecessary struggles by being polite. That is the purpose of politeness. The most common dominance battles occur when one person takes the superior role and, by so doing, defines a hierarchy that the other cannot abide. Sometimes, this happens by accident, or at least not with conscious intent. Intended or not, the results are the same.

SURVIVAL SOLUTION *36*

Learn the Rules of Dominance—That's an Order

All of us respond emotionally to the rules of dominance even if we cannot directly state them. Here are the ones you are most likely to encounter at work:

The Dominant Order; the Submissive Obey. This rule is simple and direct, at least on the surface. The boss gives the orders, and the subordinates follow them. Below the surface, there is more to it. Being told what to do is, in effect, a put-down. We do not like it even from people who have the right to give orders. We absolutely will not tolerate it from people such as a spouse or coworker who have no formal authority over us.

We always get irritated when someone tells us what to do, especially when we do not recognize that person as having ascendancy. For a few years, as adolescents, we refuse to acknowledge that anyone has ascendancy. When this condition persists beyond the early twenties, it is known as *having authority issues.*

Actually, even the meekest of us have authority issues. Nobody likes being told what to do. That's why only the most inexperienced or insensitive bosses rely on direct orders.

The Dominant Talk; the Submissive Listen. We have to listen to our superiors, but they do not have to listen to us. This explains the almost universal dislike of long-windedness, as well as how annoyed we get when people look at their watches or their BlackBerries while we are talking.

The Dominant Ask Questions; the Submissive Answer. As we first saw in Scenario 16, the person asking questions is asserting dominance over the person answering them. Most of us habitually answer questions when they are asked, regardless of how irritated it makes us. It is the assertion of dominance that gets to us, whether we realize it or not. In most disagreements, the questioner immediately has the upper hand. This is how your mother managed to win so many arguments with you. This is also why your three-year-old's habit of asking, "Why?" after everything you say is so exasperating. It is also the reason you eventually answer, "Because I said so!" even when you swore to yourself that you never would.

This is also why psychologists answer questions with questions.

The rules about asking for information at work can be very subtle. When your boss concludes a speech and asks if there are any questions, be careful. Subordinates can request clarification, but not justification. Be sure you know the difference.

The Dominant Joke; the Submissive Laugh. At work, laughing at jokes has much more to do with who is telling the joke than with how funny it is. Always remember Freud's pronouncement about humor being aggression in disguise.

The Dominant Are Right; the Submissive Are Wrong. It is no accident that right and wrong mean both correct and incorrect, and good and evil. The concepts are inextricable because ascendancy is ascendancy, regardless of what hierarchy we happen to be talking about. This is why in most companies, if there is a dispute between you and your boss, upper management will support your boss regardless of who is objectively right.

If you are dealing with someone who is at approximately the same hierarchical level as you are, being right is a Pyrrhic victory. If you win, you will suffer almost as much as if you lose. Every time you are right, the person who was wrong will be waiting for a chance to even the score. This ongoing struggle destroys working relationships, friendships, and marriages.

The battle to be right takes on an infinite number of forms. One popular way of asserting dominance is by diagnosing. This is why people get so defensive at being called defensive.

The Dominant Get the Last Word; the Submissive Leave in Silence. This rule is the reason for so many ill-chosen parting shots, and why people who cannot win in any other way leave arguments in a huff.

The secret to dealing effectively with difficult situations at work is knowing what situation you are actually dealing with. If you don't recognize the dominance struggles beneath conflicts, you are likely to repeat them until you do. To improve your skills in this area, use the feeling of irritation as a cue to ask yourself whether confusion over dominance is the underlying cause of your distress. In the next scenario, you'll find some more specifics.

SURVIVAL SCENARIO *37* Indirect Insults

You've worked hard on your report for the department meeting. It is short, sweet, and to the point, with killer graphics. Your delivery is perfect. It ought to be, since you've rehearsed it about fifty times. People are listening and nodding; they're laughing in all the right places. You ought to be thrilled, but there's one thing that is spoiling it for you, actually two things: Roger and Chris from sales (yes, the same two colleagues from earlier scenarios). They're at the back of the room talking to each other. Twice, Roger has glanced at his watch, and Chris keeps playing with his BlackBerry. You know that these guys can be real assholes, but still, their rude behavior seems to annoy you far more than you think it should. Why can't you just let it go?

You can't let it go because their behavior is an example of a particularly potent nonverbal insult that is difficult to ignore. Their rudeness is communicating directly to the primitive areas of your brain, saying that they think they are better than you are.

Perhaps I ought to explain.

When people think of nonverbal communication, they usually associate it with body language: Is the person leaning forward? Are her arms crossed? Does he make eye contact? Stuff like that. Body language actually yields far less reliable and important information than many other forms of nonverbal communication. It's just easier to notice and talk about.

The really important nonverbal communications have to do with dominance, territory, and sometimes sexuality, parts of our behavior that are mediated by lower brain areas. These messages are sent and received below the level of awareness, but they still come through loud and clear. We are always sending and receiving messages about who we are and what's ours.

In the world of business, the most important nonverbal communications are the signals regarding relative status. We automatically behave differently toward people we consider superiors, peers, or inferiors. Most often, we are not sending these messages consciously; we just act in ways we feel are appropriate to the situation.

In receiving these messages about relative status, you are either reassured by how other people act, in which case you don't notice how they act at all, or you are unsettled far beyond what you'd expect from a "little thing like that." This is why Roger's and Chris's rudeness is so disconcerting. It is insulting when a person of higher status points out just how far above us he thinks he is.

SURVIVAL SOLUTION *37*
Responding to Indirect Put-Downs

Can you imagine how you'd feel if Roger, or any other upper-level manager, came up to you and said, "Now, see here, peasant, I'm worth so much more than you that it's not even funny." Even if the statement is true, it's absolutely un-American to point it out. No one with an egalitarian conscience more developed than that of Louis XVI would think of saying something like this directly.

Saying it indirectly is another story. People of higher status do rub in the fact that they consider themselves better than you in hundreds of nonverbal ways. Usually, they don't mean to; their superiority just comes out. If you point it out directly or make too much of it, you will irritate these people, because you are attempting to take the dominant position over them, which they cannot allow. The way to deal with these subtle insults more effectively is by delicately bringing them into the offender's awareness by asking a few well-chosen questions. Here are some of the annoying things that high-status people are known to do and some ways to respond:

They Make You Wait. The message here is that their time is more valuable than yours. Maybe it is, but it's rude of them to point it out. As with all status messages, you need to recognize your own feelings and know their source. Their treatment of you might make you angry, but you cannot respond in anger. Instead, before your next meeting is scheduled to occur, say something like this: "I know you're busy and you're sometimes delayed. How long should I wait before I assume you're not coming?" Any answer at all will help to clarify the situation, add to the other person's feeling of importance, and will not get you into hot water for complaining.

They Interrupt or Don't Listen. When you encounter an uncooperative listener, respond by coming to a dead stop and holding your silence for a couple of beats longer than it takes to draw a breath. The other party will notice the pause more than anything you might say—and then will usually ask you to go on. You have to try this to see how well it works.

They Forget What They Said to You or Forget to Tell You Things You Need to Know. Dominant people don't have to remember what they say to underlings. They say it's not personal, but you cannot help but take it personally. If you were the chairman of the board, they'd remember. The only thing an underling can do is remind them the next time, or ask for the needed information. E-mail is a perfect vehicle for this. Send one right after they speak to you. Use the subject line carefully, because that may be all they read. Make the message deferent, thanking them for clarification or requesting an update as soon as they get the information.

They Look at Their Watches While You're Making a Presentation. Respond to this with a general time update, something like this: "It's now two fifteen. I have three more topics to cover, and I expect we'll be out of here by two thirty." Do not look at the offending party when you say this. Everyone else will, however. Again, you'll have to try this to see how well it works. Needless to say, you need to stick to your time line and finish when you say you will.

They Pick on You. In the barnyard, high-status chickens can peck those of a lower status without being pecked in return. This can happen on the job as well. Your best response is to ask for illumination. Always do this without an audience, to avoid embarrassment. Ask: "When you said [fill in the comment], I felt kind of upset, almost as if I had been put down. Was that your intention?" Again, any answer at all will clarify the situation.

We resent these signals of higher status, but we live with them from our superiors. When they are sent by peers, subordinates, or (heaven help us) spouses and children, then we are ready to go to war. If you confront someone about signaling that they are of higher status, they will always protest that they didn't mean it that way. They will be right, at least from their point of view. Nonverbal communication is usually unconscious. That doesn't mean it isn't there.

You may not be able to change other people, but you can pay attention to your own reactions and know their source. Also, pay attention to your own actions. Whether you intend to send status messages or not, you do, just like everyone else. People hear these messages loud and clear. It's up to you to monitor your communications. Nonverbal messages can be a way of insulting someone without saying a word.

SURVIVAL SCENARIO 38

From the Psych Lab to You: The Unbreakable Rules of Human Behavior

How do you get people to do what you want them to do? Why are some people better at sticking to a diet than you are? Why do people make the same mistakes over and over even though they are punished for them? These are a few of the questions that psychological research can actually answer.

Psychology has been studying human behavior for almost a hundred and fifty years now. Aside from a lot of speculation about the role of mothers, we have also discovered certain rules that seem to hold up in both lab rats and humans no matter what the setting. These rules are kind of like the behavioral laws of gravity—people follow them whether they know about them or not. If you know them, you can organize your job and your life so that they work for you instead of against you.

SURVIVAL SOLUTION 38
Better Living Through Psychology: Using the Unbreakable Rules to Control Other People's Behavior

In the following few scenarios, we'll go through the basic rules of human behavior derived from years of psychological research. They may sound simple and obvious, but they are about as close to mind control as you can get without using electrodes. Use them to do good; ignore them at your peril.

If You Want Something to Happen Again, Reward It. The principle of positive reinforcement is both the simplest and most powerful rule psychology has yet discovered. Unfortunately, most people, including psychologists, forget to use it. Inherent in this rule is the idea that what people do is caused not by what precedes an action, but by what happened when they did something similar in the past. This is not the way we usually think about causation. Most of us assume that telling people what you want them to do is what makes them do it. The telling may be helpful in letting them know what you want, but the actual cause is whether they have previously been rewarded for following instructions. Whatever the behavior is, if you want them to do it again, reward them now.

Also inherent in the rule is the idea that if you ask people to do something and do not reward them, they will be less likely to do what you ask in the future. Here in a nutshell is the reason for most management problems, whether we are talking about managing others or managing yourself. If there are no rewards, nothing happens.

Rewards Can Be Tangible or Intangible. Money and food pellets are tangible rewards. They work well but may be difficult to administer in day-to-day settings. For most behaviors, the rewards are intangible and psychological. At the top of the list is attention, either positive or negative. Positive attention such as praise is a powerful reward, but negative attention runs a close second, as any parent or teacher can tell you. Essentially, the more attention that is paid to anything, the more likely it is to happen again, which is why lecturing about bad behavior, whether to others or yourself, usually ensures that the unwanted behavior will be repeated.

Rewards can be external, coming from other people or events, but for most adults, rewards are internal in the form of statements we make to ourselves inside our heads. The ability to motivate ourselves with internal rewards is one of the capacities that make us adults. Success is the external reward that results from praising ourselves for persistence.

Other intangible rewards are less verbal but are even more powerful. Finishing a task, called closure, actually fires reward centers in our brains. Escape from a frightening situation is also a huge reward, but it has unintended side effects: the more often you escape, the greater the fear, and the fewer rewards you experience for dealing effectively with frightening situations.

The Sooner the Reward, the Better. More immediate rewards always take precedence over rewards that may come later. A dish of ice cream now is more powerful than a half-pound weight loss at the end of the week, unless you keep praising yourself for sticking to your diet. The only way people can accomplish long-term goals is with a series of short-term rewards, usually internal. It is the power of the rewards in the present, not the size of the future goal, that will determine what happens.

If You Want Something to Stop Happening, Remove the Rewards.
Since attention is such a powerful reward, removing it will decrease
the frequency of many negative behaviors. This is why ignoring tantrums works. Once you decide to use ignoring as a strategy, you have
to stick with it; otherwise, you will just be teaching persistence. In the
face of ignoring, there is almost always what is called an *extinction
burst*. Tantrums or other unwanted behaviors usually become louder
and longer before they cease. An extinction burst means that your
strategy is having an effect, not that it has failed.

Some negative behaviors, such as bingeing on Oreos or dipping
into the till can not be ignored. Removing the rewards by making the
behaviors physically impossible—not bringing Oreos into the house,
and putting a lock on the till—are much better strategies than punishing infractions after they occur.

**Something That Is Rewarded Occasionally Will Keep Happening
Indefinitely.** Think of this as the slot machine principle. The most
powerful rewards that keep behaviors going longest are those that
happen infrequently and unpredictably. This is why you have to stick
with ignoring once you start—and not succumb to the pressure and
inadvertently reward the negative behavior with attention. The principle of intermittent reinforcement also explains why occasional heartfelt praise works better than continuous gushing.

Punishment Does Not Work. Despite its popularity, punishment
is usually an ineffective strategy, because its effects are completely
unpredictable. The most common effect of punishment is a decrease
of all behavior in the presence of the punisher. An example is the office
suddenly getting quiet when the punitive boss walks through. Simi-
larly, regardless of how fast we were driving, we automatically slow
down when we see a police car. Punishment can also lead to retaliation, and to the development of all sorts of creative strategies to avoid
getting caught.

Internal punishment usually results in the acceptance of a negative self-image rather than a change to more positive behavior. What's one more bad deed if you already see yourself as a bad person?

SURVIVAL SCENARIO 39 Psychological Effects That Affect Everyone

Dave, the VP, has devised yet another "New Program" that seems to consist mostly of motivational hype and a lot of needless paperwork. In the break room, everyone laughed about it, saying it would never work, but it did. After a few weeks, performance in the whole division had improved. The program makes no sense, but it did what it was supposed to do. What gives? Does Dave actually know something about management that everybody else doesn't?

Actually, what is happening here is the result of something about management that Dave doesn't know, but you should. It's called the Hawthorne effect. In addition to the rules of behavior discussed in the preceding scenario, psychological researchers have uncovered several persistent patterns that appear in many different work settings.

Knowing these patterns may help to explain Dave's inexplicable success as well as a few other confusing phenomena you may see at work. Forewarned is forearmed.

SURVIVAL SOLUTION 39
Let Psychology Work for You, Not Against You

Here are some important psychological effects that affect your job and your life:

The Hawthorne Effect. The success of Dave's ridiculous program is based on one of the first principles ever discovered by industrial psychology. In 1924, a series of studies was done at Western Electric's Hawthorne Works in Cicero, Illinois, to determine the effects of changes in lighting on productivity. The researchers discovered that any change increased productivity but that the improvements didn't last. The term *Hawthorne effect* was applied years later by Henry Landsberger on reanalysis of the data.

The Hawthorne effect, stated simply, is that whatever you do will improve performance for a short time. There are many reasons for this improvement, but all are temporary and transient. The Hawthorne effect also explains the temporary boost in performance after one of Dave's motivational orgies.

In order to tell whether a program actually works, you have to take measurements over an extended period.

The Halo Effect. People who look good and act positively are seen as smarter, nicer, more competent, and better in every way than people who are less attractive and less positive. This effect shows up everywhere from schools, to offices, to online dating services. Never mind that appearance may have little correlation with substance or performance. Appearance is what counts. If you want to be hired, be promoted, or be respected, you need to look and act like the people who make decisions about you look and act. Use the knowledge of the halo effect carefully, and remember that people with halos around them can sometimes be devils in disguise.

The Anxiety Effect. Study after study has shown that a little anxiety improves performance but that a lot of anxiety destroys it. A small amount of worry causes people to be vigilant and careful; more worry causes confusion and self-protective behaviors that are usually self-destructive. This effect has implications for management. If people feel that their jobs are in peril, they usually devote more effort to covering their asses than to doing the work.

The anxiety effect also relates to your own performance in a variety of situations. Under stress, the oldest, best-learned response is most likely to occur. People go back to bad habits when the pressure increases. You might have noticed that your tennis stroke or golf swing deteriorates in a tough match. The way to beat this effect is with what psychologists call overlearning. The technique is simple: practice, practice, practice, then practice some more until the new behavior becomes automatic. In the next section, we will see how to use this technique in a number of stressful situations.

The Zeigarnik Effect. Unfinished tasks are remembered better than finished tasks. That's the Zeigarnik effect, which occurs because the brain has an automatic tickler file that reminds you of things you haven't done, often at the most inconvenient time, like when you are trying to sleep. In successful people, the Zeigarnik effect is very strong. Since many of the functions we have to do at work are continuous processes with no clear end point, our tickler files are usually overflowing. The way around the problems caused by an overactive Zeigarnik effect can involve transferring your to-do list to a fancy planner or computer program. These aids are often more efficient than memory alone, but their most important psychological benefit is in assigning an arbitrary end point to tasks, so your brain doesn't have to continually remind you of what's been left undone from one day to the next. If you want to sleep well, fill out your to-do list before you go to bed.

SURVIVAL SCENARIO 40 The Philosophy of Bad Decisions

Thanks to my good friend Dr. Bill Casey for showing me the unlikely connection between philosophy and business and for helping me to elucidate it here.

Sometimes managers makes such resoundingly bad decisions that you wonder what they were thinking and, somewhat wistfully, if there is anything anybody can say to make them change their minds.

As the preceding scenario illustrated, Dave, the VP of your division, manages with posters and motivational tapes. Some of his policies, such as having people sign out office supplies or sign up for breaks, are de-motivating, to say the least. He says these draconian measures prevent the pilfering and abuse of breaks he has seen with his own eyes.

Kyle, your boss's boss, quotes from the bestseller of the month. He tries to stay on the cutting edge, which means every time he reads a new book, he changes procedures for his whole department.

Roger, the hothead in sales (last seen in Scenario 37), claims he manages by intuition. Based on his vast experience, he knows that people who are too sure of their jobs don't put out the kind of effort it takes to make the department competitive. He regularly calls his people in for little heart-to-heart talks designed to improve performance, using roughly the same techniques the Spanish Inquisition used to improve faith.

If anyone will actually listen, you may be able to have some effect on ill-considered decisions by asking a question borrowed from philosophy class: How do you know what you know? Epistemology is the branch of philosophy that studies the advantages and disadvantages of different ways of knowing. Often, bad decisions are the result of not using the appropriate epistemological position for the job at hand. Will Rogers said it this way: "What we don't know can't hurt us. It's what we do know that ain't so." Computer programmers put it even more concisely: Garbage in, garbage out.

SURVIVAL SOLUTION *40*
When People Make Bad Decisions, Question Their Logic

Bear in mind that in philosophy, as in real life, questions are usually more powerful than statements. Questions get people thinking; statements get them defensive.

Bad decisions are often the residue of using the wrong source of knowledge for the situation. Here are some of the ways of knowing that are frequently used and abused at the office, accompanied by suggestions for thought-provoking questions to ask about them:

When People See Things with Their Own Eyes, Ask for Numbers.
There is nothing as convincing as direct sensory experience, even
though we're aware that what something looks like may not be what
it is. For instance, our senses tell us we live on a flat Earth with a universe of sun and stars revolving around it. Without measurements, we
cannot know differently.

A more insidious problem lies in the fact that we have no inborn
statistical sense. To Dave, the VP, a single instance of pilfering or one
employee lingering at the coffee machine justifies a whole management philosophy. He doesn't see that most people are doing what they
are supposed to do without barbed wire encircling their cubicles.

The questions you might ask to cast doubt on his way of knowing
are *How many?* and *How much?* In business, managers are used to
carefully accounting for anything having to do with money, but they
often are much less precise in dealing with people. Asking for specific
numbers and a cost-benefit analysis may help managers like Dave to
shift to a more appropriate epistemological position. There is no point
in attacking Dave's outrage over people's ripping off the company or
his assumption that the prospect of harsh vengeance will deter crime.
They, like his belief in the power of motivation, are religious convic-
tions; logic will have no effect. The point of vulnerability is whether
his restrictive programs actually save money.

When People Quote Authorities, Ask for Chapter and Verse. Most
management books contain plenty of useful information that is completely ignored in favor of factoids and catchy lines that support what
managers already believe. When Kyle quotes from the guru du jour,
ask for more information that will require him to delve more deeply
into the text. For example: "How exactly does it say we're supposed
get from good to great?" It often helps to have a copy of the book he is
reading so you can quote some of the lines that Kyle may have forgotten. It wouldn't hurt to remind him that it was he who inspired you to
read the book.

When People Cite Experience and Intuition, Ask if There Are Other Possibilities. Intuition is a more acceptable label than emotion. Roger's sadistic management style is based on his own anger over things that don't go his way and the enjoyment he gets out of inflicting his anger on others.

Useful intuitions are based on immersion in information, not ignorance and personal hang-ups. Ask someone like Roger what he thinks about other approaches to motivating sales forces. For this exercise, it might help to brush up using a management 101 text. As you bring up other theories, he will probably deride them as weak and stupid, unwittingly revealing that he knows nothing about them.

Don't try this strategy one-on-one. Bullies like Roger are far more dangerous when there are no witnesses. Behind closed doors they will have no compunctions about attacking you for any reason. In public, they have to at least present a façade of reason, so they like to goad people into emotional responses as a justification for attacking them. Anger is their point of vulnerability. Calmly asking sensible questions as Roger gets more and more irate can expose both his ignorance and his irrationality. One of the best ways to end bullying behavior at the office is through the pressure of public opinion.

Bad decisions are often based on information derived from an inadequate source. Your best protection lies in asking questions subtly designed to point out that business decisions are most effective when they are made from an epistemological position based on rational analysis of hard data. Who would have thought that philosophy could be this useful?

SURVIVAL SCENARIO *41* Mushroom Management

Your boss seems to be adept at the arcane art of mushroom management. Most of the time, she keeps you in the dark, and occasionally she throws on another load of manure. She never tells you what's going on, and when she does say something relevant, it's usually contrary to what she said last week.

If you think that mushroom management is the result of a character flaw in your boss, either deceptiveness or stubborn unwillingness to share information, you're probably wrong. Most likely, the real problem is with the information itself and perhaps with your understanding of how business communications actually work. In several scenarios that follow, we will be discussing more malevolent management deceptions. Here, let's consider the more common communication problems that are caused by misunderstanding.

If, when you think of communication, you envision some boardroom or CEO's office where a group of authority figures who know what's going on in your company are gathered, it's easy to imagine that if your boss would just go talk to them and come back and tell you what they said, the communication problems would cease. Sadly, this is not the case. In fact, this sort of information sharing, if it were possible, would probably lead to more confusion rather than less. There are two reasons for this.

First, nobody knows everything that's going on, because there is no *everything* to know. People at different levels of the company know about different things. Sales reps see the smiles and frowns on their customers' faces. Accountants see numbers and spreadsheets. Production people see the manufacturing process. HR people see the interactions of individuals and groups, and the maintenance department sees the mess everybody else leaves for them to clean up. The reality of even a small, relatively simple business is in constant flux. What happens depends on hundreds of factors, market forces, the cost of materials, the availability of parts, the payment of debts, the latest governmental regulations, how soon the auditors are coming, and whether a butterfly flaps its wings in China. In the time it takes to explain what's going on, what's going on has changed into something else.

The second reason is that businesses, like everything else in the real world, are rarely run according to a coherent and consistent plan. Think about what you intended to do at work today and how it differed from what actually happed. Now multiply that factor by the number of employees in your business. Things change constantly, and people must change their focus. Humans plan and God laughs.

SURVIVAL SOLUTION *41*
How to Get Out from Under the Manure

Much of what you hear at work will be confusing and inconsistent. Don't take this personally, because it is not directed at you.

Unless You Have Clear Evidence, Do Not Assume Purposeful Deception. The more your boss tells you about what's going on, the more inconsistencies you will hear. Usually, this is not an attempt to confuse you; it is an accurate representation of how things actually are. We expect our managers to know what's going on and to have some definite answers to our questions. Our managers try to oblige. We sometimes hear their answers as more definite and certain than they actually are (and, truth be told, some managers pretend to know more than they do). Details about the day-to-day job are probably the least important information you can get from management.

Bear in mind that everything you hear is someone's interpretation of events and information. What the best managers pay attention to are not the details of how various components fit together. They try to figure out which of those seem to be reliable indicators of the way things are going. This set of facts is probably what the CEO pays attention to and can communicate. This is the kind of information that your boss hears about at all those management meetings and what you'll hear more of if you ask to be included in the communication loop.

Stay with the Confusion; Eventually, You'll Begin to See Some Patterns Emerge. This is what's meant by "seeing the big picture." Once you can see it, you have a chance to play a part in it.

Don't Ask for More Than You Want. If figuring things out and making connections on your own are not for you, and all you want to know is information on what's happening that is relevant to your job, don't ask for more communication. What you would hear is apt to be inconsistent and frustrating. You will need to ask specific questions about what you need to know. More general communication from your boss may not supply what you're looking for.

Yes, there are managers who manipulate the truth and treat people like mushrooms to maintain their own power. They are probably rarer than you think. But if mushroom management is what you expect to see, you won't be disappointed.

SURVIVAL SCENARIO *42* Secrets

The work from the company's second-biggest customer just seemed to dry up all of a sudden, and nobody seems to know why. Actually, it's more like the people who do know aren't saying. There's a lot of speculation, but specific information is hard to come by. Obviously, the problem was with upper management, because if it had been anywhere near your level, heads would have rolled. This loss of business will affect everyone. Why is it being kept secret?

What are the secrets where you work? It may be salary information, the real budget, the circuitry for the newest product, plans for the next reorganization, the actual amount of cost overruns, the contaminant count on a batch of waste, or the mistakes and peccadilloes of people in power.

If you ask an upper manager why certain matters are kept confidential, the answer will likely relate to security, that secrets protect from lawsuits, industrial espionage, unfavorable negotiating positions, or drops in stock prices based on misinformation. This is all well and good; business is like war, so it makes sense to withhold information from outsiders and potential enemies. But what if the enemies actually work in the company?

Secrecy is a slippery slope. Executives can slide from covering up information that might be harmful to the company to covering up information that might prove embarrassing to them. At first, the slide begins unconsciously—a little positive spin, a few particulars glossed over here and there. Later, when not having to explain embarrassing details seems to make life easier, secrecy can become part and parcel of management philosophy.

This sort of reflexive secrecy is the doorway through which all sorts of deception and dysfunctionality may enter. A little harmless spin doctoring can turn into outright paranoia, in which everyone, both inside and outside the company, is treated as a potential enemy. Obviously, there are some companies in which this has already happened. We will discuss them in the next few scenarios. Most places, however, have not descended quite so far. In these, your actions with regard to secrecy may still have a positive effect.

SURVIVAL SOLUTION *42*
How to Keep Secrecy from Being Kept Secret

In most companies, reflexive secrecy has not become a fixed element of the culture. Executives and managers are trying it out here and there. If it works for them, they will continue on without thinking about the implications. You want to get them to start thinking before it is too late.

When confronted with secrets at work, you need to know how far into institutional paranoia the organization has descended without branding yourself as an enemy or a malcontent. If things have not slid too far, you might want to become a force for moving them in the opposite direction. Here are two simple ideas:

Ask, "Is This a Secret?" In a surprising number of cases, managers do not realize that not mentioning things is the same as keeping them secret. This may sound silly, but all of us fool ourselves with semantics in this way. By asking if particular information is secret, you are encouraging conscious decision rather than mere reflex. It is much harder to fool yourelf into keeping a secret if they have to admit that it is a secret.

If It Is a Secret, Ask Why. Asking for a rationale may start people thinking about the implications of secrecy, including the effect of treating people who are purportedly on the same team as if they were enemies. This could not hurt, and it may well help.

The answer may also give an idea about how far down the slippery slope of secrecy and distrust your company has slid. As in all survival situations, forewarned is forearmed.

SURVIVAL SCENARIO 43 Cargo Cult Cultures

On Friday afternoon, the VP addresses the quarterly meeting, reaffirming the organization's commitment to total quality and integrity. He praises leadership and management innovations. He quotes slogans from business bestsellers and outlines a radical new five-point program that pretty much boils down to "Quit bitching, and do more with less."

After his talk, you break into small groups with your managers to discuss how the new program will be implemented in your department. Monday morning, it will be business as usual.

World War II abruptly brought civilization to primitive tribesmen in New Guinea in the form of wondrous manufactured goods delivered from heaven by great metal birds. The tribesmen knew a good thing when they saw one and began to adopt some of the rituals that the white men used to entreat the gods for cargo. They built decoy planes of sticks and leaves to attract the real ones down from the sky. Wearing carved headphones, they waved palm fronds in the air in dances that resembled semaphore. Thus, with great creativity, they copied the trappings of civilization and totally missed the essence.

Very few cargo cults still exist in remote areas of the South Pacific, but they seem to be catching on in corporate America, where businesses adopt the titles and trappings of new management approaches without actually changing what they do.

Over the past fifty years, the thrust of new management approaches, regardless of what they are called, has been remarkably similar. Most recommend long-term planning, sharing authority, listening to workers, an end to fear tactics, and moving decisions to lower levels in the corporate hierarchy. Somehow, the basic ideas at the center of these programs have been ignored or forgotten, leaving only slogans, motivational rallies, and gilt-framed mission statements. Beneath the trappings, it's business as usual, with rank still having all its privileges, a myopic focus on the next quarter's bottom line, and people in the trenches cowering in fear that they will lose their jobs. Management is by what is easiest for managers to do, rather than by what works best.

In corporate jungles, managers move people's cheese, recite the Seven Habits, and intone about going from Good to Great. The essence that these rituals represent has long since disappeared into the mists of expediency. Only the names remain.

SURVIVAL SOLUTION *43*
What to Do if the Management of Your Company Is Made of Sticks and Leaves

A surprising number of cargo cults exist in American business, especially in the smaller and midsize companies, where most people work. Upper-level managers all talk the talk, but only a precious few actually walk the walk. This is not because they are bad people, do not take their jobs seriously, or are clinging to the privileges of rank. Most often, it is because they are too busy to take the time to really study the theory and practice of management. All they have time for is a general impression and a few bullet points. In their jobs, action is rewarded, and deep thinking is looked on with suspicion when there is so much work to do.

The best management ideas are often expressed in rather vague language; they require a good deal of thought and interpretation before they can be implemented day to day. (If you don't believe me, Google Deming's fourteen-point Total Quality Management Program or Covey's Seven Habits.) Chances are that your manager doesn't have time for all that thinking. You might have to help. Carefully read the texts that management cites, and ask thought-provoking questions about how exactly the programs might be implemented in your setting. Focus on what should be done in specific situations.

You will notice that I said to ask questions, not make pronouncements. Your managers will not allow you to tell them what to do even if you are channeling Peter Drucker or W. Edwards Deming. There are valuable ideas in a lot of those books; all you can do is encourage a more careful reading. It may not change anything, but it beats building planes out of sticks and leaves.

SURVIVAL SCENARIO *44* Dysfunctional Companies

In the break room, you are discussing yet another instance of management's saying one thing and doing another and how if anybody brings it up, nobody will listen.

"What do you expect?" a colleague says. "This company is like one big dysfunctional family."

Is your company dysfunctional? Of course it is. To a certain extent, every company is dysfunctional, at least according to the psychological definition of the term. Bear in mind that in the world of psychology, we focus on what's wrong with people; there is no such thing as *totally healthy*, whether you are referring to individuals or organizations. Human beings are by nature inconsistent and hypocritical, and when you group them together, the inconsistencies multiply. Diagnosing psychopathology is easier than understanding it, but you have to start somewhere.

In a dysfunctional family, therapists say, there's an elephant—usually a drunken abusive parent—in the parlor, but no one ever mentions it. To appear sane, you have to pretend that the elephant is invisible—and that drives you crazy.

The process of ignoring elephants is, of course, pathological, but it is so pervasive when people live or work together that it must be considered normal, at least in the statistical sense. There are invisible elephants everywhere.

At your office, there are problems that are never acknowledged because they might prove embarrassing to people who have enough clout to prevent their discussion, or because any official recognition that a problem exists might create grounds for a lawsuit. The greatest temptation of power is that it can be used to avoid personal discomfort. Virtually everyone with power succumbs to this temptation sooner or later. This is one of the main reasons hierarchical organizations seem so crazy, especially when you're looking at them from the bottom up. People with power use it to edit reality. Every day, things happen that hurt people, are bad for morale, and are bad for business, but nobody with the power to do anything about them seems to notice. If you have the temerity to point out these problems, it is likely to be you, not the problem, that will be taken care of. This sequence is dysfunctional, but it is also the way of the world.

Every organization has its invisible elephants. To survive and stay sane, you must first know what they are. That's the simple part. Most every gripe session you'll ever attend is about how people with power say one thing and do another.

The company's website says the commitment to quality and customer service is absolute, but the first question anybody ever asks is how it can be done cheaper.

Everybody talks about teamwork, but only the star players get the rewards. Speaking of star players, why is it that they don't have to follow the same rules as everyone else?

They tell you there should be balance between work and home but ask you to work late three nights out of five. If you go home early, you can abandon any ideas you may have had about promotion. The list of examples is endless.

SURVIVAL SOLUTION *44*
The Care and Feeding of Invisible Elephants

The following are some typical invisible elephants you are likely to encounter at the office, along with some suggestions about how to deftly make your way around them:

Negative Comments Are Regarded More as Indications of Defects in the Personality of the Speaker Than Actual Observations of Reality. Messengers of bad news are, at the very least, seen as having bad attitudes. In some places, they are still executed. This distortion is so pervasive in the world of business that it should be considered the rule rather than the exception. The only way around this particular elephant is suggesting solutions without mentioning the problems that they solve. Criticisms should be phrased to suggest that even though we're doing great now, with a few specific changes we could do better. This is a good rule to follow for any criticism at any time: Say what you want to happen, rather than what is happening that you don't want.

History Is Regularly Edited to Make Executive Decisions More Correct—and Make Correct Decisions More Executive—Than They Actually Were. In business, one of the main uses of power is to amass more power. One way this is done is by taking credit for the good things that happen and blaming others for the bad. This is also the way of the world. If you want credit for your efforts, you will have to share it with those above you, or they will take it away from you. Always say something like, "We couldn't have done it without the boss's clever ideas." If there is blame to hand out, it will always follow the first law of plumbing: crap flows downward. Rather than passing it on or trying to push it back uphill, endeavor to be the first to suggest solutions.

Double Messages Are Delivered with a Completely Straight Face. If the VP says you *can* do it cheaper and better at the same time, ask how. At meetings, press for details as if you were asking for wisdom from a great teacher. In the lecture that follows, there may be something to learn, but if there isn't, it will become clear to everyone without your having to point it out.

Conspicuously Posted Vision or Value Statements Are Made up of Important-Sounding but Vague Words such as *Excellence* and *Quality* That Are Never Specifically Defined or Measured. Some signs are merely decorations. The only way around this elephant is to ignore it in the same way you ignore tasteless paintings or those glossy photos of racing yachts and flying eagles.

Problems Are Solved by Bringing in Motivational Speakers. Often this is done in a huge orgy of positive thinking that eats up the entire training budget for the whole year. The elephant here is the implication that if people were really motivated, there wouldn't be any problems. Even though there are few things as de-motivating as motivational speakers, you must still show some respect for other people's religious beliefs. Attend the rally, and politely decline the Kool-Aid afterward. Put in requests for real training early, before the budget is used up.

The Company Fails the *Dilbert* Test. If reading, posting, or laughing at *Dilbert* strips, being a fan of "The Office," or expressing amusement at those irreverent jokes and cartoons that appear in your in-box is considered a subversive activity, be careful! There are huge elephants in your organization that are not to be mentioned. Ever. Maybe it's time to look for another job. An organization that cannot laugh at itself is headed for trouble.

If invisible elephants are getting in the way of progress at your company, remember: the rules of logic do not apply. Even though a particular elephant is apparent to you, that doesn't mean that other people see it, or that they will admit to it if they do. Unless you can find five other people who will swear in court that they see the elephant, chances are good that it will stay hidden. If you mention it, you will merely go the way of the buffalo.

SURVIVAL SCENARIO 45 Theory X

Dave, the VP, sets the tone for managing your whole division. He seems to believe that everyone who works for the company is lazy, dishonest, and unmotivated. At his insistence, every paper clip is accounted for, and even though many tasks are electronic, no one is allowed to work from home, because there is no way to check up on them. If he could, he'd have all employees strip-searched when they leave work to be sure they are not making off with office supplies.

There is a name for managers like Dave, but it's not the one you're thinking. Back in the 1960s, Douglas McGregor, a professor at MIT, described two very different management philosophies, which he called Theory X and Theory Y. McGregor inferred managers' philosophies from what they did, noting that their actions were often diametrically opposed to what they said they believed.

Regardless of what they say, Theory X managers like Dave act as if they believe that workers are inherently lazy and untrustworthy and that they will not do what they should unless they are closely supervised and controlled. Such managers organize hierarchical systems with a narrow span of control at each level, with most decisions being made at the very top. When there are complaints or something goes wrong, they tend to blame the individual rather than the system. "Bad apples" are either summarily fired or hounded unmercifully until they leave. People are promoted based on dollars saved or earned, or on motivation, which under Theory X means unquestioning support of the system.

Theory Y managers act as if they trust workers and assume that people want to perform well and will if they are given the opportunity. Theory Y managers espouse flatter organizations, greater freedom, and individual control over tasks. They see the manager's job as setting priorities and removing barriers to performance.

Each theory is a self-fulfilling prophecy. People managed according to Theory X quickly become as surly and shiftless as they are expected to be.

Even in McGregor's day, few managers verbally endorsed Theory X, but from that time to this, a surprising number of managers act as if it is what they believe. Theory X is the style that results when managers simply follow their instincts for dominance rather than thinking about what they are doing. This behavior is tolerated because in many places, real management is only about money. Managing people is so unimportant that it can be done on autopilot.

SURVIVAL SOLUTION *45*
Living Under Theory X

If Dave's management style sounds familiar, the problem is systemic and it is not likely to change unless there is a major overhaul at the top level. In many organizations, even if a Theory X manager's bosses don't agree with his style, they may tolerate it if he makes his financial goals. Survival will be tough if you expect things to be different. Here are some ideas that may help keep you sane:

Accept Things the Way They Are or Leave. If you work in a Theory X organization, division, or department, you need to accept the fact that it is what it is. You are your numbers. Morale is not a factor; how you or anybody else feels is of no concern. You will have to play by these unwritten rules to survive. You will not change the organization; gradually, it will change you. Since one of the tenets of Theory X is that people work only for the money, such organizations tend to pay better than other places you might go. Before the golden handcuffs close around your wrists, you must carefully assess the value of your soul.

Don't Be a Rebel Without a Clue. Unless you are the CEO, trying to change things will be like banging your head against the wall. Never mind that there have been quite a few innovations in management theory since the end of the nineteenth century; where you work, they don't apply. Theory X managers have a way of turning even the most up-to-date techniques into command and control.

Complaining may brand you as one of those "bad apples," but worse than that, it will tear you apart internally. No amount of humor or ironic detachment will protect you. You will not be able to stand aside and pretend that you are not a part of the way things are. Accept them or leave. There is no middle ground.

SURVIVAL SCENARIO 46
How Theory X Stays Alive in a Theory Y World

Even though Theory X has been thoroughly discredited as a management style, it still lives on in a surprising number of companies. Most often, it is disguised as Theory Y.

Dave, in jeans and rolled-up sleeves, is soliciting input at one of his motivational extravaganzas. "No idea is too big or too small," he says.

Every idea will be transcribed on an electronic screen, printed and handed out to all participants, and forgotten within a week. Next year, the same people will bring up the same ideas again, and they will meet the same fate.

You wonder to yourself, "Does anyone see the irony here?"

Being a Theory X manager in the modern world is not easy. In the old days, you could just kick butt and take names. Now you have to work hard to look like a participatory manager while still keeping all the important decisions to yourself.

Why would anyone want to be a Theory X manager when for years the research has shown that more participatory management styles lead to more successful companies?

The answer is that Theory X management is the automatic result of personal distrust. In an environment of high internal competition, what is best for business may not be what upper-level managers perceive as best for their own careers. As you ascend the corporate ladder, competition becomes fierce for fewer and fewer positions, and decisions about who moves up become more and more subjective. One negative opinion can stop your advancement cold. For managers on the way up, the consequences of even small mistakes are so high that many feel forced to spend more effort managing their own reputations than they do managing their departments. They hold on to personal control because there are very few people they can trust to guard their backs. Distrust resonates throughout their departments. Information is restricted, decisions are made at higher and higher levels, and loyalty becomes more important than performance. At the same time, they pay lip service to more enlightened approaches to management.

To people who work in the department, the incongruity between the talk and the walk is confusing to say the least—yet another invisible elephant to clean up after.

As I have said, Theory X—no matter how it is disguised—becomes a self-fulfilling prophecy. If you treat people as if they can't be trusted, they quickly get the message that it's every man for himself, and they act accordingly. This is, of course, destructive to business performance, yet, strangely enough, it sometimes enhances managers' reputations as being hard-nosed enough to get rid of troublemakers, even when it is their management style that creates the troublemakers to get rid of.

Theory X environments are difficult and dangerous places to work, especially if they are disguised as something more trusting and participatory. To protect yourself and stay sane, you need to recognize them for what they are before you become one of the troublemakers who get the ax.

SURVIVAL SOLUTION *46*
How to Recognize Theory X in Disguise

These days, nobody openly advocates Theory X, but many companies and divisions are still run the old-fashioned way while being dressed up to look more up to date. Here's how managers hold on to Theory X without being too noticeable:

They Never Admit to Anything That Sounds Like Theory X. In public, always talk about the high quality of workers and the wonderful job they are doing. Day to day in the office, these high-quality workers find that they have almost no leeway in how they do their jobs.

Information Is Closely Managed. Despite very little hard data, everything is always great and looking better. When negative information cannot be covered up, it is attributed to market forces or underlings. Abu Ghraib, anyone?

Money Is Always Tight. Cost control is the be-all and end-all of management. Regardless of how profitable an enterprise is, there is almost never enough money for new ideas that come up from the bottom. Somehow, there always seems to be plenty of money for the new programs that are generated constantly by upper management.

Input Is Solicited but Has Little Effect on Decisions. Suggestions may be actively sought in many ways, from staging elaborate input meetings to calling people into the office for fireside chats. There are never any firm promises made. The response is always, "I'll get back to you," or "We'll take that into consideration," never an outright yes or no.

Larger meetings are often favored, because they are less specific. With enough people talking, one person might come up with an idea similar to what the manager planned to do in the first place. This will be pointed out later when people accuse the manager of not acting on input. Responsibility is delegated without authority. There may be plenty of projects, but they seldom have independent budgets. People must always check back with the boss before they do anything that costs money.

Loyalty Is Rewarded More Than Ability and Performance. Really loyal people don't need to participate. They know their superiors are right and will go along with what they say. People whose loyalty doesn't measure up are usually driven out rather than fired. They lose key jobs, get bad reviews, and are generally taken out of the loop. This turn of events often causes these so-called troublemakers to get mad enough to quit or to do something that can lead to disciplinary action.

Does this sound familiar? Self-defeating as this management style is, it is not unusual. If this sounds like your company, you need to know what you are dealing with, and make your decisions accordingly.

SURVIVAL SCENARIO 47 Authority Issues Smell Like Teen Spirit

Candice, the new hire in marketing, seems nice enough, but what is it with all the piercings and green-tipped hair? Doesn't she recognize the kind of the impression she's making?

Sandi is a rebel without a clue. She does things her own way, regardless of what anyone says. Nobody tells her what to do. She teases you about sucking up. Why can't she see the dollar-and-cents value in pleasing your boss?

Carl thinks he's a stand-up comedian, but he's not that funny. His idea of humor is sarcasm and calling everything stupid, especially management decisions. He may be right, but his presentation sucks.

Colin is never prepared. He puts everything off until the last minute. Why won't he plan ahead?

How about those guys in IT? You can't just call them to fix your computer; you have to e-mail them with the model number, the serial number, and a precise statement of the problem written in geek, or they won't even lift a finger to help you.

By far, the most frequent behavior pattern that causes trouble for people at work is what psychologists refer to as authority issues. In plain English, this means not liking to be told what to do and letting it show in your words and actions—in other words, acting like a teenager.

It is a normal human tendency to deal with difficult situations in the present as if they were similar situations in the past, at an earlier stage of personal development. This phenomenon, which therapists call *transference*, is responsible for many of our worst choices, especially when we revert back to adolescence. All around you at work, there are people who are letting their inner teenagers make decisions for them. Let's hope you aren't one of them.

SURVIVAL SOLUTION *47*
Deal Firmly but Lovingly with Inner Teenagers

To deal effectively with inner teenagers, you have to understand how adolescent rebellion works.

We all need an identity of our own. We need to know who we are and what we want, and we must set basic ground rules for running our lives. When we are children, our parents supply these ground rules. As adults, we must create them for ourselves. In between, there is a tremendous confusion known as adolescence. Our first attempt to resolve this confusion is by being absolutely and obnoxiously certain about what we don't want, which is mainly what our parents want for us. Only later, as maturity sets in, we begin to discover what we want for ourselves.

Knowing who we are and what we want, as opposed to what other people want us to want, is by no means easy. This is why so many of us, in moments of conflict with others, revisit our adolescence. We may not be sure what we want to happen, but we are 100 percent certain that we don't want someone else telling us what to do.

Nobody likes being told what to do. In our culture, which was built on rebellion and prizes individual rights, our inner teenagers are seldom very far from the surface. They need to be recognized and respected, but they should not be allowed to run our lives.

It always takes two to make an authority issue: one playing the parent, and one playing the rebellious teenager. There is no percentage in being either one of them. Here's how to avoid going back to the bad old days:

Recognize the Signs That an Inner Teenager Is Vying for Control. Your inner teenager is the last person you want making your business decisions. Here are some signs that can warn you that he or she is doing your thinking for you:

- ◆ **Sarcasm.** Sarcasm is the adolescent's lame attempt at humor. Carl, the office comedian, could be the poster child.

- ◆ **Being conspicuously different.** Green-haired Candice would say that how she looks is no indication of how well she does her job. Actually, it's an indication of a good deal more than that. To teenagers, there is no issue larger than being allowed to look however they want to. Candice is literally wearing her immaturity on her head.

- ◆ **Confusion of respect with reverence.** Sandi, the I-do-it-my-way rebel, thinks that trying to please authority figures is gratuitous sucking up, rather than the number one priority on everyone's job description. Just as teenagers make self-destructive choices to demonstrate that their parents don't control them, Sandi is destroying her career to show that her boss is not the boss of her.

◆ **Not doing homework.** Teenagers have a hard time making themselves do what they don't want to do. Like Colin, they put things off until the last minute or don't get to them at all.

◆ **Contrariness.** Nobody is immune to spontaneous reversion to adolescence. Consider your attitude about the guys in IT. If you want your computer fixed, you know what you have to do. Do you need to make an issue of it? We all have inner teenagers, and if we let them choose our words and actions, they usually make our jobs more difficult than they need to be.

When you encounter an inner teenager at work, resist the impulse to act like a parent.

From time immemorial, parents have been making adolescent rebellion a bigger issue than it needs to be by getting angry at rebellious behavior and acting on that anger with punishment or long-winded lectures. This strategy is always unsuccessful, but that doesn't seem to stop anyone from using it.

Resolve conflicts with inner teenagers by focusing on what each of you wants to happen.

After adolescence, the next developmental stage is knowing who you are and what you want. The way to avoid power struggles with teenagers is to ask for more mature behavior from them and from yourself.

Decide What You Want to Happen. If what you want is for them to treat you with respect even when you are acting like an indignant parent, dream on. You may get respect by handling conflicts with restraint and maturity, which you'll never be able to muster if you're acting in anger. If you want respect, calm down and work it through again.

What you really want is to teach teenagers that to get what they want, they need to act differently. There is no point in lecturing, as this is a conclusion that they must draw inside their own heads. Instead of telling them what to think, simply ask them what they want to happen, and then ask how they are trying to achieve that goal.

That's it. If you respect inner teenagers by treating them like adults, you are more likely to get a little respect back.

SURVIVAL SCENARIO 48   Now That You Know the Rules, How Will You Use Them?

You've studied this section carefully and have compiled—and written down—a list of your company's unwritten rules. Now what?

Nothing is random. All that people and organizations do has rules and follows patterns. In this section, we have looked at rules—written, unwritten, psychological, philosophical, and even imaginary. The purpose of this section is to help you to understand how the systems you are part of operate so that you can operate within them more effectively. Most of the rules discussed here are like gravity: they affect you whether you agree with them or not. Some may have surprised you, and some may just be written versions of what you have suspected all along. No doubt you have found a few scenarios that apply to your company, and you may be eager to share what you've learned with others, perhaps even with your managers. Do so carefully!

If, after reading this section, you show this book to your boss and say, "This company is dysfunctional. It says so right here. The halls are full of invisible elephants, and nothing anybody says is the way it really is. Our management is pure Theory X, and those motivational rallies are nothing but waving palm fronds in the air."

You may find that though you have more to say, your boss's face is turning bright red, and smoke seems to be coming out of his ears.

Before you dig this hole too deeply, remember the rules of hierarchy, and that people with power hate being analyzed by underlings, and that they can be downright mean if you try to point out elephants in the hallway that they would rather not discuss. Regardless of how accurate some of these characterizations may be, please remember that people will not be able to see themselves in them as clearly as you do.

SURVIVAL SOLUTION *48*
How to Get People to See Themselves Without Making Them Angry at You

You can use your knowledge to be a voice of reason in your company, but you have to do it reasonably, from within the system, not outside it, and definitely not from above it. Here are some suggestions:

Know Your Goal. The most important goal in dealing with dysfunctional systems is to get people to think about what they are doing and why. If you tell them, then the ideas are yours, not theirs.

Ask Questions; Don't Make Statements. All the goals you want to accomplish happen inside other people's minds, which are like fortresses, heavily defended against frontal attacks. You will be much more effective sneaking in the side door with questions designed to get them to explain to you how things operate. With a little luck, they may notice some of the inconsistencies and begin to question themselves.

Part 4

Worst-Case Scenarios

SHIT HAPPENS. What do you do when it hits the fan?

Facing change, getting chewed out, losing your job, or speaking in front of a group, each scenario in this section represents the worst case for someone. It is not the external reality that makes these situations so disastrous and difficult but the internal fears, doubts, and conflicts that they awaken. This section will offer advice on how to survive the most frightening things that can happen at work, the ones that require you to wrestle with your own demons. Go on if you dare.

SURVIVAL SCENARIO 49 Change

Why do they need to reorganize? Things were fine the way they were. It was clear whom you reported to and who was on your team. Now, all of a sudden, you find yourself working in three different departments with three different bosses. You just shake your head as you look over the plan. How can they imagine that this will ever work?

It may not, so then it will change again.

Change is hard, but change is the only certainty in business. The economy fluctuates; one technology succeeds another; market patterns shift. To stay viable, all businesses must change with the times.

Unfortunately, businesses are composed of people, and people don't accept change very well. Change itself is a major stressor. Stressors are like exercise: moderate amounts can make you stronger; large amounts can wear you out. People differ in their abilities to handle change. Some thrive on it, and others are overwhelmed by it. Which group you fall into will be determined by how you think and what you do.

SURVIVAL SOLUTION 49
How to Handle Change

Most people can improve on their abilities to handle change. Here are some suggestions:

Anticipate Change. You know things can't stay the same forever, but that's an abstraction that won't do you much good. Take a hard look at your business and try to figure out the direction things are moving. Where is the money coming from, and where is it going? What is the competition doing? Changes within companies are often responses to economic forces from outside. The more you know about what those forces are, the less likely you are to be blindsided by change. As in most survival situations, forewarned is forearmed.

Pay Attention to the Talk Inside Your Head. The main determinant of how well you will handle any difficult situation is what you are telling yourself about it inside your head. Listen closely to not only accentuate the positive and eliminate the negative, but also to recognize your own reactions and take them seriously. You are the one you have to convince, and you can do that only by taking your own hopes and fears seriously. The purpose of everything is to have a good life. Only you can decide what that is, and where you decide it will be inside your own head.

Go Through the Stages. Regardless of what the change is, we pass through emotional stages before finally shifting from one reality to another. The intensity of reaction may differ from person to person, but nobody avoids the emotional upheavals completely. The stages to expect are as follows:

- ◆ **Shock and denial.** At first, you will have difficulty getting your mind around the new reality. It can be hard to think about it at all. You may even find yourself pretending that it will all go away.

- ◆ **Sadness.** Sadness is the natural response to loss. Whatever the change, you will find yourself missing some of the old ways. You may have to shed a few tears before you move on. (To all the tough guys and gals reading this, the tears can be figurative; they don't have to be literal. All you have to do is acknowledge the feeling of loss.)

- ◆ **Fear.** We are all afraid of the unknown, even the toughest of us. Real bravery is not the absence of fear, but the resolve to move forward even when we are scared to death.

- ◆ **Anger.** There is a natural tendency to get angry and assign blame for anything we consider bad. Anger and blame are self-fueling. The more we play them over in our minds, the stronger they get. They may begin as a way of understanding a complex and difficult situation, but they can quickly become a more easily understood substitute for understanding and, eventually, an end in themselves.

- ◆ **Guilt and negotiating.** We all tend to think that if we had only done something differently, things would not be so bad now. We may resolve to work harder and become better people, as a way of alleviating this guilt. This strategy may work well as a way of preparing for the future, but it will not bring back the past.

- ◆ **Acceptance.** Eventually, we accept the change and move on into the future. The emotional stages we go through are the process by which this is accomplished. The stages are different views of the same reality. No one of them is complete in itself. Your final acceptance will have elements of all of them.

The textbooks say that the stages occur one after the other in a straight line. In real life, it's more like a game of Twister, with your left foot in anger, your right elbow in guilt, and your butt hovering over fear. If you feel that you are being pulled in many different directions at once, that means you are doing it right.

Don't Get Stuck. As you are going through the stages, you need to realize that your emotions are in a state of normal upheaval. You need to feel what you feel, but you don't have to act on those feelings. It's best to go through all the stages before you make any lasting decisions about what you are going to do.

Sometimes it's easy to get stuck in a particular stage to the exclusion of others. At work, anger is where most people can get caught. In difficult times, limit your consumption of gripe sessions and inflammatory rumors in the same way you would limit that third beer.

Develop a Tolerance for Not Knowing. One of the most stressful parts of change for most people is the uncertainty. As competent individuals, we expect ourselves to know what is going on and what is likely to happen. Sometimes, in the midst of change, it is impossible to know—for you, your boss, or anyone. Don't beat yourself up for not being able to predict the future, and don't jump to conclusions with insufficient data.

Accept Support. Support is important. When change places demands on you, it is often easy to focus all your attention on the job and forget friends and family. The people you care about can be islands of stability in a sea of change. Set your course toward them.

Blame Is Not the Answer. It's always easiest to see the bad sides of changes as foisted on you by someone else. Blaming the economy, the administration, management, or the home office may make you feel better for a little while, but in the long run, it makes you feel worse. Even if people are plotting against you, you can handle it better if you don't get paranoid.

Take Rumors with a Grain of Salt. In the midst of changes, you will hear all sorts of rumors (not that you won't at other times, but during times of change, you may be more likely to believe them). Spreading rumors is just a way some people have of dealing with uncertainty. Verify your facts, and don't succumb to the temptation to believe the worst of everyone.

Know You Are in Charge of Your Own Feelings. No one can make you feel bad; you have to do that yourself. How you feel depends on how you talk to yourself inside your head. Pay attention to those thoughts: which ones help you feel what you want to feel, and which ones hurt? If your thoughts are not helping, don't be afraid to disagree with yourself and start changing the way you think.

Set Priorities, and Stick to Them. Contrary to popular belief, there can be only one emergency at a time. It's easy to be distracted from your overall goals by smaller issues that come up suddenly. This is especially true if these smaller problems can be solved readily. Paying attention to all the little stuff at the expense of the overall plan can give you a false sense of accomplishment.

Schedule Fun. When you're stressed out, it's easy to put off doing the things that you enjoy. Don't. The things you enjoy restore you and recharge your batteries. During times of change, you need all the restoration you can get.

Take Care of Yourself. Eat, sleep, exercise; take time to relax. You wouldn't expect your office machinery to run without regular maintenance. Don't expect that of yourself.

SURVIVAL SCENARIO 50 Decisions, Decisions

You've been offered a promotion to a supervisory position. That means you'd be in management. It's an honor, but it's also pretty scary. You never expected this to come so early in your career, but now you have to decide. You lie awake at night with the plusses and minuses shouting each other down in your mind. Neither side is winning. You begin to wonder if you are cut out for this at all. Management is supposed to be about making decisions, and you have no idea how to pick one side or the other. This is one of the hardest choices you've ever had to make. How do you decide?

First of all, relax. You aren't the only person who has trouble deciding. Even though management is about making decisions, most managers are not really certain about the process itself. Most of the decisions we have to make are fairly unbalanced; one side is clearly better than another. It is only when the positives and negatives are about equal, or when the whole array of implications is too vast for our minds to get around, that we have to stop and ask ourselves how to decide, rather than just deciding. The fact that you're struggling means you are doing it right, at least up to this point. The real trick is moving on from here.

SURVIVAL SOLUTION 50
How to Make a Decision

Making a decision is not about predicting the future; nobody can do that. It is about making a choice and, by your subsequent actions, turning it into the right choice. The word *decide* comes from the Latin root meaning "to cut." That is the first and most important thing you have to understand about the process of decision making. Your task is to pick one course and disconnect yourself from the other. Here are some suggestions for making the cut:

Know Your Options. The first step in making a decision is to clearly understand the possibilities. In some cases, there are more than two alternatives. Before you make a choice, you need to know clearly what choice you have to make.

Know Who Wants What. I am always surprised at how many decisions are made based on what people think they ought to want, or on what other people want them to want. Many of us, especially women, have been socialized to consider everybody else's needs but our own. Since you are awake in the middle of the night already, use the time to carefully consider whom your decision must please. If you are not at the top of the list, keep thinking.

Trust Your Gut, but Don't Let It Make the Decision for You. The first thing your gut will tell you is to avoid the possibility that scares you the most. The worst mistake you can make is to let fear alone determine your course. Usually, the path with the greatest risk also has the biggest rewards, so you don't want to cut it off merely because it scares you. Neither do you want to jump one way or another to avoid the time and trouble it takes to make a real decision.

The way to use your gut most profitably is by asking yourself which of the positives attracts you the most, not which of the negatives is the scariest. Decisions made based on moving away from something that you fear or that you wish to avoid seldom work, because there really is no *away*. Psychologically speaking, safety is an expensive illusion. If your fear makes your decisions, you will regret it. As John Greenleaf Whittier wrote, "For all sad words of tongue or pen, / The saddest are these: 'It might have been!'"

Immerse Yourself, but Don't Drown. Do research, run numbers, talk to people, list the positives and negatives. By all means, gather what information you can, but realize that there is a limit to how much you can know beforehand. Unless the right answer jumps out at you as a result of your research, you'll soon get to a point of diminishing returns, where extra information adds nothing useful. The problem is that gathering information is much easier than deciding, so it's easy to fool yourself into thinking that one more fact will tip the balance in one direction or the other.

Set a Time Line. Some decisions have a built-in date by which they must be made. Many others have some indeterminate point in the future at which one possibility dies on the vine, and the decision is made by doing nothing. To avoid reaching this point, set a time by which you will have to jump one way or another, rather than merely falling into the only alternative that's left.

Jump. Eventually, you will have to make a choice. The more conscious and clear it is, the more likely it is to work out well.

Make Your Decision the Right One. Once you have made your choice, there is no turning back. Some alternatives are gone forever. Mourn them if you must, but pick your actions based on the direction you are heading rather than on where you've been.

SURVIVAL SCENARIO 51 Toxic Gossip

Did you hear that Jim's big project crashed and burned? What a *putz*! The word is, he lost a lot of money. A whole lot. It won't make any differences as long as he's married to the boss's daughter.

Have you seen Carol's neck brace? Last week, wasn't she wearing one of those carpal tunnel things? Next week, if she shows up, she'll probably be in a wheelchair. I heard she's not marking down even half of the sick leave she's taking.

Alex is threatened by competent women. Everybody knows he's not the sharpest tool in the shed, but he treats the women who work for him as if they're the idiots. One after another, he gives them unmitigated crap about everything they do. Finally, they get pissed off enough to leave.

Gwen is such a bitch! Anytime you say anything to her, she takes it as criticism and blows up at you. It's like 24-7 PMS.

Old Sergeant Ted still thinks he's in the marines. Everything has to be "done by the book"—his book. If you disagree, he thinks you should be shot for insubordination.

Mike burned out years ago, and now he's just putting in time. Even when his eyes are open, his brain is asleep.

At work, gossiping about coworkers is a major source of entertainment. It's more fun than the company softball team, and you don't have to be a jock to play.

Gossip is also a major source of conflict and morale problems, particularly when it moves from being a vehicle for dissemination of general information to one for disseminating people's negative opinions of others. Once that gets started, it's hard to stop. You hear a few rumors about yourself or one of your friends, and it makes you angry, especially because they're a pack of lies. You try to find the source and set the record straight and, in the process, end up spreading stories about the people who are spreading stories about you.

At any given time, there are ten or twelve little wars going on, and rumors are the weapons. The result is that nobody trusts anybody except a couple of close allies, and people regularly feel hurt, angry, and insulted by what they hear. Everything is second- or thirdhand, so there's no way to resolve anything.

SURVIVAL SOLUTION *51*
What You Can Do About Gossip

There are generally two kinds of gossip in any company, with no clear dividing line between them. One is general information about events and decisions, and the other is negative anecdotes and judgments about people. Obviously, the second kind is the one that causes trouble. Your goal is to get yourself out of that loop and, by your lack of participation, decrease the overall level of hurtful gossip in your office. True, you will miss out on a few juicy tidbits, but I believe that will be a small price to pay for the decreased stress and the enhancement to your reputation as one who stands above the fray. If the rewards are not greater than what you have to give up, all these techniques are reversible. Here are my suggestions:

Carefully Assess the Gossip You Hear and the People Who Spread It. With a little thought, you can separate the neutral gossip from the toxic and the people who are merely spreading information from the ones who are trying to stir things up. Pay close attention, and analyze what you are hearing rather than just going with the flow.

Speak for Yourself. This is the most important rule. Most toxic rumors are about injustices done to other people, spread by people who convince themselves that they are standing up for others. They don't see what they are doing as an aggressive act, but as a defense against what someone else has done. Thus, the pattern is perpetuated. If you make it a rule to speak only for yourself and listen only to people speaking for themselves, most of the worst abuses can never happen.

Do Not Respond. Moment to moment, what keeps people gossiping is the listener's response. Watch people and see all the encouragement rumormongers get from nods, smiles, open mouths, and leaning conspiratorially closer, not to mention adding embellishments. Gossip is a performance. If there is no audience response, the show is over. If all you do is act uninterested—you know, like your dad when he was reading the paper—gossipers will go and find someone who is more fun, and this may be enough to get you out of the negative loop.

Take special care to not respond when you hear negative stories about yourself or your friends.

This is the part that takes real effort of will. People who share negative stories about you are generally not doing it out of friendship. They want a reaction. They'd like you to get mad and maybe retaliate, which will give them more to talk about. There is nothing about this pattern that will in any way benefit you.

Answer Bad with Good. Whenever gossips say something negative about someone, say something positive. It will drive rumormongers crazy and let them know that you are definitely unwilling to play their game.

Spread Positive Gossip. If the idea of positive gossip seems like an oxymoron, that is all the more reason to try this technique. It couldn't hurt and may help.

If You Have Something Negative to Say, Talk Directly and in Private. When you do this, don't tell them what they did that was bad. Instead, tell them your reaction and ask if that was their intention. For example: "When you made the comment about my report, I felt put down. Was that what you meant to do?" Also, you can tell them what you would like them to do instead. Don't set up a situation in which they have to admit they were wrong in order for you to get what you want.

If you work in an office where gossip and backbiting make it difficult to come in most mornings, realize that it takes two to tango. If enough people follow the advice set down here, most of the worst rumors will simply die on the grapevine. It has to start with you.

SURVIVAL SCENARIO 52 The Perils of Perfectionism

When people say they are perfectionists, I never know if they're bragging or admitting a shortcoming. To them, perfectionism means they work hard and drive themselves to produce the best possible product.

What could be wrong with that? In fact, if everybody were more perfectionistic, then the world wouldn't be so full of shoddy work. Right?

Actually, I think it's perfectionists who are responsible for most of the shoddy work. Here's how it happens, with Gwen from Scenario 27:

Gwen is a perfectionist. She accepts only the best of herself and her employees. That means she criticizes everything. If you do something for Gwen that's 99 percent right, she's going to focus on the 1 percent that's wrong. That's the way she treats herself, so she feels justified in making the same demands of others.

Mistakes to her are unacceptable, almost like crimes. In her scheme of things, they are indications of a pervasive and dangerous mental state. If people allow themselves to make little mistakes, they will allow themselves to make big ones. This cannot be tolerated, and it's Gwen's God-given duty to nip this kind of thing in the bud.

The upshot is that Gwen hands out a lot of criticism and no praise. She thinks that if people get bigheaded, they won't be as careful. Most of Gwen's conversations with her employees, her family, and herself involve telling people what they are doing wrong. On the receiving end, her well-intentioned criticism is indistinguishable from cruelty. After a few unsuccessful attempts to please Gwen, her employees believe that whatever they do is going to be criticized unmercifully; why bother trying to get it right? They certainly are not inspired to go the extra mile for her. They would, however, go much further than that to avoid her.

This is the pattern by which perfectionism creates shoddy work. The only way people can get back at perfectionists is indirectly (and most often unconsciously) by goofing up. This, of course, makes Gwen criticize even harder, which leads to more unconscious retaliation. Her employees are not choosing to do shoddy work to spite her. It's just that people's minds work less well when they are working for people who frighten them or make them angry.

It's difficult to estimate how many mistakes one perfectionist can create.

Even though Gwen is right most of the time, that doesn't make her happy. You'd think that a perfectionist could at least take some joy in a job well done. She just can't. No job is done well enough. For her, life always has a tiny dent in its door, just big enough to keep her from enjoying it. Unfortunately, when Gwen is not happy, nobody's happy.

SURVIVAL SOLUTION 52
The Perfect Cure for Perfectionism

Right about now, I know some perfectionists are thinking, "So, perfectionism is a bad thing, huh? What am I supposed to do, just slap things together and not worry about it?"

Not quite. Have you ever thought about what the opposite of perfectionism might be? No, it's not sloppiness. It's efficiency.

Efficiency means maximizing the gain for the minimum amount of resources expended. For people like Gwen, the more they drive themselves and others crazy, the less they accomplish.

In the world of the perfectionist, there is no concept of degree. Things are either right or wrong. If they are wrong, it has to be pointed out. The importance of the task and the size of the mistake are seldom factors. No mistake is too small to criticize.

If you are a perfectionist and would like to change, this is your lucky day. The cure is simple, but the trick is you must do it perfectly. That shouldn't be a problem. Here's what you need to do:

Give Four Sincere Compliments for Every Criticism—to Yourself as Well as to Others. This may not increase the number of compliments you hand out, but it will surely cut down on the number of criticisms. They'll cost too much, because every time you want to criticize, you'll have to think up four positive accompaniments.

Criticize Only the Biggest Mistake Made on a Given Day. The second part of the cure is more difficult, but it must be done perfectly too. If you are a perfectionist who is cutting down on criticizing, you will undoubtedly expect that, since you are not pointing out people's mistakes and telling people how to do things, they will goof up more often. When you notice this happening—and you will—allow yourself to comment only on the most egregious goof-up that occurs that day. For the rest, keep them a secret that you take with you to your grave.

The purpose of this part of the cure is helping you to decide which mistake is most important. It's not easy, but if you're willing to try hard, you may be able to do it well. Nobody can do it perfectly.

SURVIVAL SCENARIO 53 When People Don't Listen

Donna has messed up again. She's smart, and she means well, but she doesn't seem to keep track of all the details. Maybe she misunderstood, or maybe she forgot. Whatever the cause, the project is delayed because her part is not done correctly. If she would only listen better and pay more attention, she could do things right the first time, but she's always got so many things going that she can't stay focused on any of them.

The worst part of it all is having to go talk to her about it. Her feelings get hurt so easily. You need to say something, but what?

Wouldn't life be simpler if people would only listen?

Actually, getting people to listen to constructive criticism requires considerable skill and forethought. You already know that you have to praise what they've done well and downplay the mistakes. You know you have to be kind, sensitive, and precise, but it takes even more than that to get people to listen.

SURVIVAL SOLUTION *53*
How to Get People to Listen to Constructive Criticism

To criticize effectively, you have to remember that people usually hear only what is consistent with what they already believe about themselves. If what you're saying doesn't fit with their basic self-image, they will think you are wrong, regardless of the facts of the case.

As in so many components of interpersonal situations, criticism is judged as much by style as it is by content. To get people to listen to constructive criticism, you have to focus on your goal, which is getting them to do something differently either now or next time. You must also choose your words carefully so as not to imply that they are bad people for making a mistake. The trick is knowing in advance what most people consider bad.

All of us carry around a set of beliefs about what a good person should be, and we try to keep our actions, or at least our perceptions of our actions, consistent with those beliefs. If anyone suggests that we are different from what we believe we should be, all we hear them saying is that we are bad.

To get people to listen to constructive criticism, what you say must be consistent with what they already believe. Most of the people you deal with at work believe the following things about themselves:

They Are Right. This belief is a given, regardless of the person or situation. There is no point wasting time trying to convince anybody that you are right and he or she is wrong. You can cite facts until you're blue in the face. The best you can hope for is an acknowledgment that the person misunderstood what was asked, told, ordered, or explained.

People also believe themselves to be reasonable and fair, that they can be convinced they have made a mistake by a logical argument or a demonstration of fact. In actual practice there is no argument or array of facts persuasive enough to convince somebody that you are right and they are wrong.

They Work Hard. One's own efforts always feel as if they are worth more than those of other people. Always remember to acknowledge how hard people are working, especially if you want them to do more.

They Always Give a Little More Than They Receive. Nobody sees him- or herself as selfish. If you want people to give more, ask. Don't waste your time trying to convince them that they are not giving enough already. If you must ask for more, acknowledge what they have already given.

They Are at Least Slightly Above Average in Intelligence. People will readily acknowledge that there are other people who are brighter than they are—say, rocket scientists. If, however, you ask them where they fall in the overall continuum, they will usually place themselves above the mean. Even when you are dealing with someone who is intellectually challenged, remember that there is no way he or she can feel the lack of something never experienced in the first place.

They May Not Always Tell the Truth, but They Are Basically Honest. Most people believe that when they supply information that is not factually accurate, it is because they didn't completely understand the question or that they forgot specific details. Even pathological liars believe they are only slightly bending the truth. Suggesting that another person has purposely been deceptive is universally treated as a grave insult, especially when it is true.

They Are Good Drivers. This belief is especially prevalent in the male of the species. Challenge it at your peril.

If you want people to hear what you have to say, structure your comments so that they are consistent with these basic beliefs. If you don't, people will either fight you or ignore you. They will definitely not listen to you.

SURVIVAL SCENARIO *54* Don't Take This Personally

"Don't take this criticism personally," a coworker says, but the words are scarcely out of the person's mouth and you already are taking it personally, even though you don't even know what the criticism is. It doesn't matter. Criticism always feels personal.

"Don't take this personally" ranks near the top of the list of useless things to say to people. That's not because there's anything wrong with the concept. It's just that, as we saw in the last scenario, unless criticism is phrased with utmost care, it is personal in that it is likely to contradict your basic beliefs about yourself. If you are taking things too personally, you are seldom consciously aware of what you're doing. Telling you not to take criticism personally will be perceived as just another personal attack.

What does it mean to take things personally? All of us have external attachments—our children, our pets, our favorite sports teams, our creations at work, our view of ourselves as good people—that we experience as if they were parts of our bodies. Psychologically, we make little distinction between verbal disparagement of these entities and physical attacks to our vital organs.

SURVIVAL SOLUTION *54*
How to Keep from Taking Criticism Personally

When it comes to criticism, we all take it personally; it's part of our psychological makeup. We're hardwired to defend who we are, what we do, and what we love. That doesn't mean we have to respond to every criticism with an instinctive, kill-or-be-killed counterattack. Luckily, we have evolved brains that are capable of overriding our primitive default settings. We just have to remember to use them. Here are some suggestions on how to keep from being seen as taking criticisms too personally:

Stop and Think Before You Say Anything. This is good advice no matter what the situation. When you feel attacked, the first utterance that pops into your head is seldom the most effective response. If you make it a practice to wait twenty-four hours before you answer criticisms, the people around you may be so surprised by your maturity and reasonableness that they will listen to you for a change.

Listen Carefully. Every criticism contains useful information as well as an attack. The trick is separating the two. Useful information gives you some ideas about how to do things differently. If you don't hear anything useful at first, keep listening until you do.

Ask for Advice Rather Than Explaining, Justifying, or Giving Answers. The explanations you think of in response to criticism will sound perfectly reasonable and at least 150 percent correct. To you. To other people, they will sound like a misguided defense against a misperceived personal attack. Most any explanation you choose will make you look even more wrong. Trust me on this. If, by sheer force of reason, your explanation actually succeeds in getting the criticism modified or withdrawn, it may feel like you've won, but it probably means that people have decided it's easier to humor you than treat you like a rational human being.

What If You Have to Criticize Someone Who Takes Things Too Personally? We discussed this in the previous scenario, but it bears repeating here: structure the situation so that he or she doesn't have to admit wrongdoing by accepting what you have to say. In Asia they'd call it allowing the person to save face. Make it clear in your comments that you understand how a reasonable and honorable person might do what he or she did. Direct your advice toward improving the situation rather than pointing out mistakes. Focus on what you want to happen rather than what's wrong with what has already happened.

Come to think of it, this is a good way to present criticism to anyone, because you never know who's going to take it personally.

SURVIVAL SCENARIO 55 Getting Chewed Out

The e-mail reads: "Come to my office immediately!" Its meaning hits your gut like a triple espresso. You're going to get chewed out.

As you march toward your rendezvous with destiny, stop. Take a deep breath, and think carefully about what you are facing. You already know the pattern; every angry authority figure in your life has chewed you out in pretty much the same way. This time, you can use what you know to protect yourself.

SURVIVAL SOLUTION 55
How to Get Chewed Out and Still Stay in One Piece

The secret to surviving a chewing out is in mentally taking a step back and observing what is going on between you and the person doing the chewing. Your best defense is not getting defensive.

Pay Attention to Form, Not Content. The best way to handle a reprimand, or any difficult interpersonal situation, is to imagine what is likely to happen and have an overall strategy for dealing with it. The biggest mistake people make in such situations is listening too closely to the specific words being spoken and not stepping back to see the overall pattern of the interaction. If you recognize the pattern, you can predict what will happen next. If you can predict, you will have some measure of control.

Understand the Effects of Anger. Angry people are not thinking clearly. These folks are following behavior sequences that are hardwired into the most ancient part of the brain: They attack; you defend. What seems like a defense to you will feel like a counterattack to them, so they will fight harder, and eventually you will get clobbered. Regardless of specific content, most angry interchanges follow this ancient preprogrammed pattern.

Unless you are willing to kill or be killed, the only effective strategy for dealing with anger is to disrupt the pattern by stepping out of it and doing the unexpected. To accomplish this, you must override your own internal programming by using the newer, more flexible parts of your brain. To survive difficult situations, you must react to emotion with thinking.

Know What to Expect. Whatever the subject, think of a chewing out as a kangaroo court in which you cannot prove yourself innocent. The harder you try, the worse your punishment will be, because the proceeding itself is the punishment. The longer it lasts, the more verbal abuse you have to endure. The only way to win is to plead guilty immediately and ask what you need to do to correct the problem.

Do Not Attempt the Impossible. Get real. Facts are irrelevant: you cannot win an argument with your boss. Don't even try. A chewing out is an expression of dominance. The rules, like those for anger, are also hardwired into the brain. Disagreement or even polite defense will be seen as a counterattack aimed at gaining ascendancy, which must be put down.

The very best you can hope for is being seen as a good employee who has made a mistake and will do what is necessary to correct it. That mistake may go down as a black mark on your record, but the quickest way to expunge it will be to take responsibility and fix the problem.

If you lose your temper when you are being chewed out, there will be two black marks.

Let Your Goal Determine Your Actions. In a chewing out, the only reasonable goal is to accept blame and move the discussion as quickly as possible toward what you must do to make amends. Angry people want to rave on and on about what a bad thing you did. Often, they haven't thought about what they want you to do to fix it. The sooner you can move them from raving to thinking, the better it will be for you.

An added benefit of this strategy is that once your boss has calmed down, he or she might see that what you did wasn't so bad after all.

Never, Ever Explain! While you are being chewed out, you will feel an almost overwhelming urge to explain what actually happened. Don't do it!

Explanations, no matter how accurate or well crafted, will be heard by an angry person as: "If you consider the situation carefully, you will see that I am right, and you are wrong. You have no reason to be angry, and anyway, someone else did it."

The urge to explain is actually a part of the primitive pattern you want to avoid. It will always make an angry person angrier. Only after the anger cools and the problem solving begins is there any chance that your boss will look at the situation differently.

There is another reason you shouldn't explain: Once you start telling the story, the temptation is strong to alter events just slightly to make them fit better. The tiniest distortion will be seen as a much more serious crime than whatever else you may have done.

Do Not Submit to Cross-Examination. If you think that the approach I'm suggesting seems like copping out, because you're not standing up for yourself, remember that discretion is the better part of valor.

The place to stand firm is in your refusal to answer a question asked more than once. Angry people want reasons to get angrier. If you aren't giving them enough, they will ask for more by repeating questions, hoping to trip you up. They might also ask you to explain why you did whatever you did, in order to attack your thinking as well as your actions. You do not have to answer such questions. Instead, turn the conversation back toward your earnest desire to correct the problem. Say: "It was my mistake, and, like any responsible person, I'm eager to do whatever I can to set it right. What would you like me to do?" Even the angriest people will find it difficult to argue with that.

Plead Guilty to the Act Itself, Not Its Implication. Angry people jump to conclusions about the motives of the people they are angry at. Often in a chewing out, your actions will be presented as evidence of disloyalty or conscious deception. If this happens, you'll be really glad that you didn't succumb to the temptation to alter details. Do not attempt to prove your honesty or loyalty. Say: "I can't convince you to trust me. You will have to look at what I do and decide for yourself."

Before You Draw Further Conclusions, Wait. Think of it this way: if you were to verbally attack someone who handled your outburst gracefully, wouldn't you feel guilty the next day?

SURVIVAL SCENARIO 56 Need for Improvement

Your boss slides the annual review form across the desk and sits back as you begin to read. A couple of *satisfactorys*, an *excellent*—so far, so good. Then your breath catches in your throat. *Need for improvement!*

That's just like an F. You have never in your life received a failing grade. Not only that, but also it's completely bogus. There were a couple of problems, but they weren't your fault, and he knows it. Why is he doing this? What does it mean? Are you going to get fired, or is he just harassing you?

You look up from the form to face your boss. Now what?

For most people, a bad review is a shock, like a punch to the gut. You will feel attacked, hurt, scared, ashamed, angry, confused, and eager to defend yourself, even though you may not know exactly what you are defending yourself against. In that difficult moment, there may be all sorts of things you want to say. None of them will help. This is a time to be quiet and listen as carefully as possible.

SURVIVAL SOLUTION *56*
How to Respond to a Bad Review

In rating you as needing improvement, your boss is sending you a message. In the initial meeting, more than anything else, you need to know what that message is and what it means. You cannot get this information if you are talking. Later, there will be time to correct errors and present your defense. Now, your job is to elicit as much information as possible. Here is what I advocate:

Say as Little as Possible. I know I've already told you to be quiet, but the urge to speak will be so strong that the advice bears repeating. Silence is your best response for several reasons. First, as we have seen in other scenarios, in emotional situations if you act on your first impulse, it is likely to make things worse. Second, as difficult as it may be, you need to consider your boss's point of view. Unless he is a total schmuck, he knows that his low rating will have a strong effect on you and has probably prepared an explanation. All you need to do to hear it is point to the spot on the form and look up. He will do the rest.

Know Your Goal. Your goal in this situation is clear. You need to find out why your boss has a negative opinion of you and to avoid doing anything in the meeting that will lower it further. Over time, you will probably want to do what you can to improve his opinion, but please realize that there is no way to accomplish that goal in the initial review meeting. Any attempt you make is likely to backfire. The most positive image you can present is strong, silent, and serious.

Absolutely, Positively Do Not Play the Specifics Game. In his explanation to you, your boss will most likely cite specific situations that will seem to you to have been misinterpreted, because he does not know all the facts or has not talked to the right people, or whatever. Do not think for a second that clarifying anything will make him change his mind. To date in human history, no boss has ever changed a general opinion because the specifics on which it was based were successfully challenged. You will get nowhere by trying to convince him that his analysis is wrong.

Listen and Take Notes. In an emotional situation, it is easy to forget or distort what you hear. Try to record as much as you can as accurately as possible.

Ask What Your Boss Would See as Improvement. If your goal is to create a more positive opinion, this is vital. Do not guess what *improvement* would look like, and when you hear what your boss says, don't try to convince him you are already doing it.

Ask for Time to Prepare Your Response. Nothing you say in that initial meeting will change anything. You will need to respond, but that should occur only after you have had time to think.

Find Out What Reviews Mean in Your Company. Ideally, you should have done your intelligence gathering on reviews before you got yours, but it's never too late to learn. In some companies, annual reviews mean nothing, while in some others, they are very important. In some companies, managers have quotas of *excellents*, *satisfactorys*, and *need for improvements* that they must meet. You need to know in some larger context what it means to get a negative review and how people have handled them in the past. There may be standard procedures; if so, you need to follow them.

In Your Response, Do Not Imply That Your Boss Is Wrong, Even if He Is. Challenging a review is usually a mistake, since it is the opinion that the review is based upon that is important, rather than the words on the paper. In more bureaucratic organizations, the words may affect your future, so there might be some percentage in trying to change them. Regardless of what you are trying to change, you cannot do it by suggesting that your boss was wrong. If there are unconsidered facts or mitigating circumstances, bring them up carefully.

Present an Action Plan for Correcting the Problem. The rating was *need for improvement*. The most important thing you can do is show how you are planning to improve. Address all the points covered in your notes.

Ask for a Feedback Meeting After a Reasonable Amount of Time. The purpose of the meeting is both to see if your boss notices your efforts to improve and to supply information to show him that he should.

A bad review is usually not the end of the world, especially if you handle it well. Again, consider the situation from your boss's point of view. As a manager, he is supposed to bring out the best in people. If you demonstrably improve, he may get an *excellent* on his annual review. In the long run, this will benefit you far more than proving him wrong.

57 ## Is Your Company Going Down the Tubes?

Times have been hard for your company. There have been several rounds of layoffs and reorganizations, but the end is nowhere in sight. You like the work you do, and so far you have held on to your job. The stress has been tremendous, and you wonder how much a business can stand. Can the company pull itself together, or is the whole thing is heading down the tubes? Should you stick it out or get while the getting is good?

Organizations, like people, have a hard time dealing with change, especially negative changes such as cutbacks, layoffs, shortfalls, reorganizations, and takeovers. When such events occur, companies need to go through a period of adjustment that can be stressful and difficult, but it is also normal, necessary, and, in many cases, productive. During the adjustment to change, it may seem as if the company is falling apart. The stress can be tremendous, but sometimes businesses can come out better and stronger for the experience. Just like individuals, companies adjust to change by going through predictable stages. To make decisions about your job, it will help to know what these stages are and assess your company's progress in moving through them. Some organizations get stuck and solidify into abnormal patterns. Others move through them and come out stronger in the end.

SURVIVAL SOLUTION *57*

Recognize the Stages a Company Goes Through in Dealing with Negative Change

Companies, like people, adjust to change by going through stages. The most reliable predictor of an ultimately successful outcome is some general recognition and discussion about what is going on. Often it helps to have the help of a consultant or a manager who has been through similar situations elsewhere. If people can talk honestly and openly about what is going on, the company is likely to move forward and heal from its wounds. If there is no official recognition of what is going on, the company can get stuck and die. Here are the stages to look for; you will have to decide if your company is moving through them or going down the tubes:

Shock. For a while, everything is confused and disorganized. The right hand doesn't know what the left hand is doing. You hear one rumor in the morning and a totally different one later in the day. The hardest thing for most people, especially managers, is not knowing. At this stage, they may speculate wildly, and their speculations are passed along as facts. The best thing to do at this stage is to sit down, talk things over, and figure them out before making big decisions. At all levels, people need to be able to say, "It's too soon to tell." Management can lose a lot of credibility at this time by making too many wrong guesses or by making promises that can't be kept. As uncomfortable as it is, the best thing to do is stay with the uncertainty. Don't believe the rumors until you've checked them out thoroughly.

Formation of Factions. From the shock stage, the company often moves into a state of defensive retreat. The hallmark of this stage is the formation of factions. There is a good deal of blaming—management by workers, workers by management. Often certain people or groups are made scapegoats. At this stage, there is usually so much animosity that everyone feels that "something has to be done." This usually means getting rid of a few malcontents at the bottom or a few incompetents at the top, depending on the speaker. Getting rid of people is an extreme measure. If it is to be done, it should be with a great deal of forethought, investigation, and communication.

Unfortunately, planning and communication are rare at this stage. Plotting and secrecy are more often the order of the day. Angry meetings outside of work are common. Stories of atrocities abound.

Sometimes management steps in and cracks down on dissent. Angry memos are common, along with meetings in which the CEO, with rolled-up sleeves, tries to put an end to rumors by explaining just how everything is and is going to be. Wrong move. Such meetings are usually perceived as a way of putting an end to discussion rather than as a form of communication. Organizations stuck at this stage can become totalitarian and intolerant of any sort of disagreement.

Big meetings are a good idea at this time, but communication should come from the bottom rather than the top. Upper-level managers should listen more than they talk. As productive as this posture is in the long run, it is painful and difficult for most managers to handle. They like to be in control. Having the meetings run by a neutral outsider can be a distinct advantage.

Overcommunication. Gradually, the organization moves into a stage of acknowledgment. Communication improves to the point of being overdone. Participation is encouraged and may even be demanded. Things move more slowly, because everybody is checking with everybody else. The focus is often more on who is doing the work than on the work itself. Further changes come slowly, and decisions may take a long time to be made. For a while, there are so many meetings that there is little time left for work. Often this is a good thing. Trust has to be rebuilt, and that doesn't happen overnight. Just as in other stages, organizations can get stuck here and develop a culture of meetings for meetings' sake.

Getting Back to Work. Finally, the focus shifts more to the task to be done than who is doing it. This is a sign of healing, which, I hasten to add, cannot be rushed. An organizational reaction to change may take several years, or even longer, depending on the size of the company. Such storms are best weathered as a group, with the knowledge that everyone is in it together.

To make decisions about your own career, you have to evaluate your company with respect to these stages and judge for yourself if it is moving forward. The more openly these patterns are discussed, the higher the probability of success. If there is no open talk, there will be little progress.

SURVIVAL SCENARIO 58 Companies That Practice Human Sacrifice

Companies that get stuck in the process of dealing with change can develop strange and dangerous rituals.

Turnover seems to be a problem at your office. Some people quit, and some just seem to be there one day and gone the next. One morning, you come in, and their cubes are empty. People call them "the disappeared." Sometimes, workers staying late see them shuffling down darkened corridors, escorted by rent-a-cops. They always seem to be carrying cardboard boxes.

Everyone wonders who will be next.

Even in this enlightened age, some primitive tribes in the jungles of American business still practice human sacrifice. When revenue streams dry, the elect meet and decide who will be offered up to appease angry gods. Never mind that sacrifices do nothing to address the problem, which is often systemic. Someone must pay the price.

SURVIVAL SOLUTION 58
How to Stay off the Sacrificial Altar

Certain kinds of organizations are most apt to practice human sacrifice during times of change and economic downturn. The first step in avoiding the ritual knife is knowing whether you work in one of those organizations. The following are the company types most likely to get rid of people to appease angry gods:

- Organizations that are dependent on national, state, or local politics
- Organizations in which large numbers of people work on commission
- Organizations that have distinct two-tier systems: us and them—they could be labor and management, office and field, administration and staff, or any two groups that could turn into warring factions in times of stress
- Family-owned businesses, especially those in which two or more family members are employed, and particularly those in which family members who have little formal responsibility spend a lot of time at the office
- Organizations that allow managers to make arbitrary personnel decisions and then always back them up no matter what the issue
- Union shops in which the union's numbers and power are in decline, which can put pressure on union leaders to make choices between protecting the union and protecting its members

In these kinds of organizations, there's usually an orthodox way to do everything, no matter how small.

Certain people are in favor, and others are beyond the pale. Which is which may have less to do with performance than with loyalty. When things go wrong, it is usually interpreted as an indication that either someone in the out-group is getting lax or someone in the in-group is fraternizing with the enemy. They become sacrificial victims and are fired or harassed into resigning. The latter is often preferred, as it avoids workers' compensation claims. The purpose of sacrifice is partly revenge and partly to drive the people who remain back into the fold. There may also be an unconscious element of appeasing angry gods, as the people who run such organizations seldom believe that their actions and decisions control how their employees perform.

If this description sounds like the place where you work, here are some suggestions:

- **Keep your résumé up to date.** Realize that no one is safe no matter how solid a position appears.

- **Make time to network.** Keep your contacts current with other people in your industry. You never know when you'll need them.

- **Develop your own way to evaluate your performance.** In such firms, praise and punishment have little to do with competence. If you are to be evaluated fairly at all, you will have to do it yourself. Having a list of goals you have accomplished will be helpful in interviewing for your next job if you are a victim. In that interview, do not talk about the politics of your previous organization. Your prospective employer will either know or not. No good can come from speaking ill of your previous job.

- **If you feel you are falling out of favor, consult an attorney *before* you are sacrificed, not *after*.** Consider plans for a lawsuit or whistle-blowing very carefully. The people you go up against will have no compunctions against lying on the stand. Next time, it could be you.

SURVIVAL SCENARIO 59   You've Lost Your Job; Don't Make It Worse

You stand there, pink slip in hand, thinking that this could be the worst day of your life. Let's hope that things don't go downhill from here.

What could be worse than being fired or laid off?

The psychological states you can get into if you let your emotional response to losing your job make life choices for you.

Losing a job, even a bad job, is traumatic. Your job is part of your identity; losing it is like losing a piece of yourself. It hurts.

For the first few days, you'll be buffeted by emotion. You'll feel slow, dull waves of sadness, cold tingles of fear, and hot gusts of anger—at your boss, at yourself, and also at the people close to you, who are both easier to get at and more likely to forgive you. These feelings are normal and are actually part of the healing process. Feel them, but don't let them dictate your actions. Your heart should have its say, but your head must rule. If you are fired or laid off, the psychological work you must do is disconnecting from the old job and moving on to a new one. This is painful and difficult enough. You can make it worse by trying to avoid it.

SURVIVAL SOLUTION *59*
How to Cope with Losing Your Job

Based on years of experience counseling people dealing with the loss of their jobs, here are some suggestions:

Avoid Alcohol, Drugs, Shopping, Television, Net Surfing, Household Chores, and Any Other Mind-Numbing Substances. The urge to make it all go away will attract you in the same way that cliffs attract lemmings. There is no escape, only delay. Think of staring blankly at a screen in the same way you think about shooting heroin.

Taking on extra chores is particularly dangerous, because they can make you feel as if you're accomplishing something even when you are avoiding more pressing actions. What's important at this stage is knowing what you feel and talking about it with people close to you. Keep sadness from turning into depression by turning outward and taking action.

When you are sad after a loss, it is easy to slide into depression. At any given moment, the two states are similar. Depression is what happens when sadness becomes a way of life, when you let the low motivation and desire to turn inward determine what you do. When you're depressed, you wait until you feel better to do the things that will make you feel better. What will make you feel better is sleeping, eating, exercise, talking to people, and doing things to solve the problem. What will make you feel worse is sitting on the couch and keeping everything inside while you're waiting to feel better.

Be Careful About What Actions You Take. For some people, anger is an antidote to sadness. Especially if you have been fired or laid off for political reasons, be circumspect about impulses toward legal action, clearing your name, or explaining what really happened to former coworkers. Any idea that keeps you connected to the company that got rid of you is likely to hurt more than it helps.

Before You Consider Legal Recourse, Talk to an Actual Lawyer, Not a Friend Who Knows Something About Law. If you lose a job, usually the most realistic and productive objective is to learn what you can from the situation, and then let it go. It is much easier to dwell on feelings about your old job rather than on plans for your new life. What is easiest is not necessarily what is best.

Don't Hide from the People Who Love You. Even if you're hurt, angry, ashamed, and frightened, you need to talk to people who care about you. If they were in pain, you'd want them to come to you.

Aside from reminding you that you're not alone, talking to friends and family is what turns feeling into thinking, which is what psychological healing is about.

Spread your troubles among several confidants so that you don't wear the best one out. Give friends permission to disagree, and try to listen when they do. They are more likely to be realistic than you are. Don't keep them up past their bedtimes unless it's absolutely necessary, and don't call them if you've had more than one drink.

Emotional support means listening to you and trying to clarify what you want to happen, not necessarily agreeing, telling you what to do, or doing things for you that you should be doing for yourself.

Let people who love you say "I told you so" before making a big deal out of it.

Beware of friends who encourage you to express your anger. You can never be sure exactly whose anger you might be expressing. You have enough problems without taking on somebody else's authority issues.

Focus on the Next Step, Not the Whole Journey. There will, of course, be many other actions you have to take regarding your financial situation and landing a new job. There are suggestions here, as well as shelves full of books, to help you with the specifics. Do some reading, and follow what seems to be sound advice, even if your emotions are saying, "Not today."

Considering how far you have to go will not help you get there; it will just make you feel overwhelmed and exhausted. Instead, pay attention to what you need to do right now. In dealing with losing a job, or in any difficult situation, how much you accomplish in a day is less important than continuing to move in the right direction.

SURVIVAL SCENARIO 60 Finding a Job

Another weary, bleary morning of checking the listings. Nothing looks particularly good. Nevertheless, you e-mail out a few résumés. You wonder why you bother, because you'll never hear anything from most of them anyway. Might as well be sending them to Mars. By noon, you're still in your pajamas, feeling worthless and scared that you'll never find a job. The kitchen floor needs stripping, so you figure you might as well do something useful that's as yucky as you feel.

Before you're done with that, your mother calls. "Since you're not working, maybe you can help me run a few errands."

Another day of job searching gone to hell.

A job search is one of the most difficult and frightening ordeals a person can go through. Daily, you must live with so many painful emotions. Fear, uselessness, uncertainty, and rejection swarm around you like biting insects, not to mention the constant worry about how the bills are going to get paid. Then there is abject terror when you do get an interview, wondering how to present yourself as bright and full of enthusiasm when you feel like crap warmed over. No wonder so many people find themselves drifting away from the search, doing household tasks and running errands for other people just to feel that they are accomplishing something, anything. Perhaps the worst part is that your agony is so commonplace. You're reluctant to share it because you think people will tire of it as quickly as you do. Or worse, they will make useless recommendations and then get offended when you don't follow up. So, like most job searchers, you suffer in silence.

SURVIVAL SOLUTION 60
Job Search Dos and Don'ts

Unfortunately, I cannot make your job search any easier or less frightening, but, having counseled hundreds of people through the ordeal, I can make some suggestions:

Make Finding a Job into Your Job. Get up, get dressed, and spend a set block of time each day conducting your search. Use the same tools you would at work—organize yourself, set goals, make a daily schedule. You'll feel more businesslike, and, since you're going to be there for the next few hours, you'll be less apt to put off the more productive but difficult tasks. It may be helpful to designate a friend or family member as your supervisor, to whom you make progress reports and from whom you can get encouragement to stay on task. Make it clear that your supervisor doesn't get to boss you around.

Another advantage to making the job search into your job is that once you have put in your work time, you can be done for the day and relax without feeling guilty about it.

Never Let Anyone Complete the Sentence That Begins, "Since You're Not Working . . ." You *are* working, every day from nine to five, or whenever. Let this be known, and stick by it. If your actions acknowledge that you aren't doing anything important, pretty soon, you'll begin to believe it.

Do the Scary Part First. The more active parts of a job search, such as calling people and setting up meetings, are much more productive than passively looking at listings and sending résumés into the void. The active parts usually are far scarier and more easily put off unless you put them at the top of your to-do list.

Network as If Your Future Depends on It. You are much more likely to get a job because you know somebody who knows somebody. The most important part of your job search is calling everyone you know, telling them you're looking for work, and asking them who they know who might know somebody. Then you call those people and arrange to talk to them. Spread your net wide and eventually you'll catch something.

Ask for Face Time. Whether it's with friends who may know people, an informational meeting, or an actual job interview, try to arrange as much in-person contact as possible. People put much more effort into face-to-face meetings than they do in to phone calls or e-mails. Also, every meeting you arrange will be good practice for the big one when it comes along.

Write Scripts for Everything. A job search is, in large part, a performance. To perform well, you first need to write a script and then rehearse your lines until you can just about say them in your sleep. There is no better remedy than preparation for the inevitable stage fright. The character you want to portray is someone more bold and confident than you are. If you can't write enough hyperbole, get some help from a pushier friend.

Manage Your Web Presence. Make sure that when they Google you, what comes up is your listing on a business site such as LinkedIn, not a graphic of you doing some stupid stunt on YouTube.

Present Yourself Creatively. Most places get hundreds of résumés that all look alike. You have to do something to make yours stand out. Whether you are present in cyberspace or not, a well-written cover letter can work wonders.

Keep your résumé short and to the point. Don't boast, pad it, or use extraneous words. Put all your creative energies into the cover letter. Think of that letter as a commercial for yourself—short and a little over the top. Some people have done well with slick little PowerPoint shows. Emphasize your personal attributes, especially social skills and reliability. Your résumé speaks to your expertise and experience. The cover letter should focus on how you always show up, how motivated you are, and how great it is to work with you. These are the qualities prospective employers will be wondering about but can't ask.

Don't be afraid to blow your own horn, but don't compare yourself to others. Avoid buzzwords and clichés. Also observe the first rule of good writing: show, don't tell. Instead of saying you have excellent social skills, write about how good you are at getting difficult people to compromise. The cover letter itself will show that you are creative and resourceful and can express yourself in writing.

So what if some places won't accept your cover letter? They may still read it before they delete it.

Play the Numbers. The more you apply, the more likely it is you'll get interviews. Check with other people who have looked for jobs in your locale to find out the approximate application-to-interview ratio. Knowing the numbers is a good way to deal with the unavoidable feelings of rejection. Getting one interview for every ten résumés might not seem like much, but in most markets, it represents remarkable success.

Talk Yourself into Doing More Rather Than Less. The natural tendency is to talk yourself out of even considering opportunities that are long shots or are not exactly what you want. If you do that, soon you'll find that you're applying for almost nothing, which is a real disadvantage in a numbers game. Every application you send is, at the very least, good practice.

Recharge Your Batteries. A job search is hard, draining work. If you're scared to death, it means you're doing it right. You will need time away from it to recharge your batteries by doing things that are personally restoring, such as exercise, hobbies, and spending time with supportive friends. If you are diligently on the job search job every workday, you can take time off in the evenings and on weekends to have some fun.

Mindless diversions like TV or computer solitaire might be moderately relaxing, but they don't recharge the internal batteries. Don't just go with the default; plan your leisure time as you would your work so you can get the most out of it.

Don't Let Fear Pick Your Job for You. Unless you're starving, if a job is not a good fit, don't take it. Trust that a better one will come along if you keep trying. Accepting a job you hate is too high a price to pay for relief and the illusion of safety.

SURVIVAL SCENARIO 61 The Interview

Omigod, you got an interview! Someone actually wants to talk to you. What do you say? What do you do? What do you wear? So much is riding on one show, it's no wonder you're feeling some stage fright.

Whether it is an actual job interview, an informational meeting, or just getting together with a friend of a friend, you need to put your heart into every performance. Your first impression is always your most important tool. Make sure you're showing yourself in the best possible light. Remember, details are what make a good interview great.

How to Stand Out in That Interview

Here are some suggestions that will help you make a lasting impression:

Know the Impression You Want to Make. You know you're great, but what, specifically, makes you great? Is it your competence? Your experience? Your creativity? Your diligence and responsibility? Your enthusiastic personality? Or is it all of the above? Whatever you have going for you, you will need to demonstrate those traits in the interview, not just mention them. You can't do this by waiting for the interviewer to ask you if you are diligent and responsible. You will have to be diligent and responsible in preparing for the interview.

Create Your Legend. Tell stories that illustrate your skills, talents, and motivation. Write descriptions of specific accomplishments, including the situation, what you did, the result, and what you learned. Keep them short and sweet, about two hundred words. These stories will provide ready-made content for almost anything an interviewer might ask you about your experience.

Play to Your Audience. Know as much as can be known about the person and company with whom you'll be interviewing. Google the hell out of every name you can find. Read every word on the company's website. Then, at the interview, find opportunities to talk about what you've learned. This last step is especially important if you know something about the achievements of your interviewer. Even if there's nothing on Google, scan the office for clues to the person's interest. If you can, work in something about the personal information that is on display, be it golf clubs, dogs, kids' drawings, or Star Wars action figures.

It's OK to drop names if you actually know someone even distantly; strive to make any personal connection you can with the interviewer or the company.

Know the position of the person you're talking with. An interview with an HR screener is different from one with a prospective boss. HR people want facts, figures, and details. Managers are generally more interested in forming a global impression about how it would be to work with you.

Rehearse Answers to Standard Interview Questions. The way to present yourself brilliantly is by first writing scripts that show off your best qualities in little stories about things you've done. Use standard interview questions as lead-ins to your prerehearsed material. Here are some questions you should expect and prepare for:

- **Tell me about yourself.** This question is a gimme. Don't waste it by retelling your résumé. If you've lived in interesting places and done interesting things, tell about them, and tie them into what will make you a great employee. This question might also be a good place to use some material from your legend.

- **What is your greatest strength?** Don't just list your strengths; tell a story that illustrates how you've used them. If you can sell, give the numbers. If you're creative, draw a mental picture of something you've created. If you're reliable, tell how you showed up and manned the phones in the great blizzard of '08.

- **What is your greatest weakness?** The only acceptable greatest weakness is that you work too hard.

- **What can you do for us?** Be ready for this one, even if it isn't asked. Put together what you know about the company and what you know about yourself, wrap them in a neat package, and tie them up with a bow. Tell the interviewer in no uncertain terms how your skills will benefit the organization. If this job is a reach beyond what you've done before, use this question to show how you will make up for lack of experience with motivation, enthusiasm, and hard work.

Expect a Few Trick Questions. A recent trend is throwing in a few curveball questions to see how applicants react to an ambiguous situation under pressure. A typical example is giving you one minute to come up with as many uses as possible for a paper clip. In my opinion, interviewers place too much faith in such questions, but that will not stop people from asking them. Be ready. Another trick question is asking you about the last lie you told. This sort of question purports to test your truthfulness. If you say you don't lie, you are lying and will probably be disqualified, because everybody lies. Tell the interviewer that you told a friend that her new jeans didn't make her butt look too big, and hope that the interview will drift back to more relevant questions.

Rehearse and Rehearse Some More. An interview is stressful; unless you've really overlearned your lines, you may forget them. Give everyone you know permission to ambush you with interview questions anytime, day or night. Don't stop rehearsing until you can actually answer in your sleep.

Overdress, Arrive Early, and Shake Hands Firmly. You can never go wrong being the most conservatively dressed person in the room. Err in the direction of drabness and formality; do not dress for a party. Guys, wear a tie. Women, dress in something your mother might wear. If the job involves creativity, go for a little personal expression. If not, don't.

Punctuality is so critical to many businesspeople that it is worth your while to arrive a full fifteen minutes early. Many people also judge character by a handshake. Whatever your demographic, practice until you can shake hands like a middle-aged white guy.

Take Control. An interview is more about style than content. You are demonstrating how you do an actual job to someone who has seen many other people attempt the same task. Don't just talk about initiative—show it. Use whatever questions are asked as vehicles to present yourself and your legend in the way you want to be seen. Your prerehearsed material will help you shine. Find creative ways to work it in.

Demonstrate That You Are a Regular Person. All the research shows that interviewers are more likely to hire someone they perceive as being like them. Unless you know something more specific, assume that business is still the province of people who value playing sports, membership in organizations, community service, and having a religion but not talking too much about it. Show that you are a member of the club.

Keep 'Em Talking. Most interviews are popularity contests. Impressing interviewers is less important than getting them to like you.

Research shows that the best way to get people to like you is to show an interest in them. Ask them questions about their jobs. If you get interviewers talking and listen attentively to what they say, they will like you and, along with that, assume that you are bright, competent, and discerning, just like they are.

Never Say Anything Negative About Your Previous Job. Everybody knows this rule, but you'd be surprised at how many people say, "I know I shouldn't say anything negative about my previous job, but . . ." Don't do it! Your prospective employer will believe that whatever you say about your old employer is what you'll be saying about him or her someday.

Ask About Money. An interview is not a time to be timid. Jobs are about being paid. Interviewers will expect you to be concerned with money. If you don't ask, they will assume, perhaps correctly, that you are a wuss. The only time it might be in bad form to ask about money is if you're interviewing with a nonprofit organization.

Ask a Few Probing Questions. Engage your interviewer with a few questions that make him or her think. Some good old standbys are: What would really impress you in an applicant? What is your turn-over rate? What sorts of opportunities for advancement does your company offer? Your interviewer will be surprised at your acumen, and you may be surprised at what you learn.

Schedule the Next Contact. Interviewers rarely call you when they say they will, and if you don't get the job, they probably won't call at all. Ask when a decision will be made, and arrange to call on that day.

Write a Thank-You Note. After an interview, send an e-mail saying how much you enjoyed the experience. Use every opportunity to stand out.

SURVIVAL SCENARIO 62 Rites of Initiation

It's your first week on the new job, and you are pushing yourself to be friendly and outgoing. People are nice enough but a little distant, especially when you ask questions. It's not that they don't answer; they just give you the feeling that it's too much bother, as if they're too busy or something. Or maybe they just don't like you.

They don't dislike you; they just haven't accepted you yet. In every company and in every group when humans get together, there are always initiation rituals. They start the minute you get in the door. You must demonstrate by your actions that you deserve to be an insider.

The common element of all initiation rituals involves sacrificing something to get into the group. The question in everyone's mind is what you do when the pressure is on. Will you be in it for yourself, or will you put the group's welfare above your own? The way they get the answer is by setting up some adversity and seeing how you handle it. In some groups, there is actual hazing. In most, though, the process is considerably more subtle, but it is just as crucial, and sometimes just as cruel.

What you sacrifice to get into the group is some of your self-importance. You have to accept teasing, you have to defer to other people's opinions, you have to listen when you feel like speaking, and most of all, you must show that you are not a pain in the ass.

There's another purpose to initiation rituals, and that is to establish your place in the pecking order. You start out at the bottom and move up slowly, regardless of your rank on the organizational chart. You don't have to take orders or bend over for a paddling. You just have to indicate subtly that you know your place.

SURVIVAL SOLUTION *62*
How to Become an Insider

Be careful; how you act in the first few weeks on the job can determine how you will be perceived for years after that. Here are some ideas to consider:

Show You Can Listen. The best way to show deference to a group is to listen and show interest. Ask about the way they do things. Ask for advice, and take it. Many people believe that the way to be successful on a new job is to dazzle people with their brilliance. Actually during the initiation time, the people around you care very little about your brilliance. They want you to show them that you value the experience and knowledge of the group. Don't tell them what you learned in your M.B.A. program, and don't bother giving opinions until you're seriously asked. When people begin asking you for your opinion, that's a sign that they regard you as an insider.

Accept Teasing. Teasing is another common initiation procedure, especially on shop floors, but it happens in boardrooms as well. The style and content differ from company to company, but the purpose is the same. You have to show that you can take it and give it back with equanimity. If you get angry or appeal to an authority, you lose. There certainly are situations when teasing exceeds the bounds of propriety, especially in situations involving racism, sexism, and the like. Before you go crying prejudice, make sure that is what you're seeing. Remember, through teasing you're being asked to sacrifice a little of your personal dignity to the group. The less seriously you take yourself, the more quickly you'll be accepted. Whatever it is, if it's legal, suck it up.

Make Alliances. Do favors for people. Find out what they need from your position, and let them know that you can supply it. In other words, sell yourself by your actions. You have to find out what their idea is about where your position fits in and how you can help the group. It may be different from your ideas, but you will have to sell changes rather than having your boss legislate them.

Don't Ask Too Many Questions. One of the main elements of initiation in most companies is demonstrating that you can figure things out for yourself. When people's answers get a bit short, they are cuing you that you are supposed to be thinking things through on your own. This is not the most efficient way to train new people, but it is how it's done in many places.

Find a Mentor. It's helpful to have somebody who is willing to be your guide and sponsor, someone who will interpret the meaning of some of the situations you encounter and will answer your questions in more detail. Your boss will usually not be appropriate as a mentor, but that is not a hard-and-fast rule. If you're lucky enough to hook up with a mentor, do what he or she tells you. This person is offering a bond that may last throughout your tenure at the company. The price of it is accepting that the mentor is the knowledgeable one who deserves to be listened to.

Initiation rites are the same the world over, whether it's a high-tech company or a primitive tribe in the Amazon. The rituals may be different, but the basic rules are the same. You have to undergo a few difficulties without complaining to become a member of the tribe.

SURVIVAL SCENARIO *63* Survivor Guilt

Safe at last. You've weathered the storm. Having gone through three rounds of layoffs, you're still here. Maybe you shouldn't feel like celebrating, but you ought to feel better than you do. You used to like your job. It isn't the greatest in the world, but you wanted to keep it, and you did. Why all of a sudden is it so hard to get up in the morning and go to work?

The condition is called survivor guilt, and it is normal among those who manage to escape the harm or misfortunes that befall the people around them. It is common in disasters of all kinds, including layoffs. The symptoms are similar to a midlevel depression—low energy and motivation, disturbances of sleep and concentration, and difficulty taking pleasure in things you once enjoyed. Often there are ruminations about whether it was wrong to keep one's job when others lost theirs. People tend to dismiss these thoughts as ridiculous, often with the encouragement of friends and family. This is unfortunate, because it is these thoughts that are at the root of the problem.

People experiencing survivor guilt tend to slog on, feeling less than enthused about their jobs and their connections to the company. They are tired much of the time. They get sick, especially on Mondays. They feel guilty about that too, but hey, if you're throwing up or running a fever, you stay home, right? Often survivor guilt is misinterpreted as a physical disorder, because feeling guilty about keeping your job seems stupid, and it definitely is not important enough to be the cause of all these symptoms.

Unfortunately, it is precisely that important.

SURVIVAL SOLUTION *63*
Surviving Survivor Guilt

By far, the most effective treatment for survivor guilt is recognizing it for what it is, knowing that it is a normal response, and, most of all, talking about it. If you're experiencing survivor guilt, here are some ideas that will help:

Know How Traumatic Events Affect People. Going through psychological trauma causes specific psychological problems that relate to the mechanics of memory. Most memories are stored in words and pictures, a kind of *Reader's Digest* condensed version of what happened; memories of traumatic events are stored whole, in high definition and Dolby sound. Your brain can hardly tell the difference between the memory and the real event, so that every time you think about it, you experience it again, complete with all the negative emotions. Flashbacks are the extreme versions of this phenomenon. For most people, thoughts about the events just keep turning over in their minds until they get a headache. A person can try diligently to block those thoughts, but they are always running in the background, like a huge open computer file sucking up all the RAM that the brain needs to function properly.

Instead of avoiding these thoughts, people need to acknowledge them and talk about them, not so much to get them off their chests, but to turn them into words so that they can be stored like other memories.

Avoid Medication. The most common medication prescribed for survivor guilt is alcohol. Generally, it is not a doctor who does the prescribing. Alcohol is so popular in this situation because it makes people stop thinking, which feels better briefly but is just the opposite of what needs to happen.

Antidepressants may also get in the way of solving the problem, by dealing with the symptoms rather than their cause. Generally, antidepressants are less useful when the cause of depression is clear.

Ignore Misguided Advice. Regardless of how many people tell you that you should feel happy about keeping your job and that your guilt is silly, ignore them. They don't know what they are talking about. You should feel whatever you feel, and start the healing process from there.

Recognize and Accept Mixed Emotions. Mixed emotions are the stuff of existence. Nobody ever feels just one way about anything. Sure, you get to keep your job, but you have to do your work and the work that the people who were laid off left behind. You may feel resentful and, at the same time, guilty for your insensitivity. You may even feel a little envious of the people who are gone. Events are forcing them to go out and look for that better job, instead of procrastinating like some people you may know.

All these feelings and more are normal. They do not mean you are crazy or lacking a conscience. The only way to make them go away is to accept them and allow yourself to experience them. The more you try to push them out of your mind, the stronger they become.

Do not force yourself to keep in touch with people who were laid off unless you want to. If you really don't want to call, don't do it out of guilt. Keep in touch with the people you really want to retain as friends. Allow yourself to let go of the rest. Don't promise to call or do lunch if you know you won't. A polite e-mail or an invitation to join you on LinkedIn couldn't hurt, but don't make promises you know you won't keep. What's the point in making yourself feel even more guilty?

Talk About All of It. Share your feelings with someone you trust. Talk until the negative feelings have less of an emotional hold.

If You Get Stuck, Consult a Therapist. Survivor guilt is a complex and many-faceted problem. If you have trouble sorting it out yourself and the symptoms persist, you may need professional help.

SURVIVAL SCENARIO 64 Golden Handcuffs

Take it from someone who spends his life dealing in human misery: the unhappiest workers in the world are not in third-world sweatshops. They are right here, feeling chained to jobs they hate but will not leave because they think they won't make as much money elsewhere.

They joke about Ned's on-the-job retirement, but there is nothing funny about it. He sits in his cube, doing as little as possible, just waiting for the day almost eight years hence when he can actually retire. Everybody knows he hates his job. If you ask him why he stays, he says that there's no way he could make this kind of money anywhere else. He says he's doing it for his wife and kids, to give them all the things they want. If you ask them, however, they'd tell you that what they want most is for him to be happy for a change. They've told him a hundred times, but he doesn't believe them, because they seem to have no problem spending the money he makes.

If you've never been there, it's hard to imagine how demoralizing it is to hold on for dear life to something you don't believe in. It's like thinking you can hold your breath eight hours a day for eight years until you can pull the plug, get that meager pension, and then be free to do whatever you want. People live through prison sentences that long all the time, right?

Actually, people in prison are better off. They don't have to pretend they have no choice, and they don't have to go to bed every Sunday night knowing they'll have to get up the next morning and go back to their cells.

People in golden handcuffs become obsessed with the annoying little details of their jobs—demanding bosses, surly coworkers, stupid customers—and at the same time convince themselves that there is no point in trying to change things. Why put any extra effort into something you hate? They deal with their job stresses by running them over and over in their minds until each little problem becomes a personal insult. The anger they feel is more than apparent to the people they work with, and, of course, leads to retaliation. Resentment always creates more material to resent.

The situation grows worse. Job performance declines, and demands increase. What was once merely bad becomes intolerable. The lucky ones get fired. For the ones trapped in jobs that can't be taken away, the fate is far worse. Every ounce of self-respect dissolves away into bitter bile. Some folks start thinking about assault weapons at this point, but most turn their anger in toward themselves.

If people do nothing to get out of a painful situation, their unconscious minds engage to try to find a way out. Alcohol is often used as a temporary solution, because it dulls the pain, but it is illness that becomes the real addiction. Sometimes by accident people discover that a back sprain or chest pains can keep them safe from the hell they have created, and then unconscious forces do the rest. When the mind retires from the fray, the body creates a real and tangible enemy from the chemistry of stress. There is nothing fake about these pains, but they are usually incurable, because they are themselves a cure. The once bright dream of retirement and freedom becomes a bed of pain that can be escaped only by early death.

SURVIVAL SOLUTION *64*
Unlock Those Golden Handcuffs

If you're chained to your job with golden handcuffs, I'll leave it to you to decide what compensation package is fair payment for your life. Here are some suggestions:

First, Talk to Your Family. Many of the people who are chained to their jobs believe they are there because their families would not be willing to live on less money. Their families may tell them this isn't true, but they don't believe it, because no one seems to be cutting back on their spending. Resentment for the family's ingratitude is just below the surface, and it's just as recognizable as resentment of the job.

If you are in this situation, talk to your family, and believe what they say.

Face Your Fear. Most people submit to the embrace of golden hand-cuffs because they are afraid of the unknown—either living on less money or the even more terrifying prospect of looking for new work. If you do not recognize the role of fear in your decision to stay with a job that you hate, maybe you should talk to a therapist. If you do recognize the fear, a therapist might help you deal with it. Please don't settle for antidepressants without therapy. This strategy will only get you in deeper.

Do the Numbers. Take a cold, hard look at your finances. A financial planner who does not sell insurance or investments might be a help here. Figure out what life would actually be like on less money. Don't guess.

Update Your Résumé Today. Keeping your résumé current is a smart business practice for anyone in any position. In this situation, getting the document into shape is a necessary first step toward finding out what else you might do. What could it hurt to send it a few places? You never know. While you're at it, check out the scenarios in this book on job search and dealing with fear

If You're Absolutely Set on Staying, Take on a Challenging Hobby. Without challenge and new learning, the mind slides into dormancy and depression. Wake it up with a hobby that pushes you to your limit. Paint, write, run a marathon, build a website, learn to play the tuba—anything that requires new skills and new knowledge.

Keep Escapism to a Minimum. Limit your TV watching, Net surfing, playing computer games, and other mind candy. Go for mental nourishment.

SURVIVAL SCENARIO *65* Procrastination

Bill was promoted to department head, and all of a sudden he has developed a time-management problem. His reports are always late, he misses meetings, and even the simplest task seem to take weeks.

Frank's boss is domineering and pushy. Somehow, the more demanding the boss gets, the slower and more forgetful Frank becomes.

Marie knows that the only way to sell insurance is to make cold calls, but every time she looks at the telephone, she thinks of a hundred other things that need doing.

If you ask them, all these people would say that their problem is procrastination. They probably have even attended a seminar or two on time management and were surprised when the techniques didn't work. The reason the time-management techniques didn't work is that procrastination is not the problem; it's actually what protects them from the problem.

Bill's procrastination protects him from his doubts about his ability to perform his new job. Frank's procrastination protects him from confronting his boss directly and getting into an altercation. Marie's procrastination protects her from feelings of rejection when she is told no.

For all three, procrastination is an expensive and inefficient way of protecting themselves. If they keep it up, they could lose their jobs. They all need to do something about their procrastination right now, but what? Maybe you've been putting off doing something about procrastination yourself.

SURVIVAL SOLUTION *65*
Don't Put Off Dealing with Procrastination

If you find yourself putting off important tasks, the first thing you need to do is recognize how what we call procrastination actually works:

Don't Call It Procrastination! The word itself is an excuse, a reason that you didn't do something, not a description of what actually happened. It is far more useful to say, "I played computer solitaire until it was too late to call," or "I spent the day rearranging my files instead of working on my report."

Recognize That Procrastination Protects You from Something. Ask yourself, "If I didn't procrastinate, what would I have to do?" Dennis the Menace said, "I'm glad I hate liver, because if I didn't hate it, I'd eat it, and I hate it."

Recognize That the Liver Is the Problem and the Procrastination Is the Defense. See procrastination as something you do rather than something that just happens.

Procrastinators don't just sleep under a tree all day. What they actually do follows a fairly typical pattern: They make promises to get other people (and themselves) off their backs. They find other things to do instead of what they're supposed to be doing, then they make excuses about why what they were supposed to do didn't get done.

The next step in dealing with procrastination is closing the back door by recognizing these strategies and actively disabling them. Here are some suggestions about how to do that:

Make Every Promise a Contingency. Most procrastinators want to please people, but they usually end up making people angrier than if they had refused to do things in the first place. If you are not going to do something, say so instead of making a promise you are unlikely to keep.

Never agree to do something without saying when it will be done and clearly specifying what you will do if the promise is not kept on time. Promises, if you use them, should have this form: "I'll have this to you by five on Thursday; if not, I'll stay here until I get it done."

Enough with the Excuses Already. Procrastination cannot operate without excuses to yourself or other people. All the excuses you can think of—"I didn't have what I needed," "The phone kept ringing," "Somebody was always interrupting," "I was too tired," even "I'll do it tomorrow"—boil down to: "I didn't do it when I was supposed to." Never explain why you didn't get something done—just say you didn't do it. This is a strategy to get yourself in gear. If you just take responsibility for not doing something and don't explain why you didn't get it done, there will be more pressure on you to act.

The third step in dealing with procrastination is recognizing the specific reason you are avoiding a particular task. Generally, there are three reasons that people put things off:

They Are Afraid. People fear rejection, criticism, and confrontation. That's why they don't look for jobs, make cold calls, ask for things they want, or object to things they don't want. It is easy to get distracted by anything that is less risky.

The Job Is Too Big. People procrastinate because they are overwhelmed by the sheer amount of work involved. This is why they don't do their taxes or get started on important projects.

The Job Is Unpleasant. People put off things that they simply don't feel like doing. Unfortunately, to be a successful adult, you have to do things you don't want to do.

The fourth step is to adopt a strategy for dealing with your reason for procrastinating:

If You Are Afraid
Admit that it is fear holding you back rather than random events.
Resolve to act anyway.
Get emotional support.
If the task requires talking, write a script and rehearse.

Commit to as many people as possible to take action at a certain time.

Use the fear-management techniques described in the next scenario.

If the Task Is Too Large or Is Unpleasant

Break it down into small steps. The first few should be much smaller than you believe you can accomplish. If you have trouble breaking the task down, get the most organized person you know to help you.

Take one step a day, at a set time. Make something pleasant, such as midmorning coffee or lunch, contingent on your taking that day's step.

Focus only on the next step, not the whole task. All jobs, no matter how big, are merely a series of next steps.

Money Makes the World Go Around. The fifth, and more devious, step if you still aren't doing what you need to do is as follows:

Get a stack of five-dollar bills, and burn one bill each time you don't do what you were supposed to do that day. Or try this: Write out several checks to an organization you detest. Put each check in a stamped envelope along with a letter of support, and give the envelopes to a friend who will mail one if not notified that the day's task is done. This is a powerful technique. All it took was one contribution to the Ku Klux Klan to cure an African American client of procrastination. Mine are addressed to the American Nazi Party.

SURVIVAL SCENARIO 66 Fears Are Like Goblins

In your dream, you are with Harry Potter. Sneaking up on you is a pack of goblins. They are big, mean, smelly dudes, with curvy teeth dripping ropes of slobber. You try to warn Harry. "Run!" you shout.

"It does no good," Harry says. "Only makes them bigger." With that, he draws his wand and walks calmly toward the goblins. "Reductio!" he intones, and the goblins begin to shrink.

Harry keeps advancing, and the goblins keep getting smaller and smaller. When they are about the size of mice, they scatter, squealing, in every direction.

Harry turns to you and beckons. You see Hogwarts in the distance.

Then you wake up.

Allow me to interpret. Dreams can be messages to you from your unconscious, the place that stores all those things you know but don't know you know. Your unconscious, disguised as Harry Potter, is telling you something important about fear: If the goblins chase you, they get bigger. If you chase them, they grow smaller.

But how do you chase goblins? How do you turn and advance on your fears instead of running from them? Harry had a wand and the *Reductio* spell. What have you got?

What it takes is courage, which is as much a learned skill as it is a personal attribute. To learn how to chase your own goblins, you have to understand exactly what fear is and how it works. It also helps to understand that without fear, there would be no need for courage.

SURVIVAL SOLUTION *66*
How to Chase Goblins

Fear is programmed into the oldest part of our brains. It is an automatic system to protect us from danger by warning us and giving us an instant jolt of energy so we can get away.

Fear teaches us to avoid danger. As soon as we feel even the barest hint of that energy jolt, we move in the other direction. This worked fine when dangers were physical and the areas to avoid were steep cliffs and dark jungle paths. Today, the dangers we face are not to our bodies, but to our psyches. We avoid conflict, rejection, and embarrassment as if they could kill us.

Fear teaches us to avoid danger so well that, over time, we turn away long before we get anywhere near anything remotely dangerous to our image of ourselves—scary things such as speaking up in a meeting, asking for what we want, or telling somebody no. This is how avoidance works. It's how we run from the goblins without knowing that's what we're doing. Sometimes the only way to know where the goblins are is by noticing big circles around places we never go on the maps of our lives. That's where the goblins live, growing bigger and stronger the farther they are from awareness. To chase them, to take back the parts of our lives that we avoid, we need to face the goblins, experience the full force of the fear response, and still move forward. This is the essence of courage. Here's how you do it:

Know You Are Afraid. The first step in learning how to face your fears is knowing you're afraid. This is more difficult than it sounds, because avoidance works so well that we seldom get close enough to what we consider dangerous to experience even the smallest jolt of fear. When we get close, we automatically retreat; we forget, we procrastinate, or we just head off in a different direction.

To know where your goblins are hiding, ask yourself what you avoid. It may be cold-calling, speaking in a group, making small talk, asking for what you want, or saying no to what you don't want. If you can't think of anything you avoid, ask a few friends. Other people usually notice what we avoid better than we do. When you find out where your goblins are, turn and face them, advancing one step at a time.

Recognize the Symptoms of Fear. Fear is very real even if the danger it signals is not. To reclaim areas of your life that the goblins have taken over, you have to recognize the symptoms and manage them, rather than using them as a cue to run away. Here are some moves based on the feelings you are likely to experience and suggestions about what to do to bring fear under control:

Exercise Regularly and Learn to Relax. Fearful people are physiologically aroused much of the time. They experience this state as being edgy or uptight, usually with no particular source. The two techniques for decreasing this generalized arousal are regular exercise and learning a technique for relaxation.

Exercise is something many people avoid, because in the beginning especially, it elicits unpleasant feelings. There is no way to be healthy—either physically or psychologically—without exercise, but to do it regularly, you have to persist in the face of discomfort or disinterest. This is why exercise is the best place to start your campaign against the goblins in your life. If you exercise, you will grow strong enough to beat them. If you don't, they will win without a fight.

As for relaxation, many techniques are available in books, recordings, videos, and yoga classes. Pick one that works for you, and practice it regularly.

Make the Unknown Known. We fear the unknown, and whatever we fear remains unknown, because we never get close enough to learn about it; then, when we finally do, we freak out. The trick is to go there in our minds before we go there physically. Learn as much as you can in advance so that the newer parts of your mind can stay in control. To think, instead of merely reacting, you need to have the rudiments of a plan. This is why there are disaster drills and why there are safety cards in airplanes. If danger for you involves saying something aloud, write a script and then rehearse it until you can say it in your sleep. Then rehearse some more so you can say it in a panic.

Limit Worrying. One of the ways we try to control fear is by imagining everything that can go wrong. Thinking about difficulties beforehand and making plans to deal with them will help. Worrying will not. Anticipating without planning will only raise your level of arousal. Limit the undisciplined use of your imagination. Exercise instead.

Rehearse While Relaxing. Before you chase the goblins, it will help to imagine exactly what you need to do. Use your relaxation technique and go through the entire sequence enough times so that you can imagine it from beginning to end without becoming unduly aroused. Then you will be ready to face the goblins in the real world.

Know What to Do When the Adrenaline Hits. Once you have lowered your general level of arousal and practiced in your imagination, you are ready to advance on actual fear. As you approach whatever you're afraid of, you will experience a jolt of adrenaline, which will raise your arousal level exponentially to give you the energy to physically run away. Your mind will interpret this jolt as an alarm, and most of your thoughts will be directed toward escape. You will need to ignore the alarm clang in your head and bloodstream and keep moving forward. In this acute phase, passive relaxation techniques won't work. Do something active to burn off the adrenaline. Walking quickly or some other exercise will help, as will telling yourself that your fear is real but that the danger is not.

Adrenaline will also affect your breathing, by tensing the muscles of your chest. It will feel as if you are not getting enough air, and you will be tempted to breathe in deliberately. This will lead to hyperventilation. Excess oxygen will make you feel weird and light-headed. You may even think that you will pass out or that you will die from a heart attack. You won't.

Virtually all the unpleasant and dangerous-seeming symptoms of fear are actually caused by adrenaline and hyperventilation. Remember this as you are advancing on your goblins, and press on. Walk more quickly, and remember to breathe out. Special Forces and SWAT teams are taught "combat breathing": breathe in to the count of three, and out to the count of six. (Yoga teaches the same technique, but in order to get these tough guys to accept it, it had to have a more belligerent name.) Other time-honored methods such as battle cries and loud singing will also prevent hyperventilation, but they may not always be appropriate at the office. Forget breathing into a paper bag; it can create more problems than it solves.

If you follow these steps, you can manage fear well enough to chase your own goblins and watch them shrink as if by magic. You won't even need to say *Reductio*.

SURVIVAL SCENARIO **67** The Fear of Speaking in Front of a Group

One-on-one, Kinesha is bright, articulate, and funny. (Kinesha kicked off Part 2.) She understands the ins and outs of the project better than anyone. You suggest that maybe she should make the presentation. Her eyes grow wide with terror. "No, thanks," she says. "I'd rather die."

In a study done several years ago, thousands of people were asked to list the things they feared most. For the majority, number one on the list was speaking in front of a group. Number six was death. This finding gives some credence to Kinesha's statement that she would rather die.

Being able to speak in front of a group is essential to success in virtually any field, yet many people structure their lives and make career choices to avoid public speaking. When you come down to it, it's not the speaking they are avoiding, but the experience of stage fright.

Perhaps you know what stage fright is like. It starts with blind panic. Your heart races, your muscles clench, your vision constricts, and you feel as if you might pass out. You forget everything you ever knew, and you just want to run screaming from the room.

In this situation, your instincts are betraying you. Your body is using the automatic protection system designed to get you out of dangerous situations, when the real protection you need is something to help you stay.

Most of us learn to fear public speaking in grade school. Remember the first time you had to speak in front of the class? Maybe you had to recite a poem you had memorized. If you're like most of us, by the time you got to the front of the room, you'd forgotten it. When you memorize something and are put in a stressful situation, you are most likely to forget the middle part. Quick, what comes after "Friends, Romans, countrymen, lend me your ears"?—or before "Give me liberty or give me death"?

As adults at work our task is not reciting a poem or answering a question about an assignment we haven't read. Now when we get up, our job is to talk to people about something we know more about than they do. But for some of us, it still feels just as terrifying as it did in the sixth grade, so we avoid it like poison. Actually, the avoidance is what's poisonous. The more we avoid the things we fear, the more frightened we get.

SURVIVAL SOLUTION 67
How to Get Over the Fear of Public Speaking

The cure for stage fright involves unlearning the fear response slowly, step by step. Here's how to do it:

Get the Feel of Being in Front of a Group. Practice this long before you ever get up to the podium. When you walk past a group of people—say, the clerical pool at work—pretend they are watching you. Stop and smile; when you get your courage up, wave and make your first speech. "Hi, everybody!" will do nicely. They will probably think you are weird, but friendly.

Practice this whenever you're around a group—in theaters, church, the bowling alley. Pretend they're watching you (don't get paranoid about it—they aren't really). Don't slink around; stand tall and smile. Pretend you're Oprah.

Make a Speech Every Night at Dinner. You probably talk at dinner anyway. Whatever you are going to say, say it standing up. The topic doesn't matter—it could be economics, politics, table manners, the traffic on the way home, or whatever. As you get better at this, ask your family to say rude things and talk to each other while you are speaking (most families will do this without being asked). Remember, you will never speak to a more difficult audience than your own family.

Whenever You Are in a Group Meeting, Say Something. It doesn't matter what you say, just speak. Say, "Good idea." Say, "Right on." Ask a question: "Can you elaborate on that point?" or "What time is this meeting supposed to end?" Get in the habit of talking.

Learn a Relaxation Technique, and Practice It Regularly. An instant one like self-hypnosis is most helpful when you're at the podium.

Imagine Yourself Talking in Front of a Group. When you are relaxed, imagine yourself giving short speeches from beginning to end. Make them up, and practice them in your mind. The technique is called desensitization, and the great thing about it is that works almost as well if you imagine yourself speaking as it does if you were practicing in front of a real group. You'll be surprised how effective imaginary practice technique can be.

Try the Real Thing. Now that you're calmer in your imagination, it's time to practice in the world outside your head. Volunteer to make an announcement; take a speech class; join Toastmasters. Every time you practice, it will get easier.

Write Your Script, and Rehearse Until You Can Say It in Your Sleep. Have friends and family members ambush you asking to hear your talk. This exercise will help you sound more natural and off the cuff.

Don't Try to Read Your Speech. You will sound stilted and will probably lose your place.

Do Warm-Up Exercises. Actors move around and recite tongue twisters before they go on. If you can do this offstage, it may help you. If you can't, instead of passively waiting to go on, begin "performing." Pretend people are watching you—nod, show enthusiasm, and, if appropriate, make positive comments, such as, "Good point."

Don't Run up to the Podium. Walk slowly, making eye contact with audience members. Practice your relaxation.

If You Blank Out, Admit It and It Will Pass More Quickly. Say, "You'll have to wait a minute while I have a panic attack." The audience will think you're joking.

Speaking of jokes, experienced speakers often have one they can use if they blank out. Here's one I use: Look down, fumble with your notes, and say, "Milk, eggs, bread, soap—oh, sorry, wrong notes." (I know it's bad, but your audience will like it. They're expecting to be bored; anything is better than that.)

If all else fails, recite your opening sentence, point to your audience, and say, "Think about that." Then leave the podium. People will see you as being dramatic, to the point, and concise. They'll never realize you were scared silly.

Thank you, and good afternoon.

SURVIVAL SCENARIO 68 When Cold Calls Send Chills Down Your Spine

You can't get new business without making cold calls. You know that, but still, it's hard to find the time. Other tasks always seem to get in the way. You provide great service for your present customers, but that doesn't get your numbers up. Tomorrow, you absolutely have to get started on those cold calls. Of course, you said that yesterday.

Cold calls are a necessity that frequently get put off in favor of less important tasks. You can call it procrastination, but, as we have seen in other scenarios, the problem is more likely to be fear, but fear of what?

Most common is the fear of going up to someone and starting a conversation.

About a quarter of all businesspeople have no trouble doing this. They are born sales reps. Since you are reading about the fear of cold calls, chances are that you are not one of them, so let's talk for a minute about what you might be.

All personalities fall on a continuum between the extremes of extroversion and introversion. These labels mean more than liking or not liking social gatherings. They refer to what people consider most real. For extroverts, reality is outside themselves, what's happening with them and other people. For introverts, reality is what happens inside the mind.

Neither end of the continuum is better than the other, but they do represent different ways of looking at the world and different native skills. Extroverts don't waste time analyzing; they just get up and do. They are good talkers but sometimes pay too little attention to how people are responding. Introverts spend a lot of time thinking and analyzing; it's what they do best. What they don't do is meaningless chatter, which is how they define the conversational glue that holds relationships together.

Introverts like ideas and often have good ones. If you want to talk about something specific, they are all there. If you want to talk about nothing, they will act bored to cover up the fact that they are frightened. They keep trying to figure out the right thing to say even when there is no right thing to say.

Here's the problem: with people you don't know, you have to say a certain amount of *nothing* before they are ready to talk about *something*, such as business. It is this little bit of nothing that introverts fear most. If you are an extreme introvert, you may be fooling yourself if you think you can handle the amount of idle chatter it takes to succeed in sales.

SURVIVAL SOLUTION *68*
Getting Over the Fear of Cold Calls

If your introversion is not extreme, the only way to get over the fear of starting conversations is to start them constantly. You will have to practice doing what comes naturally to extroverts. Never go to work without packing a few nothings to talk about into your head, in the same way you'd throw a couple of cookies in with your lunch. To find nothings, read the paper and watch sports and prime-time shows. If all else fails, there's always the Weather Channel. Never miss an opportunity to use the nothings you packed to start a conversation. If you practice this part diligently, the rest will be easy.

In addition to starting conversations, there are many other things to fear about cold calls. Rejection is a big one, but there are a number of others, including chagrin over being seen as one of those typical uncouth salespeople or, God forbid, a telemarketer. To get over your fears, you have to know what they are and face them. Here are some suggestions that may help:

Resolve Any Conflicts You May Have About Your Product. Some salespeople and telemarketers use deceptive tactics to sell products that aren't worth the money. If you think that's what you're doing, and you have some integrity, you're going to have a hard time with selling. If you're not convinced, you'll have a hard time convincing other people, and you might as well try to sell something you like better.

Know Your Goal. The goal in a cold call is not to make a sale, but to engage the person sufficiently that he or she will accept another call. It usually takes several calls to make a sale.

Know Why Customers Like Your Product. If you like your product, you're probably knowledgeable about all its technical specifications, but that will not lead to compelling cold-call conversations with prospective customers. Ask your current customers why they like your product. Use their words to talk about it.

Write a Script. Unless you are very good at improvising, in which case you probably wouldn't be reading this survival solution, you will need a script for your performance. Write one that hits the high points of the message you are trying to get across or the questions you want answered. An effective way to do this is by incorporating some of the stories your satisfied customers have told you.

Don't Waste Time on "How Are You?" You have about a second and a half to engage someone in a cold call. Don't waste it on a throwaway line. The very best opening line is one that shows that you know something about the person you are talking to. Google away and see what you can come up with. Another possibility is asking a question to which the answer is most likely to be yes.

Practice, and Practice Some More. Nothing beats experience in getting over fear of any kind. For cold calls, in addition to practicing your regular script with a friend or family member, try practicing making the worst cold call you possibly can. Try to put in every mistake you can think of. Studies have shown that practicing mistakes consciously can make them less likely to happen. Do your practicing under the most adverse conditions you can think of. If you're a jogger or a walker, practice when you're out of breath. For a more sedentary person, you might try practicing lying down or bending over. The more difficult and unusual the practice, the easier it will be to do the real thing.

Learn How to Relax. You can learn by many methods, and the market abounds with relaxation books, CDs, and DVDs. You can learn meditation, yoga, or any of a host of other techniques. All of these methods work, but you have to find one that works for you and then practice with it until you know how to do it on demand.

Do Calls One at a Time. Don't think of the hundreds of cold calls you have to do; take each one separately. Start out small, with goals of making two or three a day, and then work up.

Take Notes. You will need them to remember what you said to people whom you call again, so keep notes of each conversation. It also helps to keep records of the resistances you meet and the strategies you used to get around them. Resolve to learn something from every cold call, whether you make a sale or not.

Call in the Morning. There are two reasons to make your calls early. First, studies show that most people in offices are more likely to be at their desks first thing. Second, if you start your day with cold calls, you are much less likely to get distracted by less important tasks.

SURVIVAL SCENARIO *69* Low Self-Esteem

"That's all well and good," you think after reading the scenarios on public speaking and cold-calling. "Maybe other people can do those things, but I have low self-esteem. I could never . . ."

Before you go on, let's consider this disorder you suffer from. Psychology has a name for everything. Unfortunately, as we saw with procrastination, naming psychological conditions makes them sound like something that happens to people rather than something they do. In the case of low self-esteem, we may be tempted to think of a deficiency of an essential humor, perhaps black bile or serotonin, rather than a patterned sequence of thoughts and actions that keeps people from trying anything that might improve their opinions of themselves.

In thirty-five years in psychology, I have heard low self-esteem given as an explanation for every human problem from poor school performance to the arrogance of world leaders. As to what low self-esteem actually means, your guess is as good as mine. I prefer the more old-fashioned term *self-confidence* to *self-esteem*, because it refers to a belief people have about what they can do, as opposed to their estimation of what they are worth.

Confident people believe they can do what needs to be done. Confidence is based at least partly on skills rather than an assessment of value. As people learn to do more, their confidence improves. I'm not sure whether learning has any effect on self-esteem.

SURVIVAL SOLUTION 69

Improve Your Confidence and Hope It Has an Effect on Your Self-Esteem

If you know what confidence is and how it works, the more confidence you will have. It's as simple as that—and as difficult. Here's what you ought to know:

Confidence Is Purely Imaginary. Confidence or lack thereof is the belief that in a certain situation, you will do something well or poorly. The more you know about the situation or whatever it is you are trying to do, the more likely you are to believe you will do well.

If you lack confidence, you probably have distorted expectations about the situations you are to face. You may believe everyone is watching you, just waiting for you to mess up so they can laugh and criticize you. Perhaps this is how it was in your family or in middle school, but now that you're grown up, things have changed. I hope you will be relieved to know that at work, no one is paying much attention to you at all.

They are all paying attention to themselves.

Confidence Is Based on Knowledge. To believe you can do something well, you must at least know exactly what it is you're supposed to do and how to do it. That's the reason this book has so many lists of instructions. That is also why so many of the instructions involve writing scripts and rehearsing. Success at anything requires planning and practice.

Less confident people imagine, incorrectly, that confident people do everything spontaneously, that their words and actions just flow out effortlessly. This is definitely not the case. Confident people practice and rehearse every bit as diligently as you should; they just don't worry as much. Perhaps they weren't teased so badly in middle school.

Confidence Is an Act. There is no difference between acting confident and being confident. I'm not talking just about being outwardly suave and debonair. I'm talking about thinking confident thoughts as well. If you don't know how to think confident thoughts, read *The Little Engine That Could,* probably the most concise statement of Western mysticism ever written.

If you think you can and have done your homework, you probably can. If you think you can't, pretend you think you can.

Confidence Is the Belief That You Can Withstand Criticism. Therapists sometimes have people write lists of affirmations and read them to themselves, in hope that this practice will raise self-esteem. I don't do this because of the many times I have seen long lists of affirmations evaporate in the face of the first criticism. Instead of silently practicing affirmations, I have my clients practice being criticized, by me and by their friends and family. The more ridiculous the criticisms, the better this technique works. By the time they actually have to do whatever it is, they've heard and laughed off far more disparagement than they will ever have to face in the real world. If you want to develop confidence, get the people who care about you to heckle you unmercifully, but with a bit of humor.

SURVIVAL SCENARIO 70 Time Pressure

Are you the kind of person who is painfully aware of time? Does it ever seem to you that the people around you operate in slow motion? Do you typically do two or even three things at once? Can you read or do paperwork while you are talking on the phone? Do you make to-do lists for yourself that require such tight scheduling that if one item takes five minutes longer than you expect, you feel hopelessly behind? Does a checkout-line wait of longer than thirty seconds make you consider leaving your purchases and walking out? Do you entertain hostile fantasies about slow drivers who happen to be in front of you? Do you ever act on these fantasies?

If any of those examples fit you, you know what I mean by time pressure.

If you experience time pressure on a regular basis, you probably already know that it has tremendous effects on your life. They aren't always bad, either. For one thing, you probably accomplish more than the people around you. Unfortunately, the people around you probably wish you would accomplish less and chill out more. You may have tried to appease them once or twice—say, on vacation—only to discover that just sitting around caused you intense anxiety.

Is time pressure really a problem? It is the dangerous component of the dread type A personality that, a few years ago, was supposed to cause heart attacks. Subsequent studies, however, have shown that the laid-back, type B folks, who used to be considered healthier, seem to have almost as many heart attacks, from which they are less likely to recover than are type As. Type Bs may also be more susceptible to other diseases.

You knew it, right? Type As are better.

Not so fast. There is a problem—ask the people who live or work with you.

SURVIVAL SOLUTION 70

How to Keep Time Pressure from Giving You a Heart Attack

If you are a high-achieving type A, time pressure is your own personal demon. When you wrestle with him yourself, it can lead to accomplishments and personal growth. When you demand that other people wrestle your demon, it leads only to heartache, literally. If you feel justified in getting angry with the people around you because they aren't as fast as you are, you are capable of all sorts of cruelty, to them and to yourself.

On the outside, you become the demon. People will hate you and fear you even if they are too afraid to say so. On the inside, you will feel frustrated, resentful, and lonely. These are the feelings that cause the heart attacks.

You don't have to become a laid-back, type B person to win the battle with your time-pressure demon. You don't even have to learn relaxation techniques or practice yoga. Though I'd highly recommend these techniques, I know you don't have time for them. If you want to keep time pressure from giving you a heart attack, there are two things you must do:

Know Whose Demon You Are Fighting. Every time you get the urge to blame someone else for slowing you down (even if you weren't going to say anything, resentment held inside is just as damaging as yelling and name-calling), repeat to yourself, "It's my problem, not his." Six hundred times ought to do for a start.

Make Your Schedules Realistic. People who live under time pressure typically make unrealistically optimistic schedules for themselves that they can keep only if there are no slow drivers, no one is ahead of them in checkout lines, and everybody in every other department does everything exactly when and how it should be done. However long you believe anything should take, multiply it by four to come up with a more realistic estimate.

You can do one more thing to go mano a mano with your time demon, but it takes more courage than most people have: whenever you drive somewhere, never change lanes unless there is a stationary object in your lane, you have to make a turn, or you have to take an exit.

The brave people who actually try this exercise discover that though it may add five or six minutes to an average commute, the experience of not having to race the other drivers on the road can change their lives. Try it if you dare.

As long as you don't inflict it on other people and yourself in word, deed, or thought, time pressure does little damage and may even do some good. I'd like to say more, but I'm in a hurry.

SURVIVAL SCENARIO 71   In the Unlikely Event That You Are Wrong

OK, you were wrong. You shouldn't have said what you said, and now you need to apologize. Well, maybe you don't. Maybe if you don't mention it and don't do it again, it will just go away. It's not as if you meant it to come out the way it did. Anyway, the whole thing wasn't your fault. Other people ought to take some responsibility too. Maybe you should explain.

Right now, the work is piling up. Let's put this off until later.

Apologizing is hard. Actually, it isn't. What's hard is thinking that you need to apologize. Most of us will readily admit to making mistakes in the abstract, but when it comes down to specifics, there is always a perfectly good explanation for what we did. If the other person would just take a minute to listen to our side of it . . .

When other people act this way, we call it "being defensive." When we act this way, we call it "being reasonable." Many reasonable people have such a hard time believing they're wrong that it makes their apologies sound less than sincere. When they try to say, "I was wrong; I'm sorry," it ends up sounding more like, "You shouldn't be upset, because I didn't intend for things to turn out the way they did, and anyway, you make mistakes, too, and here are a few examples."

The whole process is automatic—the rear end just sort of covers itself, whether the person speaking plans it or not.

SURVIVAL SOLUTION *71*
How to Apologize

Here are some ideas on making more effective apologies, in the unlikely event you are ever wrong:

Consider Your Goal. Do you want the other person to forgive you, or do you want to be right? The two strategies require very different choices of words. People will be far less likely to forgive you if they have to acknowledge their own mistakes to do so.

Pay Attention to Your Emotional State. If you feel more angry than guilty, ask yourself at whom you're angry and why. Even if you're angry at yourself for making a mistake, that anger will leak into your apology. Deal with your anger; calm yourself down before you try to apologize.

Less Is More. "I was wrong; I'm sorry" is about right. It's that next sentence, beginning with *but*, that starts sounding defensive.

Accept Responsibility for the Consequences of Your Act as Well as the Act Itself. Even if the consequences were not what you thought they should be—someone got angry or hurt because he or she misunderstood what you said—remember that you are apologizing for what happened because of what you did, not what you intended to happen. Nobody makes mistakes on purpose, but everybody makes mistakes.

Make Amends. If you made a mess, clean it up. Ask what the other person would like you to do to make things better.

Wait Before Discussing the Issue Further. Apologize, offer to make amends, and then leave. Schedule some time the next day for further processing if it's needed. An apology has maximum effectiveness when it stands by itself.

Forgive the Other Person for Being Right. If you keep thinking of all the things the offended party should have apologized to you for but didn't, you'll eventually try to get even. Accept the fact that, in this instance, the other person was right and you were wrong. Learn from it, and get on with your life.

Forgive Yourself for Being Wrong. People really do learn from mistakes, but first they have to be brave enough to admit that they made them. When you have that kind of courage, apologies are easy.

SURVIVAL SCENARIO 72 Normal Depression

For the past week, it's been hard to get out of bed. You wonder where your motivation has gone. You drag yourself into work, but besides that, all you do is sleep and eat. You don't feel sad exactly, just empty. Maybe the stress is getting to you.

Occasional low-level depression is a normal part of living. I'm not talking about being disabled by sadness; the most common symptom of normal depression among businesspeople is a general decrease in motivation and interest. Irritability is also common, as are concentration difficulties, changes in appetite, and waking in the middle of the night and not being able to go back to sleep. The most common thought patterns are some variant of "What's the point?" or "I know I should be more interested in what's going on, but I just don't feel like it." People usually see a distinct difference in their capacity to get involved with things that they used to enjoy.

Needless to say, if such symptoms are intense, if the sleep disturbance lasts more than a week, or if these negative feelings recur with no apparent cause, you should see your doctor or mental health professional.

Normal depression usually has a readily observable cause, often work-related. The most typical causes are as follows:

- **Loss or setback.** If you are reprimanded, if you're passed over for a promotion, or if your department has a really bad quarter, it's not unusual to experience a drop in mood. You don't need a psychologist to tell you this.

- **Letdown.** Low-level depression is common after a period of intense effort or high stress. The symptoms usually occur after the stress is over, when people think they should be feeling better. The worst holiday depression shows up in mid-January.

- **Boredom.** People need stimulation to feel good about their lives. If your job isn't challenging enough, it can get depressing.

- **Self-medication.** Over time, three or four of cups of coffee to stimulate you during the day and a glass or two of wine to relax you at night can deplete the brain chemicals needed to stabilize mood.

SURVIVAL SOLUTION *72*
Don't Let Depression Depress You

If you're experiencing some normal depression, here are some things to do before going on Prozac. These techniques will also work for prevention.

Don't wait until you feel better to do the things that will make you feel better. Depression causes a decline in motivation. To get over it, you have to do things to pull yourself out of the dumps even if you don't feel like it. If you can't do it on your own, get a friend to serve as your designated butt kicker.

Exercise. You've heard it a million times: regular exercise can help almost everything that can go wrong with a human being.

Practice a Relaxation Technique. Meditation, yoga, relaxation tapes, self-hypnosis, or whatever, learn a structured technique for inducing physical relaxation, and practice it daily. Even at the office.

Say No to Drugs. Cut back on caffeine, alcohol, and other mood-altering substances. You don't have to cut them out; just stop using them as daily medication. After a few days, you ought to feel a difference.

Say No to Television Too. If you're depressed, television is your worst enemy. It fills time and gives back nothing useful. Ditto mindless Net surfing and computer games. Resting does not cure mental fatigue. It is far more calming to do a twenty-minute relaxation exercise and spend the rest of the evening with family or friends than it is to plop down in front of an electronic screen for three hours.

Talk to People Even If You Don't Feel Like It. Isolating yourself will make you feel worse. Spend time with people doing something other than complaining.

Take on a Challenge. Learn something new, take on new job responsibilities, or do anything that makes you feel a little bit scared. Force yourself to grow a little; it's better than being depressed.

Schedule Regular Fun. There should always be a couple of events in your appointment book to look forward to—not necessarily a trip to Hawaii, but a movie, a shopping trip, lunch with a friend, or maybe a day fishing. If it's not in your appointment book, it won't get done.

If you try these techniques and don't feel better after about two weeks, see a professional. See a professional also if a friend or family member thinks you should. With depression, one of the first things to go is your judgment.

SURVIVAL SCENARIO *73* Do You Have a Drinking Problem?

Before you read further, know for better or worse that this scenario has nothing to do with twelve-step programs.

You know who you are. And you know what you've been wondering at four A.M. when you can't get back to sleep, or in the headachy but not quite hung-over morning that follows, when you just can't wake up: Do I drink too much?

It's probably not the sort of question you'd want to ask out loud. You know as well as I do that the answer you'd get would depend mostly on the preconceived notions of the person you happen to ask. To an AA member, everyone who drinks is an alcoholic. To a heavy drinker, if you can still stand up, there's no problem.

In your own mind, you try to figure it out based on all the things you've heard. You can't be an alcoholic. You don't crave alcohol. You've never missed any work. You don't have blackouts. You haven't been arrested for drunken driving, and you can certainly name at least three people who drink more than you do. You've even read that a couple of drinks a day will protect you from heart disease. So, there's no problem—right?

The universe gives back no answer. All you're left with are those doubts that twist and squirm through your mind in the middle of the night.

You know the dangers, but the idea of life without alcohol is unimaginable. Scary. Empty.

"I'll cut down," you think. You repeat the words over and over. Gradually, they lull you to sleep.

You aren't alone. At this moment, all around you, thousands of responsible businesspeople are silently struggling with their doubts and fears about alcohol.

How to Know for Sure Whether Your Drinking Is a Problem

Here are some ideas about how to answer the question for yourself in the privacy of your own heart:

Never Again Go Without Counting. From now on, you need to know exactly how much you drink. Always. Alcohol creates a bleary uncertainty about where the second drink stops and the third begins. There are a million tricks—larger glasses or six-pack cans, "freshening up," losing your drink when it's almost done, going for higher alcohol content, or simple forgetting. Either give up the tricks or give up drinking right now. A drink, by the way, is the equivalent of one ounce of eighty-proof liquor, one twelve-ounce can of beer, or one eight-ounce glass of wine.

Set Absolute Limits. You need to set limits for how many days out of the week you drink and for how much you drink in one day. The amounts may vary. Drinking every day won't hurt you if it's one drink per day and, occasionally, two or three over the course of an evening. I'd be suspicious of any limits higher than ten per week or three per day. No saving up. If these limits seem absurdly low, forget this solution and talk to someone qualified to evaluate an alcohol problem.

The Day You Exceed Your Limit the Third Time Is the Day You Give It Up, Once and for All. If you can't follow these rules to the letter, you have a problem that requires talking to a professional about what to do next.

Don't Drive If You've Had More Than One Drink. Even if you've had only one, it's still not a good idea.

Beware of Self-Medication. If you have problems with anxiety, depression, or anger and think alcohol is helping you, or if you have been told that drinking is dangerous to your health, forget what I've written here. Discuss your drinking with a qualified person.

Obviously, this scenario is no substitute for talking with a professional. I've written it for those of you who aren't ready to go public but still want some concrete way to determine whether you have a drinking problem.

You know who you are.

SURVIVAL SCENARIO 74 Flirting with Doom

Never in your wildest dreams did you intend to have an affair. One thing kind of led to another, and it just happened. It started as a hug after a particularly stressful week; that turned into a kiss, and it went on from there. Now, since you're both involved with other people, you have some tough questions to answer. Then there is the whole issue of how it will affect things at the office. Maybe one of you will have to leave. Normally, you're such a sensible person. How did you get involved in something like this?

An office romance can be a beautiful, wonderful thing—or it can wreck your career and your life. It is amazing that something this important almost always happens by accident. The people involved are rarely out looking out looking for affairs (or sexual harassment complaints); they just happen, or at least that's how it feels.

How it feels is not necessarily how it is. Courtship behavior in humans, as in most other animal species, follows predictable and easily recognizable patterns. It is a dance that is engraved upon our brains. No conscious thought is required; one step leads to another. Most kids in junior high know the steps and will readily tease their peers for engaging in them. In offices, people may be doing the same dance, but somehow they think it's just a "meaningful business relationship" and has nothing to do with sex or anything like that. Until it's too late.

SURVIVAL SOLUTION 74
Recognize the Steps in the Courtship Dance
Before You Try Them out at the Office

Before I go further, I feel I should warn you. No other subject that I have written or spoken about has stirred up so much negative comment as what you are about to read. People get very angry at me for pointing out that the harmless friendship they so value is, at its heart, sexual. Then they have to make a difficult choice: knowing the nature of the relationship, do they stop, continue, or pretend that I don't know what I'm talking about. Most choose number three, often with considerable animosity.

The following are the steps in the dance of office courtship. Read on if you're sure you can control your temper.

Noticing. The pattern begins with seeing the other person as different or special. It's not necessarily sexual attraction, but attraction it is.

Display. You notice the person, you want him or her to notice you. Birds use bright feathers and funny dances. In the office, it's more likely to be perceptive questions, witty comments, carefully assembled outfits, or new clothes that highlight the fact that someone was finally able to sweat off those extra five pounds.

"Accidental" Meetings. Reasons appear for going places a certain person happens to be—such as developing a sudden, all-consuming interest in a part of the business that heretofore has not been of much concern. (She just explains marketing so well.)

Planned Meetings, Calls, and Texting. Suddenly the job requires a close working relationship. At first, shared projects are discussed in the office; later, it's on cell phones, at restaurants, or during lunchtime walks on beautiful spring days. At this point, conversation drifts from work to more personal topics. For most people, the listening and understanding they get at this stage are far more seductive than mere sex.

Banter. In the fourth grade, boys chase the girls they like and hit them. Grown-ups in offices use teasing, joking, and playful aggression as signals of interest. It's as if Katharine Hepburn and Spencer Tracy suddenly appear in the accounting department.

This is a dangerous stage if the attention is unwanted. Returning the fire, laughing at the jokes, or anything short of running away screaming will be interpreted as a sign of reciprocal interest. The line between politeness and encouragement is so thin that it may require a jury to determine whether it actually exists. If you're being showered with unwanted humorous attention, talk it over with someone in authority immediately. Misunderstanding the nature of this stage is the source of many sexual harassment complaints.

Gifts. In the animal world, it's a fresh-killed chipmunk. In the office, it's a studio card, a sticky-note wishing luck on the day of the big presentation, or anything from the store downstairs with the balloons and bears.

Touching. Neck rub, anyone? This is the point at which things become overtly sexual. If you don't believe it, ask yourself how you'd feel about someone's giving your spouse a neck rub.

Confiding. At this stage, people start to believe they can tell each other everything, and do. By far, the most common way accidental sexual contact begins is with a heartfelt hug to console someone who is going through a difficult time.

These are the steps; make of them what you will. I fear this scenario will make some people feel that I've taken something beautiful and pure and dragged it through the dirt. I know there are times that all the interactions I've written about here can occur and mean nothing. I also know there are some office romances that work out beautifully. I assure you I'm not in the least cynical about love. I merely think it's far too important to fly into on automatic pilot.

SURVIVAL SCENARIO 75 Office Romances That Can Warm Your Heart

Despite the fact that experts like me warn against office romances, you're dating someone at work, and it seems to be going quite well. You sometimes worry about hidden problems down the road. How do you know if this romance will warm your heart or blow up in your face?

Actually, only a small percentage of office liaisons create problems for anyone. But when they do create problems, things can blow up, such as careers, marriages, and families. As the preceding scenario warned, the accidental romances are particularly explosive.

The kind of office romance that warms the heart is a classic win-win situation. The people involved feel there is a balance between what they give and what they get. If that perception changes, one or the other terminates the relationship. There may be sadness and heartache, but these aftereffects are confined to the lovers themselves and perhaps a few sympathetic friends. Even if the relationship ends, the perception of balance remains. The people involved, though temporarily hurt, would agree that it's better to have loved and lost than never to have loved at all.

What I'm describing here is a normal dating relationship that happens to be between two people who work together. By far, the greatest number of office romances fit this pattern. Coworkers may be dating, but the boundaries between love and work remain clear.

In the kind of office romance that blows up in people's faces, there is a blurring of those all-important boundaries between the office and the romance. At some level, people feel that there is an imbalance between what they're giving and what they're getting—either from their work or from each other. Instead of terminating the unbalanced relationship with the job or the lover, they cross the boundaries and try to use the job to fix the relationship or to use the relationship to fix the job. That's when the sparks start to fly.

How do you tell the difference between the good kind of office romance and the bad kind?

From decades of sifting through the ashes of love, I've discovered five tests that seem to reliably predict which office romances will be successful and which are likely to go up in smoke—sometimes taking the rest of the office with them.

SURVIVAL SOLUTION 75
How to Tell Which Office Romances Will Blow Up in Your Face

If both people can answer *yes* to the five questions that follow, chances are good that their relationship will be a win-win situation for them and for the people who work with them. With every *no* answer, the danger of explosion increases exponentially.

1. **Can you date openly?** Whatever reasons people have for not acknowledging their relationship can weigh it down with paranoia and distrust. Infatuation turns into love by answering difficult questions. The big ones here are: What will happen if you're caught, and what will you do then? No one is too careful to get caught.

2. **Are you at approximately the same level in the organization?** Romances between people at different levels seem to cause the most damage to the most people, especially if one of them has decision-making authority over the other. Love is blind, and power often does what it can without thinking

about whether it should. Put the two together and you have an explosive situation of the first magnitude.

3. **Are you willing to discuss problems, real or imagined, that your relationship may cause for the people who work with you?** For love at work to be successful, the people involved have to be willing to consider the possibility that the people who work with them may not be as enthused about their relationship as they are. There are a number of reasons, short of puritanical outrage, that coworkers might be concerned about an office romance. You have to have forbearance enough to discuss them.

4. **Can everything you're doing and saying at work be done or said in public?** Groping in elevators or oval offices is what gives office romance a bad name. Do I need to say more?

5. **Do you unequivocally grant the other person the right to say no?** Relationships get ugly when one person says no to something and the other person refuses to hear it. This is especially true if someone is saying no to the relationship itself. Here, in a simple unbalanced equation, is the formula for everything from sexual harassment suits to crimes of passion.

If an office romance can pass these five tests, it will probably warm your heart. If not, stand back, because sooner or later it's going to blow sky-high.

SURVIVAL SCENARIO 76   What Part of No Did You Not Understand?

Kinesha (who was last observed in Scenario 67) really didn't want to be on the safety committee. It's not that she considered it unimportant; it

is just that she is overwhelmed with other tasks, and the safety committee requires a lot of time in meetings. She didn't want to be on it, and
she even said no when the committee chair approached her. But, here
she sits at seven thirty P.M. when everybody else has gone home, eating a burger from McDonald's at her desk and reading an eighty-page
pamphlet called Everything You Always Wanted to Know About Fire
Exits. As she reads, her mind drifts to how she got on the committee in
the first place.

Diane, the committee chair, approached her three months ago asking her to fill a vacancy. Kinesha smiled and said she didn't think she
had the time, since she was feeling overextended already. Diane asked
her what was taking up all her time, and Kinesha mentioned some of
the projects she was involved in, the other committees, the report she
was working on, and some other loose ends here and there.

Diane was not convinced; she tried to be helpful. She gave Kinesha
a smile and a lot of ideas about how to delegate tasks, what to put
off, and how to be better organized. She even volunteered to speak to
Kinesha's boss to get a little time freed up so Kinesha could serve on
the committee.

Pretty soon, Kinesha felt boxed in. Somehow Diane had found ways
around all of the reasons Kinesha gave her for not participating. All the
support had been knocked out from under her, so she now felt she had
to say yes.

Kinesha feels manipulated, but she's not quite sure how it happened. She said no, but somehow it didn't work.

SURVIVAL SOLUTION 76
Saying No Once Is Seldom Enough

Kinesha fell into one of the oldest traps known to humankind. Instead
of taking no for an answer, Diane asked her why not, and Kinesha
answered. This ploy miraculously changed the focus of the discussion
from whether Kinesha would serve to whether her reasons for not serving were valid. Diane was able to decimate each of the reasons. Since

all her stated reasons were blown out of the water, Kinesha would have to change her no to a yes or risk seeming irrational. This manipulative technique is extremely effective because nice, polite people believe they are not allowed to say no unless they have a good reason.

Most of the people who claim to have a hard time saying no really don't have a hard time saying no the first time. The problem is with saying no the second time, after someone has asked their reasons and suggested that they aren't adequate.

There are two ways to avoid the trap that Kinesha fell into:

1. **Say no the second time, after your reasons have been decimated.** You have to be able to do this whether or not you feel you are being impolite or even irrational.

2. **Say no the second time before giving your reasons.** In most situations where people are asking you to do something, the question is whether you want to do it. They have a right to a yes-or-no answer. You don't necessarily have to say why not.

If You Must Give Reasons, Be Vague. It's much better to say that you have too much to do already. If the person continues to press and demand more information, you can be pretty sure that he or she is trying to manipulate rather than understand.

Counterattack. If the person keeps asking why not, you might say, "It sounds like you are suggesting I don't have a good reason for saying no. Is that what you believe?" By bringing the process into the open, you maneuver the manipulator into the position of being the impolite person. Manipulation cuts two ways.

Most people who are trying to manipulate you can't do it unless you give them the information they need to work with. If you don't give it to them, they can't maneuver you into the unpleasant position of having to say no twice and feeling unreasonable for doing so.

SURVIVAL SCENARIO 77 Losing It

You've been working sixty-hour weeks, living on coffee and dough-nuts, trying to keep this hellacious project organized and on track. The whole thing has been one foul-up after another. Just when you think you can't take any more, something else goes wrong. Computers crash, software malfunctions, supplies are on back order, and you're getting absolutely no cooperation from other departments, even though every-one knows how critical this project is.

Today was the final straw. At the staff meeting, the IT manager complained about how rude you'd been to a couple of the deadbeats who work for him. You lost it then and there. You told him in no uncer-tain terms how incompetent and passive-aggressive his people have been throughout this project. How dare they complain about you! And another thing . . .

You look around the room, which has suddenly grown very quiet. A couple of people are staring at you with their mouths open. Most everybody else is shuffling through papers or checking their BlackBerries.

You lose it, and you lose.

Make no mistake; unless you are at the very top of the dominance hierarchy, an emotional outburst is poisonous to your career. Even if you are at the top of the food chain, only outbursts of anger with as few witnesses as possible will be tolerated for very long. Regardless of who you are, male or female, you are allowed no more than one small tear for a fallen hero or a terminally ill child. In most places, any other loss of emotional control, no matter how loud, intimidating, or even justified, will brand you as weak and raise questions about your fitness for promotions.

There are organizations and departments in which anger and ver-bal abuse are tolerated. If this is the case where you work, feel free to ignore the advice I offer here, but do remember that those who live by the sword die by it.

If you work anywhere else, no matter how much pressure you're under, it is in your best interest to do everything you can to avoid losing control at work. It's not the pressure itself that can cause you to blow; it's how you handle it.

<u>**SURVIVAL SOLUTION**</u> 77
How to Keep from Losing It, and How to Minimize the Damage if You Do

The time to do something about emotional outbursts is before they happen. Here are some suggestions:

Pay Attention to Your Thoughts. Emotional outbursts don't come out of nowhere. They start with a spark of frustration or indignation, which is then fanned into flames by internal repetitions of lists of all the things that have gone wrong or been done wrong.

When a new problem comes up and you find yourself repeating a list of all the foul-ups that have come before it, or when your particular nemesis does the same old thing and you find yourself repeating all of his prior transgressions, you are setting yourself up to explode. This is the time to control yourself by paying attention to these internal repetitions and disrupting them, rather than playing them over and over. Do not wait for the next incident to push you over the edge.

The Most Important Time to Manage Stress Is When You Don't Have Time. It always amazes me that when people are under stress, the first activities they drop from their repertoires are the techniques they use to manage stress. They don't have time to exercise and eat right. They stop meditating, miss yoga class, don't get massages, and cancel their golf games. This is about as close to insanity as most sane people get.

Watch the Sugar, Caffeine, and Alcohol. When people work long hours under pressure, they tend to adopt habits that make them more susceptible to emotional outbursts. Sugar and caffeine for energy during the day, followed by alcohol to relax at night, is a common but dangerous regimen. These substances upset the chemical balance your brain needs to stay resilient under stress.

If you don't have the time or the inclination to follow this advice, and you do find yourself in the midst of an emotional outburst at work, here are some things to remember:

Shut Up. Now. Once the outburst starts, the sooner you stop it, the better. Sit down. Leave the room. Do whatever it takes to stop yourself. Do not attempt to explain or justify yourself. Any attempt will only intensify your emotion. Minimize the damage by using every bit of willpower you have to sit down and shut up.

Afterward, Do Not Apologize. An apology will make you look weaker still. Your best bet is to say nothing unless you are asked. Then, a simple statement that your outburst rose out of a strong desire to do the best job possible is more than enough.

Do Not Explain Your Position Further Until You Have Written a Script. If you try to explain without writing a script, you are likely to use the same words, which will tap into the same emotions, which you may still find difficult to control. If you must explain, your script should present in different words a simple statement of what you want to happen. Do not attempt to justify something for which there is no justification.

Just Go Back to Work and Do the Best Job You Can. The overall goal is to make the incident a temporary aberration rather than a defining moment. You can do that by getting it together and getting back to work as quickly as possible.

SURVIVAL SCENARIO 78 Relocation Blues

Everybody says you have a bright future in your company. The marketing manager has talked to you about a job that may open up in the next few months, and you were looking forward to it—until your boss offered you a promotion. The bad news is it's in Peoria. You've been there, and it's really not your kind of town. Your friends and family are here; your kids have just started school. It's just not a good time to make a move. You'd like to say no and just wait for that marketing job, but you wonder about the ramifications. How do you decide whether to accept the offer or decline?

If you work for a large corporation, moving up usually means moving to another place. It's not just an issue of a job's coming open in Peoria that fits your talents and skills. Relocation is part of the culture of large corporations, and you can't really be leadership material until you've moved a couple of times—think sea duty in the navy.

What if you don't want to go?

Early in your career, it's possible to misunderstand relocation by paying more attention to the position or the place than to the meaning of the action. You're not being offered a specific job so much as a chance to prove yourself by accepting the ritual transfer. Don't let the fact that you're really waiting for a job in marketing, or that they don't ski in Peoria, cloud your judgment. In most corporations, you can say no to relocation only once, and then the offers stop coming.

To make matters more confusing, your boss will probably say that the transfer is optional, that something in Boise might open up in a few months. She isn't lying, but what she's saying is only part of the truth. To know the rest of it, talk to a few people who have turned down more than one relocation. If you can't find any, take that as your answer.

SURVIVAL SOLUTION *78*
Should You Stay or Should You Go?

How do you decide when to say no to relocation? Here are some things to think about:

Consider the Stage of Your Career. When you're in your twenties or thirties, it's hard to imagine yourself as a stodgy fifty-year-old with teenage kids who want to graduate from high school with their friends, and a spouse who has finally found a good job and a social network. It will happen, whether you can imagine it or not. Later in your career, your option to refuse may be more important, and a refusal may be more understandable to the middle-aged people who decide your future.

Consider the Place. The whole relocation issue becomes even more complicated when you consider the fact that where you're being transferred can also make a big difference in the trajectory of your career. Headquarters is always good, as is any place where there's an exciting new project. Stable, long-running operations away from big cities may be the corporate equivalent of Siberia—people go there and get forgotten. It's also possible that you're being sent to the hinterlands so you can show your stuff. How dynamic is the operation where they want to send you? Before you make a decision, make sure you know what your choices mean. Check it out carefully with a few veterans.

Consider the Stage of Your Life. Speaking of veterans—for you stodgy fifty-year-olds, the issues involved in deciding whether to relocate are different. Every transfer may lose you something outside of work that you may not be able to replace. Is it worth the disruption? You have to weigh your choices just as carefully as those youngsters do, but the questions you ask yourself are harder.

Consider Whether You're Moving up or Sideways. Are you still on the way up? Are the relocations you're being offered promotions, or are they lateral moves needed to fill up holes? If you're not bound for upper management, you need to take a close look at what happens to people at your level as they build up seniority. Corporate loyalty is no longer what it once was. Fifty is a little old to still be marching along like a good soldier, especially if there aren't many sixty-year-old soldiers around.

In the end, relocation is your decision. Choose wisely.

SURVIVAL SCENARIO *79* Blame

Earnings at your company have been way down these past three quarters. What's the problem, and what should be done about it?

People in marketing say that if the guys in sales got off their rear ends and moved more product, this would never have happened. Maybe a new sales manager would do the job better and would get some of the lead out of the department.

Sales reps say they can't sell products that are overpriced, are obsolete, and don't work. They think the bean counters upstairs are to blame. They pulled way back on quality control and research to cut costs, but they had to increase prices to pay for their huge new computer system and God knows how many layers of management. A little cost cutting upstairs would be a help.

The bean counters in finance are aghast at the exorbitant costs of doing business in this state. Do you have any idea what we are paying in health insurance and workers' compensation? How about what it costs to stay in compliance with safety and environmental standards? "Get rid of meddling legislators and ridiculous regulations!" they say. "Then this business and the whole economy would take off."

If that's not bad enough, look at the figures on material wastage in the factory, not to mention overall levels of worker productivity. Maybe a management shake-up at the plant would help get things back on track. The managers at the plant have a lot to answer for.

The plant managers say they don't have time to answer. They are busy filling out reports for central office. Besides, the workers they get don't know work ethic from a hole in the ground. You have to send them an engraved invitation just to get them to come in. If you get three-hours-a-day's worth of work out of them, you're doing well. With all the worry about lawsuits from the human resources department, you can't even fire the bad apples anymore. They know they can get away with murder. If we got rid of a few problem workers, that would send the right kind of message to the rest of them—shape up or watch out.

The crew on the shop floor say the problem is that they have to spend all their time fixing equipment that should have been replaced a decade ago. What do they expect in a plant that is obsolete, unsafe, and understaffed? The foremen are more interested in kicking butt and taking names than seeing if any work gets done. The real problem is the whole philosophy of management in this company. The guys upstairs in the boardroom are the ones that should be tossed out on their ears.

Upstairs, at the board meeting, it was decided that what the company needs is a fresh approach to management. A new CEO sweeps clean, they always say.

So it goes.

SURVIVAL SOLUTION *79*
If Blame Is the Answer, You're Asking the Wrong Question

The real problem at your company is the approach to problem solving. When things go wrong, instead of figuring out what can be done about it, everybody looks for someone else to blame. The primitive parts of our brains are programmed to equate punishing the guy who made the mistake with solving the problem. In many businesses, this primitive thinking is elevated to company policy.

Blaming leads to company-wide paranoia and a culture where covering your own rear end is more important than doing the job. That's what's really running up the costs.

Everybody is doing two jobs instead of one—whatever he or she is supposed to be doing and making sure that if any mistakes are made, they are blamed on someone else.

Let the blaming stop with you, now. We learn from mistakes, or at least we can if we try. In companies where problem solving consists of punishing or getting rid of the people who make the mistakes, nobody learns anything. They just keep making the same mistakes. The only thing that changes is who gets punished for them.

Mistakes, yours and everyone else's, are not sins. If your company's culture is one of blame, it is not just because the board and the CEO decreed it; it is because everyone, top to bottom, participates and perpetuates the same pattern. You may not be in charge, but what you do has an effect on the people around you, and it certainly has an effect on how much harm the general insanity does to you. If you want to stay sane, take a tip from Gandhi: be the change that you wish to see. When someone makes a mistake, fix the problem, not the blame. Let it start with your own mistakes.

SURVIVAL SCENARIO 80 Learning from Mistakes

Norris is a political pundit, or so he assumes. Rush says it, Norris believes it; that's all there is to it. Actually, there's more to it than that. Norris delights in quoting the master's bons mots about how stupid liberals are. He wonders why a guy as bright and funny as he is doesn't get promoted. Must be a liberal conspiracy.

Adam is behind in entering his management information reports. Way behind, to the point of probation. Nobody ever seemed to care, and then bam! One day they want to see it all. Even though he stayed up two nights in a row, he couldn't come anywhere near catching up. He wishes he'd been given more advance notice.

You lost your temper and yelled at the IT manager. Remember? It was just a few scenarios ago.

Everybody makes mistakes, which is a good thing, because we learn far more from our mistakes than we do from our successes. Success teaches us to keep doing the same thing over and over, until it becomes a mistake. If we are willing to learn, mistakes can teach us to think differently.

If the best conclusion we can come up with is, "Don't do that again," the life lesson is wasted, because there is no usable information. Unless we figure out the thoughts and perceptions that led us to believe that the mistake was a correct response to the situation, we are doomed to keep whacking our foreheads and wondering why we keep doing what we told ourselves we shouldn't do.

SURVIVAL SOLUTION *80*
How to Learn What Mistakes Are Trying to Teach You

Learning from mistakes is hard, because they keep getting confused with sins. Making mistakes is something good people are not supposed to do. It is far easier to rationalize and justify than it is to learn. If you are willing to take the hard road, here is how to learn from your mistakes:

Admit You Made a Mistake. By this I mean admit to yourself. As to admitting it to others, that is up to you. As we have seen, there are cultures in which mistakes are punished as much in the real world as they are in your mind.

Figure out Exactly What the Mistake Was. Mistakes usually arise from a misperception that leads to erroneous action.

Norris mistakenly believes that everyone thinks making fun of other people is as hilarious as he does. Adam needs to realize that he was given advance notice about his reports when he was told he was supposed to do them. And you, did you learn only to keep your mouth shut, or did your outburst teach you to cut back on caffeine and stop skipping yoga class?

Make a Plan and Follow It. Learning from your mistakes is do-it-yourself therapy. To be successful, therapy must have two distinct phases: *insight* and *working through*. Insight involves gaining an emotional grasp of the thoughts and actions that caused the problem. Working through means doing what it takes to fix it. Neither is sufficient by itself. Learning from your mistakes, as with everything else that is valuable in this world, requires thought, effort, and commitment. Oh yeah, and courage.

Part 5

Useful Workplace Skills

IN THIS SECTION, you will learn a few tricks that will help you to get ahead or, in some cases, just get by.

<table>
<tr><td>SURVIVAL
SCENARIO</td><td>81</td><td>**Doing a Good Job and Succeeding
Are Not Necessarily the Same Thing**</td></tr>
</table>

Chuck, in the cube next to yours, has been with the company more than twenty years. He does his job really well. He's great at calming down angry customers, and when new people come on board, he's always the guy they pick to train them. He volunteers for all kinds of committees, such as safety and morale, and is always coming up with positive suggestions. Chuck does a good job, but he's been in the same place for almost twenty years. He always seems to be second in line for promotions. It's beginning to get to him.

One of the most damaging illusions that people hold about whatever occupation they happen to be in is that if they do a good job, they will be successful. In general, doing a good job means competently managing what is below you in the organizational hierarchy. Success comes from managing the people above you. The skills involved are usually very different, so it's not a good idea to mistake one for the other.

How to Tell the Difference Between Doing a Good Job and Succeeding

There are some precepts that Chuck hasn't learned about the realities of business. If your definition of success involves moving up the ladder, you need to make a few distinctions that Chuck missed.

The following activities are all part of doing a good job but will probably have nothing to do with whether you will advance in the corporate hierarchy:

- **Working directly with customers.** In most companies, customer service is an important corporate goal, but it is not accomplished by important corporate people. Selling is a possible exception. If you want to get ahead and you have to deal with customers, it is much better to be close to the people who buy your product than to the people who use it.

- **Serving on committees and task forces with people at your own level.** These committees solve problems, organize work, and get things done. They don't yield much in the way of glory to their participants.

- **Training.** Training is an absolute necessity, but in the corporate world, they believe the old adage: If you can, do. If you can't, teach.

- **Coming up with ideas that improve quality or morale but cost money.** If you're the owner or CEO, you can do this and be praised for it. If you're anybody else, it will be taken as evidence that you don't understand what business is all about.

The following activities may have little to do with doing a good job, but they will lead to corporate advancement:

◆ **Bringing in new business.** It doesn't have to be much business or even good business. In the corporate world, it is always the rainmakers who are on top of the heap. Compared with bringing in new business, winning the Nobel Prize is small potatoes.

◆ **Cost cutting.** Cost cutting is a divinely ordained task of management. Do it often and conspicuously to show that you are leadership material. At meetings, always be the one who asks if it can be done cheaper. If you want to get ahead, never talk about cost cutting and executive salaries in the same breath.

◆ **Doing anything with people of higher rank.** This is especially true if you are the person in front of the room with the PowerPoint and killer graphics. If not, be the one who asks if it can be done cheaper.

◆ **Taking the management side on controversial issues.** Doing a good job often involves cooperation and compromise. Getting ahead involves looking after your own interests. It may be sad, but it's true. Promotions are not awarded by popular vote.

◆ **Generating text.** Most anything other than simple e-mails that goes out with your name on it will enhance your reputation. Reports, policies and procedures, goal statements, mission statements, quality-improvement plans, and pieces about corporate values are all good choices. Avoid documents explaining government regulations, because they will cause people to mistake you for the government.

- ◆ **Socializing.** Promotions go to the people who are out shaking hands, not the ones sitting in their offices merely doing a good job.

In the corporate world, doing a good job and succeeding involve different tasks and different skills. Both are necessary, but you should never believe you are doing one when you're actually doing the other.

SURVIVAL SCENARIO 82

A Good Attitude Is like Pornography: It Can't Be Defined, but People Know It When They See It

In your division, any promotion or raise must meet with Dave, the VP. (Dave and his management style were introduced back in Scenario 5.) What he looks for is motivation and a good attitude. He can't tell you what they are exactly, but rest assured, he knows who has them and who doesn't.

Make no mistake about this: If you want to get by in business, being perceived as having a good attitude is more important than competence.

Throughout your career, people will be making important judgments about what is going on inside your head without having any way of actually knowing; they will be making inferences based on what you say and what you do. It will be these inferences, as much as any objective accomplishments, that determine the trajectory of your career.

Sure, you can do the work, but if you want to get ahead, you have to be perceived as having a good attitude. How do you do that? Let's ask your boss:

"Well," she says, "a good attitude means having a strong work ethic, being willing to go the extra mile, thinking proactively, playing well with others, and having a positive influence on the group."

Does that tell you what you want to know? If it does, go on to the next scenario. If not, read on.

A good attitude is like pornography: it is very difficult to define, but people know it when they see it, or at least think they do. They can spot a bad attitude even more quickly.

Based on many years of experience working with businesses, I believe there are unwritten rules about how to conduct yourself successfully in any job. You can break any of these rules without getting fired, but they are still absolutely critical.

These rules pertain to the basic behaviors that distinguish an insider from an outsider, one of us from one of them. Following these rules will not assure you of success, but not following them will ensure failure.

SURVIVAL SOLUTION *82*
How to Fake a Good Attitude If You Don't Have One Already

An attitude is something that's inside. What shows is your behavior, what you do. These are the kinds of things that you need to do so that the people who make decisions about you will think that you have a good attitude, regardless of what you actually feel:

Come In. Yes, I know you get eight hours of sick leave per month, but that does not mean you have to use it. Nothing marks you as a real outsider any better than regular use of all your sick leave. Anybody can be sick once in a while, but regularly missing a day or two here and there is the mark of someone who really doesn't know what working is all about. If there is anything that enrages employers more than regular absences, it is regular absences on Mondays and Fridays.

Identify with the Company. Act, speak, and behave as if what's good for the company is good for you. If you act as if your boss is your adversary, you're asking for trouble as well as displaying the fact that your own problems with authority are more important to you than doing a good job.

Have a Professional Appearance. Yes, I know that the clothes you choose, the color of your hair, and whether you have tats and piercings have nothing to do with how well you do your job. Bear in mind, however, that every company has its own standards for dress, and it's best to conform to them. Don't wear anything that will call more attention to your appearance than to your abilities. The last thing you want to be thought of as is the guy with the ring in his nose or the gal in the flip-flops.

Be Pleasant. Make a conscious effort to get along with the people with whom you work. If you're upset with someone, try as best you can to resolve the dispute directly with the individual. Do not take your problems to everyone you meet in the hallway, and for God's sake, don't take them to your boss. And please: eliminate snorting and eye rolling as a means of expressing displeasure.

Accept Direction and Criticism. It would be nice if your boss were more positive, but in work, as in poker, you need to play the hand that you're dealt. There is no point in whining.

Do Your Job as If It Were Worth Doing. Know enough about your job to know everything that's involved. If you cut the grass, don't make them have to tell you that the project involves raking and edging too. Do the whole thing, and do it as well as you can. That means both the parts that are regularly checked and the parts that aren't.

Know Your Boss's Priorities, and Follow Them. Never mind if they are wrong or look wrong to you. The way to succeed at your job is to see it from your boss's point of view rather than from your own. When you run things, you will get to call the shots.

Be Circumspect with the Ideas You Put Forward. Make suggestions about how things could be done better, but realize that in the world of business, everything has a price tag. Even if something is a good idea, what usually determines whether it will be accepted is what it costs.

Don't Make Them Have to Tell You Everything. Watch what successful people are doing, and imitate them. That's the way to really get ahead, because most of the important things about work are never told to you directly.

Have a Sense of Humor. Be able to laugh, especially about yourself. No one likes to work with people who take themselves too seriously. Be able to take mild joking about your politics, your religion, your illnesses, your allergies, your pets, and your children.

Come in on Time. Regularly. Always. I know I said it before, but it's important enough to repeat.

SURVIVAL SCENARIO *83* Do You Have to Suck up to Get Ahead?

The short answer to this question is yes. Unless you want to be miserable throughout your entire career, you need to make a good impression on the people above you. They need to like you and feel that you like them.

The longer answer involves posing another question: What is sucking up, and why does it fill some people with existential dread?

Let's consider Dale and Eric, two guys who work in the same department. First let's look at Dale. There he is in the break room, kidding around with a couple of managers. Even he would say he's not the brightest bulb in the chandelier, but he makes up for it in motivation. He's always positive, and he's always volunteering for something.

He's even been known to bring his boss coffee. That's right: Dale is a suck-up.

Now let's look at Eric, who's at his desk working, exactly where he should be. He's bright and competent, but behind his back, some people call him "Mr. Attitude." Not his friends: they see him as a warm, caring person who's always there when times get rough. He's quick with a joke, and the jumper cables on that old Jeep of his have started more cars in the company lot than Triple A.

Managers see a totally different side. Eric's boss thinks he has a chip on his shoulder. Some days, it seems to her that all she hears from him are grunts and monosyllables. She wonders why Eric hates her and how much longer she can take having him in her department. Other managers steer clear of him too, even when they have a project that could benefit from his talents.

Eric does not suck up. He sees himself as a man of principle. I see him as an overgrown teenager.

SURVIVAL SOLUTION *83*
No, You Have to Suck up to Get *Anything*

As a general rule, people don't put themselves out much for people who they think hate them. Even if you do hate your boss, there is absolutely no percentage in letting her know it. If you have compunctions about sucking up—and you do if that term is a regular part of your vocabulary—here are a few suggestions:

Ask Yourself Why You Call It "Sucking Up." If you substitute "treating managers like human beings," the absurdity of the situation becomes clearer. As people, managers are no different from your coworkers. What is different is the way you feel about them.

Ask Yourself Where You Got the Idea That People in Authority Are the Enemy. There is no way to put this gently. You might be an overgrown teenager.

At about age thirteen, a biological time bomb goes off inside our heads as we begin the difficult transition from dependence on our parents to dependence on ourselves. We start thinking things like "You can't tell me what to do," and that people in authority don't know what they're talking about and cannot be trusted. We learn to trust our friends and eventually to trust ourselves. As we eventually mature, our parents, teachers, and bosses seem less like evil incarnate and more like regular people.

The problem is that some people can get stuck in their teenage mind-sets well into their eighties. Some of this failure to budge is cultural. America was founded by a rebellion, and most of our heroes are people who did their own thing no matter what the authorities thought.

If you have some question as to whether you are a hero or a teenager, check it out with a few close friends. Another clue is that heroes accept the consequences of their choices with equanimity; teenagers think the world is unfair.

Grow Up. There is definitely value both in complying and in doing things your own way. It takes a very mature person to decide when to cooperate and when to stand up for principles. Each situation has to be evaluated on its own merits rather than living your entire life by one rule that applies to all situations. Anybody who has a hard-and-fast rule about sucking up, or who calls any attempt at being friendly to higher-ups brownnosing, is showing a little immaturity. Often, treating your boss like a friend can work out to your benefit. Maybe you ought to try it.

SURVIVAL SCENARIO *84* We Are All in Sales

At the edge of a savanna, two Neanderthals meet. One has a spear, and the other has a crude basket full of roots and berries. They look over each other's wares doubtfully. They point and gesticulate until the trade is made. Commerce is born.

Let's fast-forward to the present day.

Barney, the sales rep, approaches his calls with a smile, a handshake, and a box of doughnuts for the folks in the office. Barney's products are as good as the next guy's, and his prices are about average too. People tend to steer their business toward him because he is such a nice guy.

James wants the promotion so bad, he can taste it. The competition is stiff, but he can handle it. He has to show his boss that he has what it takes to be a leader. He knows what she values: positive attitude, creative ideas, high motivation, and an ability to get along with the rest of the team. He also knows he has all the qualifications; he just needs to structure things so that his boss will be as sure of that fact as he is.

Tom runs a papermaking machine that is so big and complicated that it is well beyond my ability to describe it. In order to keep it producing, he needs the help of about ten other guys on the floor. Sure, it's their job to help him, but he knows that he gets quicker and better help if he doesn't push people around and if he always remembers to thank them.

The personnel officer smiles and says, "Tell me about yourself." Connie is on; she has rehearsed and is ready to convince anyone who cares to listen that she's the right person for the job.

Mack, from engineering, has a new idea that might save a bundle in the manufacturing process. He's got a few sketches and some rough projections to show Willis, the production manager. He knows he needs Willis in his corner if this idea is going to go anywhere.

Marlene, the attorney, is meeting with some new clients. This could be a very big case. Will she get it? It depends on what they think of her. Aside from the air of professional competence that she usually projects, she makes a special effort to show that she can listen and be concerned with what her clients want. They need her on this case because she cares.

Richard approaches the pulpit, and he looks the congregation straight in the eye. He is firm in his belief that the practice of Christian charity is what it takes to make the world a better place. The Bible says it. Richard believes it. Now all he has to do is convince the flock. This is going to be one . . . heaven . . . of a sermon.

Aaron knows particle physics, that's for sure. You don't get to be assistant professor without knowing your stuff. But it takes more than that to get tenure. He's polishing up the grant proposal he will be sending to the NSF in the morning. Without grants, there will be no research; without research, no publication; and without publication, no tenure. It is as simple as that.

SURVIVAL SOLUTION *84*
If You Don't Think Your Job Requires Selling, Think Again

All these stories have one thing in common, and it is the one activity that everyone from cave dweller to president needs to engage in to be successful: selling. Good ideas by themselves are never enough; they have to be promoted. The people who recognize this fact and put it into their daily lives at work are the ones who succeed.

Here is an important idea to consider: *The world of business is based on selling.* Sales is a skill that everyone needs. If you think your job doesn't require selling, then there is probably something about it that you don't understand. Whatever you do, there is always something that you have to sell to somebody.

Get out there and sell!

SURVIVAL SCENARIO *85* Negotiation

You are off to a meeting with a supplier. Your boss claps you on the back and says, "Be tough! This is an important negotiation." You give him a thumbs-up sign as you go out the door. Inside, you're wondering what exactly it means to be a tough negotiator. Should you be carrying a big stick?

Businesspeople don't talk; they negotiate. Even though there are many excellent books and articles on the subject, the idea most people have is that negotiation is an aggressive act. A tough negotiator is seen as the kind of person who sets out a position and says, "Take it or leave it." Actually these people only look tough. What they're doing is really weakness of mind dressed up in boots and a cowboy hat. They lose a lot of business for the sake of vanity.

Actually, the toughest negotiators are the people who listen best. They figure out what the people they're dealing with really want so that they can make them an offer they literally can't refuse. The key to being a good negotiator is not so much what you say or do; it's how well you listen and think.

SURVIVAL SOLUTION *85*
How to Be a Tough Negotiator

The first and last rule of negotiation is: Let the other guys talk. The second is: When they talk, listen. The biggest mistake most negotiators make is thinking so much about their response that they miss important and useful information. There is always time to stop and listen. While you're listening, asking yourself the following questions will make you a better negotiator:

- **With whom are you actually negotiating?** In most cases, your opponents are representing other people besides themselves. Sometimes what a negotiator wants and what his or her constituency wants may be different. It's always easier to deal with a person than with a representative.

◆ **What are your goals for your company and for yourself?**
You'll never get anything unless you know what you want. Are you in it for the money, a good deal, a strategic alliance, or do you merely want to carve another notch on your BlackBerry? All negotiators have goals for themselves as well as their companies. Some want to win. Some want approval. Some want to be feared. These personal goals may influence them almost as much as their company goals—more if they are unaware of them.

Always be honest with yourself about what you want for yourself, lest your personal goals be used to distract you. Think clearly about your goals, and set priorities. Know what a successful outcome would be for your company and for you. If they are not one and the same, rethink. You are most vulnerable when you are itching to win but aren't quite sure what winning is.

◆ **What are the other guy's goals?** How do your opponents define success? If you're thinking that all they want is to get as much as they can for as little as possible, you need to delve deeper; everybody wants that. To figure out other negotiators' personal goals, you must read between the lines of everything they say and do. The most effective way to use what you observe is by giving something without giving in.

People who want to win can't resist scoring points. Let them. Take a hard stand, and then back down in some less important areas. For negotiators who want to be the smartest guys in the room, make a few mistakes. They will find it hard to resist correcting you. Act pissed, but know inside that you are gaining control by giving them what they secretly want.

Some negotiators want to be seen as fair and reasonable. They want your approval, so why not give it? Compliment them on being reasonable. For negotiators who want to intimidate you, surreptitiously chew antacids. It gets them every time.

- **What is the outside pressure on you?** What would your boss consider barely adequate, and what would knock his socks off? What would he call losing the farm?

- **What limits are there on your decision-making authority?** Often people feel they get into a negotiating situation representing someone else and they really don't have the authority to make any decisions.

- **What is the pressure on your opponent?** Always try to phrase your proposals in such a way that they would sound good to whomever your opponent represents. He or she will have to make a presentation. Why not supply the material?

- **On what premises do you agree?** Start out from a common goal, and then move on to the items about which you have differing opinions. Focus on the points of similarity between your goals and your opponent's goals.

- **What might be considered a win-win?** Everybody tells you to go for the win-win, but they don't necessarily tell you what that would look like. Think about what would happen if you both got exactly what you wanted for your companies and yourselves. Go for that.

- **Is any of this personal?** If you're scared, angry, or upset, or if you have an ax to grind, put off the negotiation until you calm down. Negotiation is best done with a cool head and an open mind.

SURVIVAL SCENARIO *86* People Skills

"Can you believe it?" Rick says to his homies in the break room. "Her highness, Queen Gwen, dinged me on my evaluation because my 'people skills need improvement.' What kind of horseshit is that? It's not like I can't do the job. My numbers are the best in the department, but it doesn't mean diddly. She says I need to be more 'sensitive'—like sugar-coating everything I say and making sure it's all nice and politically correct, so it doesn't offend anybody. 'People skills' is a bunch of crap, if you ask me."

There's something inherently unmasculine about admitting there's anything important that we don't know, so us guys often pretend that what we don't understand isn't important. Nowhere is this more apparent than with people skills. We were out on the football field communicating by punching each other on the shoulder while the girls were at home learning how to keep a conversation going. Now, as adults, we're stuck having to pretend that people skills aren't important because we don't have any.

People skills require mastering difficult tasks that, when they are done well, make our customers and coworkers feel they are being heard, understood, and valued. There's no way you can convince me that isn't important for success in whatever you may be doing besides football. The grim fact of it is: people skills is a competitive sport, and we're losing. To girls.

SURVIVAL SOLUTION *86*
A People-Skills Workout for Guys

Guys, it's time to get off our butts and get into training! Add this people-skills workout to your routine today:

Warm-Up: Listening. When other people are talking, pay attention to what they say well enough to repeat it back. Do not begin composing your reply until the other person has finished talking. Don't try any of the other exercises until you get this warm-up down pat.

Exercise 1: Making Small Talk. The basis of all people skills is the ability to keep a conversation going. This means showing an interest even if you're not interested. It is accomplished by asking questions about what the other person is saying and by sharing anecdotes about similar thoughts and experiences in your own life. You do this not because the content of the conversation is particularly important, but because you want the other person to feel important. Act as attentive as you'd like your kids to be when you're explaining the value of work ethic or how to throw a baseball.

In this exercise, appearing interested makes all the difference. Never look at your watch, your computer screen, the newspaper, or the TV when another person is talking.

Exercise 2: Using Praise. Praising is not normal behavior for an adult male. It's a lot easier for us to criticize people for what they do wrong than it is to praise them for what they do right. Still, praise is the most important motivator there is, so we need to build up a tolerance. Start small, and work up to four times as many positive comments as negative. This one is tough; you may want to check with your doctor before you try it. We don't want any heart attacks.

Exercise 3: Remembering. If you forget a name or a conversation, you're saying that the person is unimportant. You may not mean it that way, but that's how it will be understood. There are few things as insulting as telling the same story twice or forgetting what someone said to you or what you said you'd do. Pay attention, and get it right the first time! If your brain isn't up to the task, take notes.

Exercise 4: Being Tactful. The essence of tact is knowing the other person's feelings well enough to present whatever you have to say in a way that is likely to be heard. This takes thinking and planning. Think carefully before you speak. No shooting from the hip.

Exercise 5: Validating Problems Before Offering Advice. Most people would rather have their difficulties acknowledged than be handed solutions. Always let people know that you understand why something is a problem before asking if they want suggestions. Advice is not a gift from the gods; always ask if it's wanted before offering it.

Exercise 6: Showing Empathy. All people skills boil down to an understanding that though other people may feel differently than you do, they still feel. Never miss a chance to demonstrate this understanding. If you don't know how people feel, it's not a problem: they will usually tell you if you ask.

Guys, go through this people-skills workout for a few weeks, and pretty soon you too can have rippling charm and rock-solid confidence. Better yet, no ninety-eight-pound girl will be able to kick sand in your face by being better at influencing your customers and coworkers than you are.

SURVIVAL SCENARIO 87 Asking for a Raise

You've been in your position for almost eight months, and you are doing far more than when you first started in this position. During your tenure, you've completed three difficult projects in record time, and you've have been given far more responsibility than other people at your level, especially one person who you found out makes almost 10 percent more than you do. The cost of living is going up much faster than your salary. If you are going to stay in this job, you'll need a raise. How are you going to get it?

There may be a lot of reasons that you need a raise or want a raise, but to actually get one, you have to answer one question in a very convincing way: Why would paying you more be a good business decision?

First, here are some approaches to avoid:

- **Make jokes about the low pay around here.** This hardly qualifies as asking for a raise, but I include it because some people joke around, hoping that the boss will take a hint and spare them the anxiety of actually asking. Maybe this kind of manipulation works for your mother, but it will not work for you. Aside from being annoying, this approach demonstrates a profound ignorance of how business decisions are actually made. You may consider your salary a joke, but to your boss, it is never a joking matter.

- **Compare your salary with someone else's.** This approach will probably make several people angry at you. Most companies consider what various people make to be their secret. Your boss will not be pleased that you know and will be even less pleased at the poor judgment you show in bringing it up. Your boss will also be irritated at the person whose salary you found out about, and that person will be angry at you for dragging him or her into your negotiation. Do I need to go further with this?

- **Explain how much you need the money.** This is the most frequently used and least effective way to ask for a raise. Why should your boss care that your expenses have gone up? Maintaining your lifestyle is not management's responsibility.

- **Argue that the cost of living has gone up faster than your salary.** The cost of doing business has gone up as well. To actually get more money, you have to tell the boss what she's buying for that money. A warm sense of having done the right thing is not an easy expenditure to justify.

◆ **Issue an ultimatum.** Nobody likes to be threatened. Unless you are completely willing to walk if you don't get the raise you want, don't even hint at the possibility. Your boss may call your bluff. If you *are* looking elsewhere, your boss is the last person you want to know about it.

SURVIVAL SOLUTION *87*
How to Get That Raise

The approaches that are more likely to work involve showing the boss what those extra dollars are buying. If you think of the problem from this angle, you're more likely to find a profitable solution. Here are some suggestions:

Set the Stage. Pay is important; don't be shy about it. Talk about money from the first day. Ask your boss how people get promotions and salary increases. She will probably tell you, and that will save you a lot of guesswork in the future.

The very best time to negotiate for a raise is before your job changes. When you are given a new assignment, point out that increased responsibilities usually involve increased compensation. The best time to cut a deal is right then. It will be harder to backfill later.

Do Your Homework. Know what is typically done in your company. Read your personnel manual. If there are procedures for applying for a raise or promotion, follow them. If people are typically given raises after an annual review, or if the company gives across-the-board percentage raises, you will have to work within that system. Many busy bosses are behind in their reviews. If yours is overdue, asking for it is a good way to open negotiations.

Know What Is Done in Other Companies. This approach can be effective if your data are accurate, verifiable, and based on your local market, especially if they show that your compensation is in the bottom half. Most companies want to pay at or just below the average rate.

You cannot base your entire approach on information from an online salary calculator or any generalized classification of jobs. Be aware that the wording of most job descriptions is only slightly less vague than the *I-Ching*; there will always be a higher-paying description that seems exactly like your job, at least to you. The same description could seem like your boss's job to her. Be aware also that online salary calculators often come out on the high side. The last things you want when negotiating for a raise are for your boss to have more accurate data than you do or to get into an argument about the semantics of a job description.

Prepare a Statement of Value. Put together a concise list of what you have done for the company beyond your day-to-day work. Document the goals accomplished, cost savings, and improvements in productivity and staff development. Make an understated estimate of the value you have added. Your main negotiating point will be to ask for a percentage of that figure. If your boss supports giving you a raise, this is what she will be asked for. It couldn't hurt to prepare her argument for her.

Create a New Position for Yourself. In most companies, there will be reasons that you can't be paid more for the job you are already doing. You may be able to get around these reasons by proposing a new position for yourself. Find something that needs doing that will have a positive impact on the bottom line, combine it with some of your old duties in an attractive package, and present it to your boss.

Negotiate. Set a meeting with your boss when you present your information to her. Be aware that if she supports you, she will be thinking of how she will justify her decision to her boss. You are, in effect, sending in an unnegotiated higher bill for services already rendered. Be ready both to use your statement of value as an example of what you can do and to negotiate a raise contingent on higher goals for the future.

If your boss says no, ask what additional information or accomplishments she would need to support your request. Based on her answer, you will know where you stand.

The common element in all successful strategies is demonstrating how the company gets more value for the extra money it's going to pay you. Like almost everything else that's important in business, getting a raise is a sales job. If you want that money, get out there and sell!

SURVIVAL SCENARIO 88 Do You Really Want to Be Creative?

Peter is creative; you can tell that from a block away. Maybe it's the black clothes and the magenta streaks in his hair. People close to him say he's a genius, but all that brainpower hasn't helped him to succeed. He's lost a couple of jobs for political reasons, and now he is struggling to hang on here. He has a hard time finishing what he starts, and often he doesn't know when to keep his mouth shut. Still, if you need an idea, he's the go-to guy.

Not too long ago, I was asked to speak at a business seminar entitled "Awakening the Creative Genius Inside You!" What they seemed to want was a bunch of experts to give peppy little talks about how to get creative juices flowing when it's time to come up with a new marketing plan. The fact that the people putting together the seminar thought that new ideas could be turned on and off like a faucet was my first clue that they really had no idea what creativity is and how it works. Creativity is a mental aberration that might be more of a curse than a blessing in the typical corporate setting.

To begin with, the process is called "creativity" only when it generates ideas that are useful, convenient, and cost-effective. The rest of the time, it's called "being weird" or "having a bad attitude." Creativity grows from the same roots as rebellion. People who like things the way they are just aren't motivated to think of anything new, nor are they well disposed to new ideas that change the way they do things.

Creativity means seeing things differently from other people, and it seldom leads to reverent thoughts about the existing order. If you are creative, be warned: even though most businesses require a good deal more reverence than they really need, you will be judged on your capacity to be reverent long before anybody will spend enough time with you to judge the quality of your ideas. When you think out of the box, there will always be someone demanding that you get back into it.

SURVIVAL SOLUTION *88*
How to Bear the Burden of Creativity

If you still want to be creative, or have to be, here are a few ideas:

Creativity Without Discipline Is like Having Wings but No Feet. Creativity is something you're born with, but before it's worth anything, you have to learn how to use it. Some of the ideas that pop into your mind will be brilliant; most will be garbage. Knowing the difference takes years of hard work. Flying is pointless if you can't land.

Remember, No Matter How Brilliant They Are, Ideas Still Have to Be Sold. Usually, the more brilliant the idea, the harder it is to sell. If you can't sell yours, all that brilliance goes to waste.

Learn to Tolerate Boredom. Creative people like to do creative things, and they tend to regard tasks that aren't exciting and new as beneath them. They are often great at starting tasks but likely to lose interest in the detail work that it takes to finish them. Always remember that it's the boring part that brings in the money.

Get Control over Your Authority Issues. Creative people don't especially like to be told what to do, and they see humor in everything, especially the behavior of people in power. This is a dangerous combination. People don't laugh at jokes about themselves or their values. Remember this if you would like to live past your adolescence.

Express Yourself in Ways That Count. Get over the need to have everything you do, say, and wear be a statement that you are an individual and different from everyone else. People have gotten that point already, believe me. More important, all those annoying attempts at self-expression detract attention from what you really do well. Learn to express your creativity in conventional ways to conventional people, and they'll see your brilliance just as clearly as they see your piercings.

Strive for Something More Than Shock Value. Any idiot can shock people. Urinating in public will do it every time. To achieve something more, you have to enter the world of your audience, rather than requiring them to enter yours. Think Shakespeare rather than Yoko Ono or Andres Serrano.

Treat Your New Idea as If You Were the Second Person Who Thought of It. The glare of a brilliant new idea can blind you to flaws in its conception. Better to assume you had the idea second, so you have to think about why it's better than the first.

Finally, a word of advice for anybody who has to work with creative people: Without those annoying creative people, there are no creative ideas. Without creative ideas, businesses die. Learn to recognize a good idea even when it is badly expressed.

SURVIVAL SCENARIO *89* Comedy Is Hard

Jeff walks into the break room with a big grin on his face, bursting to tell the latest joke he read on the Internet. This one is about Mexicans, but he has a whole collection about African Americans and women as well. It never seems to bother him that most people in the room aren't laughing.

Some workplace humor just isn't funny. I'm not talking about dusty old jokes told with poor timing, but the psychological fact that humor has its roots in aggression.

Aggression against some people is very funny—imagine a pie thrown right in your stuffed-shirt boss's face just at the moment he is being most pompous. Now, that's entertainment! Cutting the powerful down to size is a time-honored task of humor.

There's some danger involved, as the powerful are not always connoisseurs of jokes. Comedy *is* hard. The danger aside, when this sort of joke is done well, it serves to level the playing field and point out that, powerful and weak, we're all in the game together.

Now imagine the boss throwing a pie in the janitor's face. Did you laugh? I hope not, because aggression by the strong against the weak is bullying, not humor. If you don't understand this point, I hope you're reincarnated as a nerd.

Humor is a positive force at work as it turns upward and inward—the old pie-in-the-face routine works even better if the boss is willing to throw the metaphorical pie at himself. If it points inward and upward, joking reinforces the connections between people. As humor turns downward, it becomes bullying. As it turns outward, by making fun of people's differences rather than their similarities, it can quickly become bigotry.

SURVIVAL SOLUTION *89*
Tips for the Aspiring Workplace Humorist

Humor at work should help solve problems rather than become a problem in itself. Productive humor concerns itself with the needs of the audience more than the needs of the person telling the joke. Also, what is appropriate at a comedy club may not go over well at the office.

At the risk of being thought of as the joke police, I offer these tips to aspiring workplace humorists who may not be getting all the laughs they expect:

+ If you have to tell people you were joking, you weren't.
+ If you don't know the difference between irony and sarcasm, don't use either. A sarcastic answer to a serious question is never funny.
+ You aren't funny if you (or people like you) aren't the butt of at least 80 percent of your jokes.
+ You aren't funny if your joke can be told around only a limited set of people. The smaller the group, the less funny it is.
+ You aren't funny if you can't appreciate a good joke simply because it was told on you.
+ Humor at work can be a stress reducer and a useful tool. It can also be an unintended weapon. Make sure you know the difference.

Pie, anyone?

SURVIVAL SCENARIO *90* Blowing Your Own Horn

A job just opened up in marketing. You want it so bad you can taste it. You know who will be making the decision, and you know you'll have to talk yourself up, but what do you say? All your life, you've prided yourself on not being conceited. How do you promote yourself without sounding like an egomaniac?

Is it possible to promote yourself without sounding conceited?

That depends on what you mean by conceited.

If you mean sounding like those stuck-up populars in your middle school who were good looking, made good grades, and still kissed up to adults: sorry, no. Stuck-up populars are exactly what you have to sound like. If you have a problem with that, maybe that's where we ought to begin.

How did you decide that what those populars were doing was bad? Did someone teach you that shyness was next to godliness? Or did you invent the idea yourself as you sat in class tight-throated with fear, knowing the answer but not daring to speak? The first step in promoting yourself well is realizing that it isn't a bad thing to do, only difficult.

SURVIVAL SOLUTION *90*
How to Promote Yourself Without Sounding Like an Egomaniac

To promote yourself effectively, you need to forget your resentment of those stuck-up populars and remember what it was they actually did. They didn't boast about themselves or put other people down (at least in public). Those heavy-handed approaches turn authority figures off just as badly as they do you. Here are some of the techniques that worked in middle school and that will work just as well for you on your job today:

Ask for What You Want. "I'd really like a part in the school play." Forget about working so hard and doing such a good job that people come to you with opportunities. In the real world, people get very little that they don't ask for.

Be Positive and Enthusiastic. "Of course I can play quarterback!" Keep your self-doubts to yourself (and maybe your best friend). Never discuss mixed feelings with someone who is considering you for a challenging task.

Compliment as a Way of Showing Interest. "I was really impressed with how the debating club performed in the finals last year. Your coaching really paid off." The most impressive thing you can say to most people is that you are impressed with them. If you want someone to look favorably on you, give the person a list of his or her achievements, not yours.

Tell Stories That Accentuate Your Past Successes. "When I was cheerleading in eighth grade . . ." List your achievements by telling stories about what happened and what you learned doing responsible tasks in the past.

Practice. None of this stuff comes naturally or spontaneously. It is all acting and has to be rehearsed. The populars knew that, and you should too.

SURVIVAL SCENARIO *91* The Zeigarnik Effect

It's two thirty A.M., and you're dead tired. Instead of sleeping, you find yourself composing your to-do list for the next day—thinking about the e-mails you need to send, the people you want to talk to, and even what you ought to pick up at the grocery store on the way home. None of these things are frightening, or even very important. You tell yourself not to think about them. You roll over and try to go back to sleep. Two minutes later, you think of a phone call you have to make tomorrow.

The reason you are lying sleepless was discovered in 1927, when an early psychologist was probing the mind by asking waiters how they remembered their customers' orders. Bluma Zeigarnik discovered that unfinished tasks are remembered better than finished tasks, and today the effect bears his name. What he found was evidence that the brain has an innate propensity to fill in what is incomplete and finish the unfinished. When you awaken in the middle of the night, your brain is being helpful by reminding you of all the unfinished tasks you took to bed and might forget by morning.

In high-achieving people, the Zeigarnik effect is particularly strong, so as you lie sleepless, you can console yourself with the realization that your brain is wired for success. If that isn't enough, maybe you ought to learn more about how the Zeigarnik effect works and how to get around it so you can get more sleep tomorrow night.

SURVIVAL SOLUTION *91*
Don't Lose Sleep over Unfinished Tasks

Along with all the rest of the programs wired into our brains, the Zeigarnik effect is a relic of simpler times, when tasks were more discrete and most of them had a discernible beginning and end. Today, most of what we do at work is an ongoing process. Nothing is ever completely finished, so the tickler files in our brains are often full to overflowing with unfinished situations. When we are not actively engaged in something else, our brain uses the opportunity to remind us of what we haven't completed. If you want to shut the tickler file and get some sleep, here's what you need to do:

Assign Arbitrary End Points to Tasks. Even though most of what you do is a continuous process involving one task after another, with no end in sight, you can and should set yourself goals that can be finished by the time you leave the office. Get into the habit of telling yourself that you've done what you needed to do today and then closing the file. When you start doing this, it's best to say it out loud to remind your brain that the task is finished for today. If you need to remember something for tomorrow, write it down on a pad or on a sticky-note. Until closing files for the night becomes a habit, you need to be very deliberate, so that your brain is reassured that the task is indeed finished.

Transfer as Much as Possible from Your Brain to an Electronic Gadget or a More Primitive Device. If you are a successful person, you can hold a lot of thoughts in your mind at the same time, but why should you? You need all the RAM you can get to come up with creative ideas or to deal with the unexpected. Why waste it on fragments you can enter in Outlook, write on a calendar, or stick to your computer screen? Writing things down in a way that closes the file until it is reopened is an excellent investment of your time, but it is a new habit that you will have to do consciously, especially if you pride yourself on your good memory and your ability to keep a lot of balls in the air at any given time.

Do a Final Transfer at Bedtime. Before you go to sleep, write down all the things you need to remember in the morning. Keep the pad by your bed in case you remember something else in the middle of the night. The sooner you bring the task to an end point by writing it down, the sooner you can get back to sleep.

See a Doctor About More Persistent Sleep Disturbances. The Zeigarnik effect will keep you awake occasionally. If you have trouble getting to sleep most nights, or if you wake up and take longer than a few minutes to fall back to sleep, check with your doctor or therapist. Sleep disturbances can be symptoms of anxiety or depression.

This scenario is finished. Good night.

SURVIVAL SCENARIO 92   When Life Looks like Easy Street, There Is Danger at Your Door

I thank Jerry Garcia for the wisdom embodied in the title of this scenario. He knew that the most dangerous place to be, in a psychological sense, is where you feel most comfortable. In an earlier scenario, I wrote that we are all standing poised at the crossroads that lead to what is scary or what is boring. If we don't take the scary road once in a while by choosing to do things that are frightening or challenging, our minds become dull, sluggish, and prone to depression.

For most of us, our jobs offer us the opportunity to challenge ourselves by doing things that are difficult, stimulating, and, yes, frightening.

"Not *my* job," thinks Kevin. "*My* job is doing the same old thing day after day. They don't let me do things that are stimulating or challenging."

Kevin's comfort zone is believing that somebody else has to provide his challenges for him.

Maybe Kevin works in the most stifling and frustrating company in town, and there are no challenges or opportunities on his job (or maybe he sits in the desk next to yours). My guess is that at least some of the stifling is in his own head.

SURVIVAL SOLUTION 92
Look for Growth and Challenge, or Wither on the Vine

Kevin is like most of us in not seeing his opportunities to grow and be challenged because they are, well, challenging. The most important challenges lie in doing things that you don't want to do. This makes sense, because the only things you can learn are the things you don't already know. The way we miss our opportunities is by convincing ourselves that what we don't already know or don't want to do is unimportant, rather than scary or difficult. If you are tired of being bored, here are some suggestions:

Look for Challenge in the Things You Complain About. There are opportunities for growth available in Kevin's job. Maybe some of the same opportunities are there in yours. Usually, the best places to look for these opportunities are in the areas you complain about the most. Many of us hide our fears and ignorance beneath things we make jokes about or look down on. For Kevin, finding the area he complains most about is easy—politics. He could learn a lot about politics if he didn't consider the concept unimportant and vaguely immoral.

In any organization of more than one person, there will be politics, whether we choose to see them or not. Politics is the set of skills required to get other people to help us accomplish our goals. Kevin is playing politics whether he knows it or not. Needless to say, he is playing poorly. By staying aloof and not trying to convince people to let him try something different, he influences people to help him accomplish his goal of remaining stuck in the same old rut.

When You Think Something Is Being Done to You, Look at What You Are Doing. Kevin, of course, sees his work situation as him plodding along and nobody offering him any opportunity to get out of his rut. What he really could use are a few lessons in how to influence people in a positive way, so that they will do the things for him that he wants done. In that area lie skills that he could develop and hone for the rest of his professional life and beyond. Unfortunately, he will never discover any of those skills in his comfortable old rut.

"Comfortable!" thinks Kevin. "I'm not comfortable; I'm miserable." That's my point.

SURVIVAL SCENARIO *93* The Office Holiday Party

It's that time of year again. The office party is coming up, and you're wondering if there is any excuse that your boss might believe. Office parties are such a drag. At least the booze is free.

Whether it's in honor of Christmas, Hanukkah, Kwanzaa, or whatever, remember: your office party is a business function and not like a soiree at a friend's house. Office parties are work. Your job is to graciously and visibly enjoy what's being put on for your benefit. If you can have fun while doing so, more power to you. If not, like every other day, do it anyway.

SURVIVAL SOLUTION *93*
Businesslike Celebration

If you are a social klutz, here are some tips that may help you endure the office party:

Go. Don't think you can skip this event because you don't like parties. Whoever's throwing this shindig believes all *normal* people like parties.

Participate, even in what you consider silly. The holiday party is no time to make a point of the fact that nobody can tell you what to do. Do whatever is on the agenda. Smile, talk, sing, dance, eat, or play volleyball. Nothing is more conspicuous than somebody sitting off in the corner being cool. Blend in and let people mistake you for a team player.

Limit the Drinking. Nurse one drink, and, after that, have sparkling water with lime. No matter what you do elsewhere, there is absolutely nothing to be gained by getting drunk at work. There will be alcoholics in the crowd who will encourage you to drink more than you want. Even if the boss is one of them, don't do it. Hold up your sparkling water and say you'll get another as soon as you finish this one. Also, if you don't approve of alcohol, you don't need to share your philosophy any more than you need to share your religion or your politics. Live and let live.

Speaking of living, friends don't let friends drive drunk.

Unless It's Employees Only, Bring Your Spouse. Show off the stability in your life. It can't hurt. Foster the illusion that the office is a big, happy family. Of course, it will probably mean you'll have to go to your spouse's holiday party too, but those are the breaks.

Work the Room. Say a few words to everyone you know, not just your three best friends. This is what socially adept people do at parties. If you don't speak to people, they may not realize it's because your religion forbids chitchat. They will think it's because you don't like them.

Avoid Talking Shop. The office party is no place for a business meeting, even if you haven't been able to get a minute of your manager's time for three weeks. Switch into social mode. In case you didn't learn how to make small talk in engineering school, ask about a person's hobbies, pets, or family. If all else fails, talk sports.

If You're Looking for Romance, Ask for a Date. The office party is a public place, subject to gossip and laws about anything that looks even vaguely sexual. If there is someone you'd like to get closer to, do it on a date. Hopefully, you will read the scenarios on office romance before you do.

If there is some reason that you can't ask for a date—say, the person is married to someone else—at least wait until after the New Year to make a move. You may change your mind.

Do Not Leave Until Twenty Minutes Before the Scheduled Ending Time. Find a babysitter whose curfew is past nine o'clock. Anyway, you used that excuse for leaving early last year.

Thank the Boss Profusely. Even if you don't like spray-cheese on Ritz crackers and dancing the limbo rock, the boss still thinks she's giving you something nice that you should enjoy. You wouldn't criticize a second-grader's finger painting, would you?

Look at the office party as a masquerade in which you are playing the role of a mature, responsible, socially skilled person who likes his or her job and coworkers. It's only three hours; then you can go home and be yourself. Happy holidays!

SURVIVAL SCENARIO 94 Congratulations on Your Promotion!

You've done it! You've read and practiced all the survival solutions in this book, and you've been promoted to management.

However . . . from the first day, you've felt as if you stumbled into the Twilight Zone. The people around you are different, but so subtly that you wonder if it's just you being oversensitive. No, something has changed . . . but you can't quite put a label on it.

People newly promoted into supervisory positions may develop a psychological disorder I call Management Shock Syndrome.

SURVIVAL SOLUTION 94

Recognize Management Shock Syndrome

The first symptom of MSS is a sense of social isolation. Your old work buddies don't hang with you as much as they used to. When they do, they seem more formal and polite. You want to say, "Hey, it's me in here. I'm still the same person." But you aren't. You can see it in your former friends' eyes. You've become one of Them.

Over the next few weeks, you begin to feel as if everything you say is blown out of proportion. If you tease or joke, or say anything to them short of lavish praise, your erstwhile friends seem all of a sudden ready make a federal case out of it.

They start making the same lame excuses that you all used to joke about handing to your old boss. Now they say them with a straight face, and they expect you to believe them.

You begin to get irritated and decide to clamp down. Pretty soon, you hear words coming out of your mouth that you swore you'd never say. You realize with a shock that you are becoming the kind of authority figure that you used to hate.

Maybe you go to your boss for advice. Since you're in management now, you figure he'll let you in on all those little secrets that the people in power seem to know. Nothing! He tells you even less than before—

except that the production quotas have been raised, and you'd better figure out how you're going to break it to the troops.

Back in your new corner cubicle, you sit down on your new chair with the six-inch-higher executive back and stare out at the office corridors that used to feel like home. They look the same, but you know that somehow they have changed forever. Any minute, you expect to hear Rod Serling's voice-over saying that you've taken a wrong turn on the road of life and entered the Twilight Zone. Fear takes over, and you're tempted by the kick-butt-and-take-names management style that's been around since the Stone Age.

Management Shock Syndrome is the silent destroyer of new managerial talent. If you're afflicted, come out of those shadows of self-doubt and into the light of understanding. You are not alone! It happens to everybody. Reality actually changes when you're promoted to management. It only seems as if you've entered the Twilight Zone.

The best cure is finding a mentor who's gotten through the disorder and become a regular person again. Ask older managers how it was for them when they were first promoted, and pick one who's willing to admit that she didn't know it all from the very beginning. Talk it over. It helps.

SURVIVAL SCENARIO *95* The Language of Management

At meetings, you listen closely to what the senior people say, hoping to surreptitiously gain a few clues about what a manager is supposed to do and how a manager is supposed to think. They act as if they all know what they're talking about, but sometimes you're not so sure. They use a lot of buzzwords; everybody seems to know what they mean, but you don't. You've even resorted to looking some of them up in the dictionary and in management textbooks. That only makes things more confusing, because the definitions don't seem to fit what people are talking about. This is not the kind of thing you can ask about. You're a manager now; you should know already.

Language is the primary tool of management. Guys on the shop floor would get into big trouble if they used their tools as imprecisely as managers use words. Beneath the jargon and buzzwords are some important concepts that need to be understood and communicated.

SURVIVAL SOLUTION *95*
Understand a Few Critical Distinctions That Every Manager Should Know

If you're a manager, your job requires you to understand the critical distinctions between words and concepts that are often used inter-changeably in day-to-day conversations at work. Let's clear the air:

Problem and Dilemma. A problem can be solved, and with luck, it goes away. Once you've figured out how to get a critical order out the door on time, the shipment is gone, and the problem with it. Dilemmas are not solved; they must be continuously balanced. More of one means less of the other. Some examples are quality versus cost, speed versus accuracy, and profit versus market share. If you "solve" a dilemma by moving too far in one direction, you create problems that can only be solved by moving in the other. If you are a manager, dilemmas are with you every day of your working life, but that's a good thing. If there weren't opposing forces to balance, there would be no need for managers.

Supervising and Managing. Supervisors organize the work and solve whatever problems get in the way of doing it. Managers balance opposing forces so that they can set clear priorities for supervisors. Supervisors see that the job gets done. Managers decide which of all the possible jobs deserves the most attention.

Adequacy and Excellence. Excellence is close to perfection. Perfection, though admirable, is frightfully expensive. It is the job of management to set the standards for adequacy and specify the jobs that are so critical to the overall goals of the business that only perfection will do.

Product and Process. Product is what you do. Process is how you do it. When a manager can clearly describe the product, he or she does not have to meddle with the process. This descriptive ability is known as "vision." Managers without vision keep tight control over process.

Sales and Marketing. Sales means persuading customers to buy the product you have already produced. Marketing is asking customers what they want to buy, so you will know what to produce in the future.

Working Hard and Doing What's Most Important. Working hard involves putting in a lot of hours and doing a lot of stuff. Doing what's most important always involves making tough choices. No amount of hard work can compensate for avoiding a difficult decision.

Delegation and Task Assignment. You delegate power, not tasks. Telling people what to do is task assignment. Giving them the power to do it is delegation.

Reverence and Respect. Whatever—and whoever—is perfect and cannot be improved deserves reverence. Anything that can be improved deserves the respect of open discussion about how it can be improved and whether it should be.

Cooperating and Competing. The difference between these two involves information. If you're sharing it, you're cooperating. If you withhold it for whatever reason, you're competing. How much information should you share with your superiors and your subordinates? It's just one of the many dilemmas a manager has to balance every day.

SURVIVAL SCENARIO 96   Breeding for the Wrong Characteristics

Why is it that the brightest and most creative people on your team
are the most difficult to manage? They can be surly, they ask difficult
questions, and they always want to do things their own way. You're
tempted to avoid them and try to get by with less talented people who
are easier to work with. You know enough not to give in to this temptation, but it definitely makes your job harder. Nobody said management was easy.

I once read an article about how show dogs are being bred for the
wrong characteristics—looks, instead of vigor, stamina, and intelligence. As a result, many breeds are experiencing alarming increases
in health and psychological problems. The article concerned me, not
just because I'm a dog lover but also because I see so many parallels in
the companies I work with. No, it isn't bad genetics, nor do I believe
business is going to the dogs. I do think that certain styles among
businesspeople are over-rewarded at the expense of other necessary
and desirable traits.

It's no secret that conformists with positive attitudes are likely to
get ahead in most businesses. Throughout this book, I have reminded
you that to stay sane and get ahead, you have to fit in, be cheerful, and
please your boss. I stand by the advice—but not necessarily the wisdom of the decisions that make the advice necessary. Businesses need
people at all levels to be flexible and creative, to anticipate problems,
and to make decisions for themselves. At some places, managers are
discovering, to their chagrin, that many of these traits have been bred
out of the strain.

How did this happen? The problem is, as usual, simply human
nature. Many actions that seem so natural that we do them without
thinking are not necessarily what's best for business. The case in point,
if you were a manager, who would you consider more intelligent and

capable: someone who usually agrees with you or someone who usually disagrees? When promotion time comes, who would you pick? Before too long, you can fill a department with people who think the way you do and agree with you. They probably share your limitations as well. If you're perfect, of course, this is not a problem. The fact is that it's easier to manage people who agree with you and are positive and cooperative. Over time, this can leave the strain you're breeding short on a few desirable but difficult traits.

Keeping the Strain Strong and Healthy

There are a few traits that every department needs to stay strong and healthy. Unfortunately, the people who display these traits are often the most difficult to manage. It takes extra time and effort, but the results are worth it. Here are some of the important attributes that managers should make an effort to nurture:

Creativity. Creativity and rebellion grow from the same roots. Both are characteristic of people who look at a situation and see it differently than other people might. Creativity can't be turned on when it's time to develop a new marketing plan and be turned off the rest of the time. This fact can make creative people exasperating. Their stubborn unwillingness to conform can make them seem more trouble than they're worth. That is, until you need a radically different approach to a problem.

Critical Thinking. People who notice problems and point them out are necessary to keeping a business healthy. These people also tend to make things uncomfortable for everyone, especially their managers. It's easy to ignore them or to pass off their complaints as nothing more than bad attitude. This teaches people that, to get ahead, they'd best keep their mouths shut. They become hesitant to look closely enough at any situation to discover problems before those problems affect the bottom line.

Initiative. Nobody likes mistakes, but they are an inevitable result when people take initiative. If a company's culture treats mistakes like sins, it will breed a strain of employees who are better at covering their tails than seizing opportunities.

The temptation is strong to hire and promote people based on how easy they are to manage rather than how well they supply the critical traits that a company needs. As with a show dog, an organization can be bred to look good but have an unhealthy tendency toward cheerful conformity and avoidance of personal risk. As a manager, you have to decide what's best for the strain that you're breeding in your department.

SURVIVAL SCENARIO 97 What's Wrong with Superwoman?

Alicia is an achiever and a wonderful, caring person besides. She prides herself on her organization skills. Without her superb ability to plan projects, she would never be able to fit so much productive activity into each day.

Work: She's a manager at a high-tech company, with a good chance of being department head before too long. Fifty hours is a short week for her.

Community service: She serves on a couple of nonprofit boards and at the moment is helping out a friend's campaign for county commissioner.

Sports: She plays a mean game of tennis (watch out for her backhand), and it is not unusual that she would ride at least a half-century on a weekend morning.

She is also able to spend quality time with her family and friends. If you'd like to do lunch, she has an opening two weeks from Tuesday, or maybe a walk this Monday at six A.M., but if you have a problem and need her to help, she'll drop everything and see you now. That's the kind of person Alicia is.

She says she owes it all to Outlook and her day planner, and she firmly believes that if you are organized, you can have it all. She has it all. Though Alicia prides herself on her superwoman image, her real motivation is service. She strongly believes in her obligation to use her talents to serve her community, her friends, and her family. She knows that is what she was put here for. She doesn't talk about this much; she just lives it. She is living a life consistent with her values. She feels good about herself, at least most of the time.

Lately, however, she has been feeling a little off; her energy is not quite what it was, and she just doesn't feel how she used to feel. It's as if something is missing. What could be missing? She has it all. But each day she seems to feel a bit more empty. What's wrong with her?

SURVIVAL SOLUTION *97*
If You Don't Take Care of Yourself, You Can't Take Care of Anyone Else

To answer the question of what's wrong with Alicia, I offer a Jewish folktale:

Two hundred years ago in Eastern Europe, it was customary for learned rabbis to travel from town to town to visit one another. So it was that Rabbi Elimelech visited Rabbi Shmelke, who was famed for his extreme scholarliness.

Rabbi Shmelke spent most of his time at his table studying the Torah and Talmud. He took little time away from his studies. What sleeping he did was by sitting up among his books with a candle between his fingers; when the candle burned down, it would awaken him, and he would resume his studies. There were, he believed, callings more important than sleep.

Concerned, Rabbi Elimelech talked Rabbi Shmelke into going into his bedroom for a "little nap." This Rabbi Shmelke did reluctantly but only out of respect for his learned colleague. While Rabbi Shmelke slept, Rabbi Elimelech had the shutters closed throughout the house so it would be dark and quiet. Rabbi Shmelke slept for almost two days.

When he awoke, he was dismayed to discover that it was almost Sabbath. He hurried to the synagogue, more than a little irritated at the trick Rabbi Elimelech had played on him. For now, though, his irritation would have to wait, since he had a congregation to teach about the ways of the Lord.

As he entered the synagogue, he noticed a clarity of mind he had not experienced in years. His sermon was vivid as never before. When he spoke of the Red Sea, the congregation pulled up their coats and skirts for fear of getting wet. His words reached out to the hearts and souls of all who heard him.

As he left the pulpit, he turned to Rabbi Elimelech to admonish him for his trick. Then he understood. He said, "Not until this day did I know that one could also serve God with sleep."

It is not just sleep that Alicia needs, though a few extra hours might not hurt. In the bustle of all the things she does for others, the person doing them is fading away. She can serve others best by taking care of herself. If she does not provide for her own needs, there will be nothing there to provide for others.

If you aspire to be superwoman, learn from Alicia and Rabbi Shmelke.

SURVIVAL SCENARIO *98* Teamwork

The framed poster by the conference room says "Teamwork" with a photo of some fancy Asian dragon boats. The poster is about the only formal training you've gotten in team management since you've been promoted. You're supposed to inspire people, but you just can't see how a pep talk would have any effect on the herd of cats in your department. Whatever became of telling people what to do and then them doing it?

Teamwork. The word gets batted around like a softball at the company picnic. What does it really mean?

Most people would agree that teamwork implies a group of people working together, pooling their resources to accomplish mutual goals, and placing their own needs secondary to the needs of the group. Easy to define, hard to do.

The problem is that people don't automatically know how to work as a team. Unless the common needs are explicitly defined, the group's needs will end up being synonymous with the desires of the most assertive team member or of the boss. People who ride over other people are seen as having leadership qualities; people who bring up problems are seen as not being team players.

Businesses are full of frustrated, somewhat unassertive people who, having thought that being part of a team meant they would have a part in making decisions, offered an opinion and then discovered that teamwork really meant keeping your mouth shut, smiling, and doing what you're told. Most often, the reason for this disconnect is not that their managers are incompetent or have control issues. The managers were just not taught how to get their people to play as a team, and no matter how many posters the employees saw and slogans they heard, they just weren't able to figure it out for themselves. By default, the managers became the kind of authority figures they said they'd never become.

SURVIVAL SOLUTION *98*
How to Encourage Teamwork

Unless something is done to prevent it, teams have a way of drifting in the direction of hierarchical management. They are easier to run that way, but their main advantage—that of having many brains working on the same problem—is canceled out for the expediency of having one brain thinking and many hands following directions. If you are a team leader, here are some suggestions for encouraging real teamwork:

Arrange Contingencies, and Enforce Them Carefully. If you want to maintain the spirit of teamwork, contingencies must be arranged so that all team members share in rewards and punishments. If there is a chance for individuals to make big career advances by showing leadership potential (read that as being bossy), it is quite likely that's what your more assertive members will do, instead of playing along with the rest of the team. As soon as one of the players starts putting his or her own needs ahead of the needs of the team and getting rewarded for it, the whole team concept is out the window.

Continually Redefine Teamwork. To keep a team functioning as a team, you have to talk regularly about the definition of teamwork on this project and in this setting. Team goals must be clearly specified, as well as each member's responsibility for meeting those goals. It has to be clear in everyone's mind which behaviors are characteristic of cooperation and which are characteristic of vying for control. It's hard to specify these behaviors in advance, but it is fairly easy to see them when they occur. That's why you have to talk about it on a regular basis. Being team leader means leading these discussions.

See That Each Member Can Be Heard. To keep a team working as a team, you also have to ensure that each member can be heard by the group at any time. If several people have become dominant, and others fear retribution if they disagree, people with alternative ideas merely keep quiet and grumble to each other as the team falls apart. It may be helpful to have some anonymous way of getting items on to the agenda, to prevent people who have problems from being singled out as having bad attitudes.

Teamwork can be a real benefit to a business, but, as with any other equipment, it continually needs to be adjusted, monitored, and improved. It also helps to know how to operate it.

SURVIVAL SCENARIO 99 The Evolution of a Manager

Since you've been promoted, you've scarcely had time to think, but when you do, you sometimes wonder what it is you're supposed to be doing. You know your goals and objectives, but beyond that, what does it mean to be a manager? You'd like to talk it over with your boss or some of the other team leaders, but there never seems to be enough time. Maybe you ought to know it already.

Managers do not spring fully armed from the head of Zeus, nor do they arise spontaneously from the ranks, nor emerge from graduate school ready plug-and-play. Managers are people, and as such, they grow, develop, and evolve. As they grow, their conceptions of what managing is evolves as well.

The process of evolution happens in silence most of the time, because the people it's happening to are far more focused on the job than on understanding the person who's doing the job—even if they are that person. Business culture is suspicious of persons who aren't too busy to reflect. As a result, most managers must reinvent themselves like lonely and imperfect wheels, smoothing their own rough edges in painful collisions with the hard realities of existence.

Observed or not, development in human beings—and managers—follows certain predictable patterns. We all move from self-conscious fits and starts to fluid grace in performing our tasks, from seeing only black and white to recognizing subtle shadings of gray, and from wanting all we can get to wanting to be useful.

People can get stuck at a particular stage and do things the same way throughout their careers. But most grow and develop. Through experience, they learn better ways to do things and better ways to think about things. This is the quiet joy of our careers—not the accolades, testimonials, and promotions, but the knowledge that we are actually getting better. One of the great thrills of life is using yourself to full potential.

SURVIVAL SOLUTION *99*

How Managers Grow and Develop

Managers grow by understanding that there are five things you can manage: money, tasks, people, image, and power. To be a mature manager, you must be able to manage all of them. Early on, people try managing only the one or two that come easiest. As they mature, they begin to realize that they have to master the difficult parts as well. What people learn about managing each of these areas develops in its own predictable way:

Managing Money. Managers who don't manage money don't last long. Cost control is the minimum. If a new manager does nothing else but stay within budget, he or she will eventually discover that merely avoiding costs does not create anything new. As managers mature, they begin to conceive of money less as treasure to be hoarded and more as a tool to be used. It takes money to make money. Managing money well involves a clear conception of what you'll get for what you spend.

Managing Tasks. As people mature, their conception of managing tasks moves from doing the job themselves, or telling other people exactly how to do it, to encouraging people to do it their own way. A beginning manager is a single person with many sets of hands. As a manager matures, he or she becomes more able to use excess heads as well as hands.

Immature managers attempt to control the process as well as the product. They manage every task as if it were the rapid, orderly production of hamburgers at a fast-food restaurant. If you manage for hamburgers, you get hamburgers. Forget new ideas and groundbreaking insights: the best that you can hope for is that your work comes out cooked on both sides.

Managing People. The simplest way of managing people is by telling them what to do. Mature managers develop a complex understanding of the people who work for them so that they can lead these people to places they never would have gone themselves. There is a huge difference between being a taskmaster and being a leader.

Managing Image. The world no longer beats a path to the door of the inventor of the better mousetrap. To get anywhere, you have to be able to promote yourself and your product. As people mature, the management of image moves from manipulating other people to think what you want them to think, to presenting yourself and your product as they really are to a market—either superiors, constituents, or customers—that really needs what you have to offer.

Managing Power. To the immature manager, power is an end in itself. It is something that you use to get your own way. The temptation is strong to use power to make life as pleasant and comfortable as possible. This is kind of like using a Ferrari only to commute to work. It looks good and feels good, but its potential is wasted on the task. The mature use of power is in creating a vision, an idea that is bigger than the person thinking it, and bringing it to life in the real world.

Maturing as a manager means moving from a conception of the world that is no larger than yourself to seeing a larger system and knowing you have an important place in it. It is the drive to attain this state of balance and usefulness, far more than greed and ambition, that is responsible for the great things that business, and people in business, can do.

SURVIVAL SCENARIO *100*   A Systems Analyst Falls Prey to the System

The following is a cautionary tale for managers. One way to look at it is as a story about how a good employee goes bad, but there's more to it than that.

Daryl is a systems analyst. Don't ask me what he does exactly, but he is good at it. He works for a large high-tech firm that also does a lot of things I don't understand.

Daryl feels frustrated in his job. That I do understand.

You see, a couple of months back, Daryl was being considered for a promotion to project manager, and he didn't get it. That wouldn't have been such a problem, but the person who did get it, Jason, was totally unqualified. Well, maybe not totally, but all the guys in the department agree that his grasp on the technical aspects of the job is slippery at best.

Speaking of slippery, that's an even bigger problem. Jason's not a total liar, but he does seem to tell people what they want to hear, especially management. When they bring up changes in procedure or suggest things that the department can do to improve, he is always the one saying, "No problem."

Sure, it is no problem to him. Most of the time, he doesn't understand what is involved, and besides, he probably won't be the one doing the work anyway. He's always getting himself appointed to committees with all the PR types from upstairs, or he's off doing lunch with someone or in some ridiculous meeting. Anything to get out of doing honest work.

Daryl just can't believe it. Why would they promote a guy like Jason, who, to be honest about it—though Daryl would never say anything like this at work—is nothing but a lazy, incompetent, political sleaze.

Daryl says it a home—constantly. Tricia, his wife, listens and agrees. She knows how upset Daryl is, and she wants to be supportive. About once a week, Daryl comes home all bent out of shape about something "the idiot"—their pet name for Jason—has done this week. He rants and raves and tells the whole story again, starting from the day Jason was hired. Tricia is getting a little tired of hearing it, but she knows how bad Daryl feels so she listens.

Then came the day another project manager position opened. Daryl figured his turn had come at last. He went up to Clara's office— she's the vice president of operations—and told her he was putting his hat in the ring. He was expecting her to give him the high sign and say, "Yeah, Daryl, your turn is coming at last."

That's not what she said. She told him she couldn't back him, something about his attitude problem and lack of sufficient people skills. Daryl burned out that day, right there in Clara's office. Of course, it took a few years before they actually swept the ashes away, when he finally took early retirement because of a back injury.

Another systems analyst falls prey to the system.

SURVIVAL SOLUTION *100*
Managing Means More Than Perpetuating the System

Ironically, Daryl the systems analyst lost out because nobody really tried to analyze the system of which he was a part.

I guess you could say that he was to blame for his own demise. Daryl saw Jason's promotion as an indication of incompetence of the people upstairs rather than a statement of their clear preference. Tough luck, Daryl. It's your own fault that you never got it.

Maybe Daryl wasn't the only one who didn't get it. He was a talented, knowledgeable, and highly skilled employee. His disaffection and burnout was a big loss to the company and one that could have been prevented if the people who managed him thought more clearly about the difference between managing and being managed.

Now that you're a manager, don't blindly perpetuate the system that drove you crazy. The easiest thing to do as a manager is to give the biggest rewards to people who figure out for themselves how to manage you. The real work of management is setting up a system that rewards what is best for the company, rather than what makes your life easiest. That takes effort, sacrifice, and, most of all, honesty. If you want people to perform well within a system, you have to know how that system operates and clearly communicate what it takes to succeed within it. This is seldom done, because it is difficult and sometimes embarrassing. It is the lack of thought and communication about what is really going on that drives employees like Daryl crazy.

This book began with suggestions about how to survive in a dysfunctional system in which people say one thing and do another. Now, I'm suggesting that you think clearly enough about what you are doing as a manager to avoid perpetuating that dysfunctional system.

Let's look at what the managers of Daryl's company could have done. Their first mistake was promoting someone who looked good to them but did not have the respect of his peers. They could have checked out how Jason was viewed and chosen someone else, I suppose, but that might not have been feasible and would not have solved the problem anyway.

A real solution would have taken more courage than that. Somebody needed to tell Daryl and other people like him what the company really valued and what he would have to do to get a promotion. Everything Daryl heard led him to believe that his hard work and competence would be rewarded. His skills were eventually wasted, because the company assumed that if he were project manager material, he would have known how to get ahead without being told.

After Jason's promotion, Daryl became more visibly disaffected and surly. Even then, nobody put two and two together and told him what he needed to do. Daryl needed a mentor, desperately, but all the mentors went to upwardly mobile, political guys like Jason, who probably didn't need them. That was a very expensive decision, considering what losing a guy like Daryl actually costs.

Daryl's story is repeated thousands of times a day. It's not just systems analysts who burn out because they don't understand the system. If you are a manager, it is your job to analyze the systems of which you are a part, see them clearly, and explain them as they really are. This is the only way to end the craziness once and for all.

SURVIVAL SCENARIO *101* Taking That Next Step

Kinesha knows she needs to stop running away and face her fear of speaking. Gwen has to let go of her need to control. Marie has to get going on her cold calls. What about you? By now, you know what you need to do to, but you knew it all along, didn't you?

I don't mean to sound like your mother, but why haven't you done it already?

This is a serious question. All of us have things in our lives that we know we should do but haven't gotten around to doing. We just keep tripping over the results of our avoidance, each time saying, "I've got to do something about this," and then doing nothing. As I've said in previous scenarios, calling it procrastination gives us no information. When facing these important issues, nobody thinks, "I'll just procrastinate," but we all do say something to ourselves that diverts our attention and enables us to avoid facing the inevitable. Before you read further, think about what you say to trick yourself into believing that now is not the time to do what you need to do.

Most of us say that we'll do it later. Well, later is here.

This is where the rubber meets the road. To be a sane and successful adult, you have to be able to make yourself do things you don't want to do. The question is how?

This is the reason you're reading a self-help book, isn't it?

SURVIVAL SOLUTION *101*

How to Make Yourself Do Things You Don't Want to Do

The following are a few basic strategies for making yourself do what needs to be done regardless of how you feel about doing it:

Accept That You Really Need to Do It. Sweep aside all the justifications and rationalizations, look at your choices with a cold eye, and see that to improve your job and your life, you really do have to face your demon, even though you are afraid or don't want to.

Just Do It. This strategy makes excellent advertising copy but is virtually useless unless you know how to do it already. It is the way people talk when they know how to do something but don't have the verbal skills to explain. It is the language that athletes use in talking with each other, which is utterly meaningless to klutzes. It is the way people who have never been addicted talk to addicts and how people who have lost their sex drive talk to hormone-intoxicated teenagers. It is sometimes as irrelevant as telling a fish to just breathe air. "Just do it" is the stock in trade of motivational speakers—many of whom are athletes, come to think of it.

The essence of the strategy is getting so stoked up with slogans that resistance is burned away by the belly fire of motivation. For some people, this works, but for most, the pyrotechnics may be bright and beautiful, but they don't last very long. If this strategy has not worked for you in the past, it probably won't now.

Know Exactly What You Need to Do Now. Motivation is no substitute for knowledge. Any endeavor can be broken down into steps that can be done a day at a time, or a minute at a time if need be. The smaller the steps and the more narrow the focus, the more successful you are likely to be. Even the most overwhelming transitions are composed of moment-to-moment decisions. If you always know what the next step is and take it, wherever you're going, you'll get there.

Do It or Else. The strategy we think of most often is punishment, which does not work at all. Getting chewed out or beating yourself up after you've made the wrong choice only makes you feel resentful or like a bad person. It is the avoidance of punishment that does the job.

As we've seen, punishment strategies don't usually work as intended, because even though there are myriad punishments for not doing what we don't want to do, it is our nature to believe either that this time we won't get caught (nobody expects to get a speeding ticket) or that punishment is unavoidable (was there ever a time that your mother had absolutely nothing to criticize?).

Also, when we think of punishment, we think of other people administering it, which rarely works the way it's supposed to. Think of how you feel when someone tries to make you feel guilty. Usually, you get angrier at them than you do at yourself. Then you feel so bad that you wonder why you bother trying anything. This is why most of us learn so little during our teenage years, and why we have such mixed feelings toward authority figures.

In order for the avoidance of punishment to be a real motivator, you have to set up the contingencies yourself. For example, you might tell people what you need to do, and give them permission to nag you if you don't do it. Make punishment inevitable if you don't do what you're supposed to, avoidable if you do, and, most important, totally under your control. If there's no one to help you, you can arrange a contingency for yourself by burning a five-dollar bill each time you fail to take the step you were supposed to take.

Do It for the Reward. There is definitely a pot of gold at the end of the rainbow: a promotion, freedom from fear, or being able to do something you could only dream about doing. The only problem is the psychological distance from here to there. Long-term rewards do not motivate us unless we remind ourselves of them every day. Then the reminders become short-term rewards, which are the only kind that work.

To make yourself do things you don't want to do, you need rewards at every step. The best rewards are kind words spoken to yourself or by those friends you have enlisted to help you on your journey. Praise and avoidance of punishment work better together than either one does by itself. Don't expect your friends to notice how well you're doing on their own. You will have to tell them and ask for their encouragement.

Do It for Someone Else. Most of us are more willing to do something difficult for someone else than we are to do it for ourselves.

This is a strategy that must be used with great care. There is good reason that people keep saying, "You can't do it for someone else; you have to do it for yourself." What they are trying to say is that if we expect gratitude or acknowledgment, then we are not really doing whatever it is for someone else; we're doing it for ourselves, but the contingency is stated only in our own minds. The other person has not agreed to praise us, promote us, or love us forever.

The only time doing it for someone else can actually work is when there are no strings attached.

Do It for the Internal Rewards. Doing things that are difficult is what makes us feel like good people. If there is such a thing as self-esteem, then this is its source. External contingencies work, but in the end, to be effective, they must be internalized. Only with practice can we discover that virtue is its own reward.

Even this noble strategy must be used with care. It is surprisingly easy to cross the line into believing that more pain leads to more emotional gain. This is the trap that impales anorexics and workaholics.

Now that you know what you have to do and how to do it, what are you waiting for? If not now, when?

Index

Protect yourself against people
who seek to destroy the emotional and psychological well-being of others

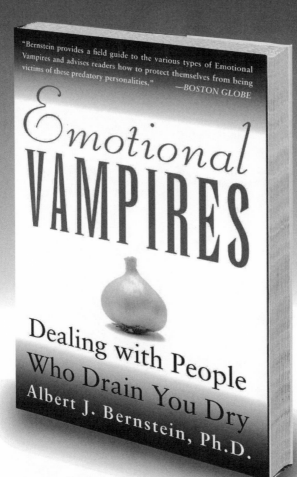

"Bernstein provides a field guide to the various types of Emotional Vampires and advises readers how to protect themselves from being victims of these predatory personalities."
—BOSTON GLOBE

Emotional VAMPIRES

Dealing with People Who Drain You Dry

Albert J. Bernstein, Ph.D.

Learn more. Mc Graw Hill Do more.

AVAILABLE EVERYWHERE BOOKS ARE SOLD